On a High Horse

Dave Oliphant

ON A HIGH HORSE:
VIEWS MOSTLY OF LATIN AMERICAN & TEXAN POETRY

Prickly Pear Press   •   Fort Worth

Publication of this book was made possible in part
by a grant from the Texas Commission on the Arts.

Prickly Pear Press
2132 Edwin St.
Fort Worth, Texas 76110

THESE forty pieces are for the many friends, professors, & colleagues I have known on & through the "Forty Acres" and are printed in this centennial year of The University of Texas at Austin.

Contents

Illustrations

Chile: The Poetry View

A jackrabbit hopped to the edge of the runway where our plane sat awaiting clearance from the tower, daylight passing through his long ears as he raised them, listening to the propellers humming in the Austin heat. Seated next to Mike Hennen, a major in Latin American affairs, and already too aware of my own limited knowledge of Spanish, the tower, the rabbit's ears, and the plane's deafening roar all served dramatically to make me know how everything I would hear in Chile might well sound like that infamous babble spoken of in the Bible.

That such should prove the case was to me a most distressing thought, for, as with all fifteen of us Chile-bound Texans (and we really are bound to Chile now, by ties much stronger than the State Department will ever know), I wanted to communicate—not convince, you understand, but communicate! I wanted to know the country's people, especially her poets. And so, during that day and night of flight, my hopes and fears grew almost unbearable by way of Houston, Miami, Panama City, and Lima, Perú. Finally, with morning and the snow-capped Andes, we descended into the valley of Santiago, suddenly there, Columbuses every one.

Before leaving Texas I had read the poems of two Chilean poets and one poetess: Nicanor Parra, Pablo Neruda, and Gabriela Mistral. In Chile I was to meet each in a different way, spending an evening with Parra at his home outside Santiago, arguing against Neruda's florid poetry with students in Valparaíso, and visiting in the north of Chile Mistral's grave in her out-of-the-way village of Vicuña. Even though Parra was the only poet with whom I came in contact, I was able through conversations with Chilean students to experience all three on rather more intimate terms than is ordinarily possible when the poets in question are either deceased (Mistral) or out of the country (Neruda).

In addition to these three poets, I also met the short story writer Luis Domínguez, whose name I had not encountered before and who has only recently been published by "Zig Zag" (in a sense the Chilean equivalent to the avant-garde publishing house of New Directions). Domínguez teaches, as does Parra, in the University of Chile, the former within its school of journalism, the latter as a physics professor with the University's Instituto Pedagógico. While living in the Instituto's dormitories, I was also able to meet many student writers, so many, in fact, that it almost seemed that everyone on campus was an aspiring young poet. Next to "futbol" (soccer, that is), poetry

Panorama, supplement to *The Daily Texan* (31 October 1965): 4-5.

I found is the national preoccupation among students. This uncommon interest in poetry has produced a surprising number of fine poets, especially considering the size of the country (population 8 million).

Nicanor Parra, the first writer I met and the one I was most interested in meeting, is little respected in his own country, as is so often the case with experimentalists, in spite of the fact that abroad he is gaining quite a wide recognition for his straightforward poems. For instance, here in the States, New Directions is soon to publish Thomas Merton translations of his work, while City Lights has already brought out a volume of his early poems which was called by one reviewer the most notable in the City Lights series. The reason for my own personal interest in Parra stems from the similarity of his work to that of Robert Creeley—a prominent leader of the hard, thin school of United States poetry. Although there were some students who championed Parra's works, the majority either knew very little about him or thought it ridiculous to mention him in the same breath with Neruda and Mistral.

During an evening spent in Parra's home, I questioned him as to the cause for the students' reaction. It seemed to him that his country's literary critics had come to consider his verse the work of an iconoclast, of a physicist out to destroy all poetry. "They still want 'beauty' and her cast of a thousand adjectives," he said. "When Allen Ginsberg was staying here with my family two years ago, he also spoke of this same problem in the States. He's a most interesting person, and a fine poet I believe." Sitting on a couch smoking his Havana cigar (Parra lived in Cuba until he was asked to leave after those involved with the Revolution discovered that he was really no political poet), he spoke of his visits to Russia and the United States (is conversant in both Russian and English), his sister's paintings (one of which hung on the wall at his back), and his latest book of poems, *Versos de salon*. This title, "Versos de salon," is ironic, he said, for the verses could never be read in a salon, which, it seems, is a proper place, but one "the poet" doesn't respect. (In referring to his own works, Parra would always say "the poet" has done such and such, as if it were some other person of whom he spoke.) Along with each new subject, we were treated to another round of Chilean wine, the drink which is so much a part of life in Parra's country that he recently wrote a poem entitled "Coplas del vino." "Coplas" are verses, but included in the look and sound of that word is "copas," cups. One of the most popular toasts we drank to in Chile was sung to a song called "Copas de vino." Parra incorporates that toast, the social function of wine drinking, and his own poetic art in this simple and moving poem. It is too long to quote in its entirety, but here are three stanzas as a "sample." Since no part of the poem has been previously translated into English, the version here is my own crude attempt. (Note: "cueca" is the national folk dance of Chile.)

> The poor takes his gulp
> to get through the debts
> his tears or strikes
> can never repay.

While the lamed by birth's
dancing the cueca,
the blind with a wine-glass
sees flashes & sparks.

When you drink wine
with sincere inspiration
it's only to be compared
to the kiss of a maid.

Seated in the poet's den, warmed by an antique German stove, drinking
wine and listening to recordings of Chilean folk songs done by his very talented sister, I found the pleasure of the occasion heightened for me when I
suddenly read a most accurate self-portrait in one of Parra's early poems: "The
nose of a mulatto boxer / Over an Aztec idol's mouth." There is certainly nothing to take the place of being present oneself, but with this description by
the poet himself, perhaps the reader will feel some of what we felt, sitting in
the presence of this most extraordinary *chileno*.

The next writer with whom I became acquainted was Luis Domínguez,
whose enthusiasm for writing his own short stories in Spanish is matched by a
high regard for United States authors, particularly Poe and Hemingway. The
bizarre quality of the one and the lucidity of the other are fully evident in
Domínguez's own collection of stories, entitled *El extravagante*. Although
my not speaking Spanish had at times been a barrier, from the first few ideas
we got across to each other through Veronica Koch, a student translator and
journalist, we quickly moved to a fascinating discussion of modern literary
techniques, of Domínguez's interest in writing an art film, and of his book of
short stories, which he said is unified by the theme of distance between the
young and old. With all we were able to communicate through Veronica, no
telling what I could have learned had I only known the author's language.

It was at this time that our exchange group moved its base of operations
to Valparaíso and Viña del Mar. Here we were accused of being part of Plan
Camelot, a Defense Department sociological study of insurrection which was
uncovered by the Chileans and which consequently involved us in many heated
discussions since we were, in their eyes, representatives of the U.S. Government. On being faced with accusations of this sort, I generally attacked Pablo
Neruda for his Lorca-influenced romanticism—the state of poetry my only
counterweapon in the face of an endless talk of politics.

Richard Romo, UT's top track star, had been serving as translator for the
group as a whole and was keeping me in good humor with his one question
for all occasions—"But does it rhyme?" It was in Valparaíso that Richard
helped me really stir up a hornet's nest. Here I was asked what I thought of
Chilean poetry, and I followed up my response with a question as to the in-
terrogator's feelings about United States poetry. This local político-poet, who
asked me in the first place, replied that he only read poetry in Spanish, and on
hearing this, I confronted him, through Richard, with the very same charge

we had had constantly thrown at us: "Why don't you take an interest in our country?" I was quite happy that for once I helped catch the Chileans off-guard (we were placed on the spot so many times it became sickening), and particularly on a point that could be related to their own policy with regard to international relations. As it was not my aim, however, to antagonize the Chileans through poetry, I left the rest to Tony Pate, our chief political trou-bleshooter, and ended my part of the exchange by reciting in broken Spanish one of Neruda's poems, "Ode to Valparaíso." Only later did I discover that my reading had made an even stronger point against the students gathered there to attack us. Many of the listeners were very impressed by what they took to be a poem *I* had written about their city. Not only did they know little about United States poetry, they even failed to recognize an ode by their own celebrated Pablo Neruda!

Viña del Mar, the sister city to Valparaíso, is a famous resort center on the Pacific, and to a weary bunch of Texans it proved itself a true place of rest. There in Viña I spent an entire week at the home of Patricio Garrido, a con-cert pianist. Each night he played Beethoven, Bach, and Chopin to my heart's content. The Chilean students, who roomed there in Patricio's home, were all as absorbed as I was, and even though they can hear his music most any time, their pleasure in his playing never seemed to wane. Their delight in architec-ture was also brought to my attention during a stay that, with respect to accommodations as well as to companionship, was the most agreeable of my entire trip. Patricio's home, built atop a hill known as Cerro Castillo, is en-closed by a high wall (typical of most Chilean homes), within which are well-kept gardens. Next door is a nunnery. The students were often kidding one of their fellows, whose room adjoined a nun's, by asking him how his hole in the wall was coming along. Patricio, in addition to his love of music and phi-losophy, also takes great pleasure in vulgarity, and so he had me write down as many dirty English words as I could call to mind, after which he repeated them aloud to the extreme joy of all the males in attendance. One afternoon we found a stranded penguin, but then, that's another story.

All in all the week in Viña brought much-needed relief from the hectic pace in Santiago (population 2½ million) and made me for the first time wish for a much longer stay in Chile than the programmed month that was fast coming to a close. On returning to Santiago I received an invitation to drive up north and view country quite different from what we had seen up to that time. With permission from our accompanying professor, I crawled over the Instituto wall one morning around 4 a.m. and was picked up by the Domín-guez translator and three of her university friends.

Driving up through the mountains in Veronica's Citroen was a welcome change in more than one way, for up to that point I had gone by bus with the group, unable to see much of the landscape or to take a closer look when I saw something worth investigating. Too, it was such a pleasure to escape the city. All of this was made possible by means of private transportation, and our first stop took in a beach of black obsidian. On that and the following night we stayed in a *residencia* in La Serena. The lady who ran the home-

4

hotel remained rather puzzled by all my nodding and pointing. The Chileans had warned me against speaking English lest she charge us more on finding in me the proverbial rich gringo.

On the first morning we awoke to roosters and church bells, the whole nation celebrating its Independence Day, September 18. Driving inland we arrived at Vicuña, the town where Gabriela Mistral was born and is now buried. There we visited a museum which houses many of her manuscripts, photographs, statements by literary critics, and signatures of visitors like ourselves who have left their names in the guestbook. Mistral's first volume of poems (*Desolación*, 1923) was published here in the United States, and in 1945 she won the Nobel Prize for Literature, having spent her entire life teaching in a town known mostly for its "pisco," a type of clear brandy. Both her poetry and the pisco are comforts to a people who labor long and hard, rarely tasting more pleasure in life than what that numbing drink can bring, or the pride they can feel from knowing how beautifully she lived and wrote among them.

Indeed, Gabriela Mistral was a poet of their own earth, warm in only a woman's way. To see her in the photos lining those museum walls is to regret not having met her on the streets of her beloved Vicuña. Had she never written a single great poem, the light out of those Indian eyes would have been poetry enough to fill anyone's life with a living fire. Yet to walk her streets was to witness the Vicuña people still reflecting her presence from the past. Soon, however, another generation, unfamiliar with her face, will supplant those who knew her personal radiance. How good it is, then, that she has left in its place another glowing form: poetry, in which they and the world can always take comfort and find a renewing spark of inspiration.

For me the trip found its perfect conclusion when Veronica Koch signed her name in the museum guestbook and appended a line in Spanish to this effect: "Gabriela, I understand you better." Within one month's time a country is not to be discovered, especially if the visitor is unable to speak the language. And yet, because of the poets and friends who opened their hearts and welcomed us into their homes, I can gratefully say, Chile, I understand you better than I ever thought possible on arriving at your Santiago airport. And though I am still painfully aware of all I missed and misunderstood from not knowing your language, what you have told me, in spite of this, proves that you are ever ready to share your finest moments with those who would seek them in your life and in your letters. *¡Hasta bien luegito!*

Trilce / Arúspice / Tebaida

Chilean poetry, like Chilean democracy, has a long and distinguished history. Going back before the founding of the Republic of Chile (1818), back before even our own Plymouth Rock, Chile was the subject of one of the New World's few epic poems, Alonso de Ercilla's *La Araucana* (1569). In the 19th and early 20th centuries this narrow but lengthy land of 2,600 miles also produced its fair share of romantic and modernist poets. But perhaps more important was the fact that Chile had already by those times such a grand literary and libertarian tradition that she attracted to her capital two of probably South America's three most influential pre-World War II writers.

It was while living as a journalist in Santiago that Rubén Darío published in 1888 his first major work, *Azul*. Ciro Alegría, another visitor to Chile, having escaped from political oppression in his native Perú, brought out his first novel, *La serpiente de oro*, in 1935, winning a prize offered in Chile by a Santiago publisher. Chile's part in encouraging great art, including the work of her own authors, assured the nation from the beginning of a position as one of the literary leaders in the New World. And out of an interest in her neighbors has come Chile's awareness of and profit from the major literary movements of the Americas.

The other great South American writer already active prior to World War II was, of course, Chile's own Pablo Neruda, 1971 winner of the Nobel Prize for literature. Joining Neruda's during those years were two other internationally known Chilean names: Vicente Huidobro, the founder and practitioner in France of *creacionismo*, and the poetess Gabriela Mistral, who won the Nobel Prize for poetry in 1945. Much has been made of the impact of these three giants on the younger generations of Chilean poets, but what is more amazing is the variety and independence of these new poets, particularly in recent years. This should come, however, as no surprise in view of the brief history already outlined. For Chile continues to live up to her unique heritage as *vanguardista*. More than just to prove an indisputable point, then, I have gathered a sampling of today's younger Chilean poets, most of them under thirty. No Neruda, but plenty of what Nicanor Parra calls giving them apples when they ask for pears.

With the big news from Chile in 1970 the election of the socialist Dr. Salvador Allende as president, many feared a loss of freedom of speech and press, but Chile has for many years allowed the communist party to exist as a politi-

Introduction to special Chilean issue of *Road Apple Review*, vol. 4, no. 1 (spring 1972): 4-8.

cal force in her democratic government. This tradition of true freedom of choice, plus an economic situation common to most of the "underdeveloped" countries of the world, has made it both possible and inescapable for the poets of Chile to live in the 20th century in a way perhaps those of other nations have yet to suffer or enjoy. An openness to political themes, a maturity in terms of socio-economic awareness, has enabled Chilean poets to face many of today's problems significantly and to write about them for the benefit of the age. This has naturally brought their poetry into contact with propaganda, and even the finest of poets have failed to distinguish between the two. But the Chilean poet has not been "sullied" by rubbing shoulders with current affairs, has definitely grown from the experience. Witness, for example, Luis Moreno Pozo's ironic "Capitalist Prayer for Che," Raúl Bruna's witty "Public Man," Enrique Lihn's subtly probing "Revolution," or Omar Lara's reply to attacks on his humanity in "Upward."

In reading the new poetry, what is probably most striking to those conscious of Chile's political situation is the fact that, even though most of these poets are active in the Unidad Popular, the poems are *not* propagandistic, are *not* weighed down by broad social programs, by ranting and raving, but are preoccupied with the inner life of a people, with daily human relations, with dreams and memories, with coming to grips with the fundamental needs of each man, and are preeminently dedicated to poetry as a means of revelation and response. The craft of poetry is practiced after the grand manner of the Chilean tradition, yet the matter of these poets's work is as vital and original as that of their more famous predecessors.

Older poets collected here include Nicanor Parra, Enrique Lihn, Jorge Teillier, and Andrés Sabella. These men have influenced the younger poets of today more closely perhaps than has even Neruda. Parra and Lihn, for example, have introduced into Chilean poetry such modern tendencies as the Kafkaesque and the Freudian. Although these may not sound revolutionary, in the hands of these two artists the result has been a poetry uniquely Chilean, and by that I mean unlike earlier Chilean poetry as well as new to the contemporary poem. Humorous reaction to the world's hang-ups is a trademark of both Parra and Lihn. These two poets have become, both technically and spiritually, the guiding lights of the younger generation. Each in his own way has revolutionized Chilean poetry, and between them they have influenced the future of the nation's literature as much as have "the big three."

Parra's influence can be felt throughout this anthology, especially in the younger poets's ability to find the humor in situations, in their outbursts of reasoned cynicism, and above all in their attraction for the "antipoetic" in language and life. As to the other older poets, Teillier is a romantic, and although his followers may not openly identify themselves as such, his influence is to be found among those returning to contemplate the past, particularly those who share, as does Jaime Quezada, Teillier's southern upbringing, with its slower pace down among the rainy, forested areas of the land. Sabella is a northerner, and his equally poetic but less vegetative verse is typical of that desert region. A quiet artist, Sabella seems not to be so well known at home or abroad, yet to the northern poets—who represent here the real promise of things to come—Sabella is a very meaningful presence and a constant inspiration as they strive to create out of the literal wasteland that makes up the Chilean north.

In speaking of himself, Lihn, for many young poets "the master," has contrasted his own work with that of Parra and Neruda, using for the purpose one of his characteristic religious metaphors. Parra, he has said, believes in nothing. Neruda, on the other hand, has long been the faithful party man (in 1970 he ran as the presidential candidate for the Communist Party of Chile). While I, Lihn says, am the doubter. He wants to believe, but so often he finds it impossible. This is quite apparent in his poetry, which consists basically of a hardnosed attitude toward the very things in life obviously fundamental to his makeup: poetry and the past. His honesty of approach and his innovative formal designs force him into many dilemmas, but out of these he has constructed an exciting, penetrating new poetry. Lihn is definitely a poet whose stature deserves international recognition.

Among the younger poets, Gonzalo Millán, Oliver Welden, Omar Lara, and Cecilia Vicuña have achieved a directness and simple profundity rare for their years. The fine poet-critic Waldo Rojas first brought Millán to my attention, and when I asked if there were others like him, Waldo replied, "I assure you there are not even a few like Gonzalo." Welden's work, though it is often Parra-like in style, has a sound all its own: hard, yet very much in the big middle of the emotional wash. Omar Lara grows on me, and I have tried to include enough poems by this young poet that he may work his magic on more "gringo" readers. And Cecilia Vicuña, hers is a fresh voice certain to find welcome wherever she goes, or perhaps not, what with her wholly impious tone. Like the spirit of her work, she has wandered off to France or Siberia and left us only a small batch of her candid poems.

Which brings me to the title of this introduction. *Trilce / Arúspice / Tebaida* are the three Chilean poetry magazines in which the majority of these poems first appeared. Named for the 1922 volume of poems by the Peruvian, César Vallejo, certainly another of the greatest South American writers before 1940, *Trilce* is no longer publishing, nor is *Arúspice*, only *Tebaida* goes on, but fortunately the last of these is expanding rapidly and its quality and coverage improving with each issue. Under the editorship of the sensitive poetess Alicia Galaz, it has become *the* poetry magazine in Chile, presenting poems from both north and south as well as from the capital. Through these three little magazines, then, has come a worthy continuation of the work of Huidobro, Mistral, and Neruda. Without claiming too much for the poetry of this land of earthquake and copper, I think I may safely say that Chilean poems, like her wines, product of a nation of but nine million, can hold their own with the best.

Latin American Literature in Translation and the "Summer of '65"

Evidence of the variety and vitality of Latin American literature has come to light in recent years through a number of special issues of small and established magazines devoted to the work of Mexican, Central American, Caribbean, and South American authors, as well as through a dramatic increase in translations of novels, short story collections, essays, and single volumes and anthologies of poetry. In an effort to survey, measure, and weigh the import of this literary explosion, a special focus on Latin American literature in translation was conceived for *Margins* one year ago. Even since that time several new and important publications have appeared and still others are in preparation. So vast, indeed, is the range and significance of Latin American literature in this century that it was immediately apparent that the survey would have to be in some way limited. Essentially, then, the focus here is on special numbers of magazines, a restriction which is not so serious as it might seem, since the overview presented by magazines is in fact comprehensive and consequential.

The various reviewers involved in this special focus demonstrate through comparisons of magazine issues or simply through their own critical predispositions that there are revealing contrasts to be observed between numbers of magazines that center on the different geographical areas; that the avant-garde is active in Uruguay; that there are definite conflicts to be found between the influence of political ideologies and artistic traditions; and that both theory and practice are included in these very useful introductions to Latin American literature compiled by magazines old and new. Not to overlook the many magazines and their editors having long provided readers with translations of Latin American literature, though not necessarily in special numbers, I took it as my own task to offer a brief survey of some of these periodicals, particularly *The Seventies* (formerly *The Fifties* and *The Sixties*) and *The Pan American Review*. For very recent and forthcoming issues I have tried to provide as much information as was available at the time of writing. In addition to these items, I have also wanted to present a rather personal account of my own discovery of Latin American literature by way of my readings of a group of noteworthy magazines published in Latin America; by means of my awareness of the contribution of *Review* magazine as an outlet for criticism, interviews, translations, and news notes related to Latin American literature; and through my own reactions to translations of what I consider key publications in the field. Since it has been my responsibility to report in passsing on an assort-

Margins, nos. 21/22 (1975): 4-12.

ment of materials, many arriving at the eleventh hour, I beg the reader's indulgence for the often disjointed character of the essay.

What has turned out to be a longstanding involvement with Latin American literature began for me in 1965 with participation in an exchange program sponsored by the Universities of Texas and Chile and the U.S. State Department. The great irony about this exchange program, which changed my entire life, was that the idea for such an exchange between "student leaders" of U.S. and Latin American universities came reportedly from Richard Nixon. It is difficult to acknowledge that something so dear to me may be owing to a person for whose ideas I have had little but contempt. It seems that following his trip to Latin America in the fifties, when his car was stoned in Venezuela, Nixon returned to the States and proposed some type of program to help improve relations between the two Americas. What his ulterior motive may have been is perhaps another question, for revenge has long prompted his every move. In any event, fate would have it that the "Summer of '65" proved to be a preview for me of coming Latin American attractions. The main feature at that time was Chile, starring Miller Williams as translator and Nicanor Parra as anti-poet *par excellence*, and with a cast of major and little magazines in their perennial supporting role.

Knowing I would be visiting Chile, I read with great interest that summer of 1965 a special section of *Motive* magazine (a publication of the Methodist Church concerned with literary and social issues). The February 1965 issue of the magazine (vol. 25, no. 5) was edited by Miller Williams, who introduced a selection of Chilean poems with an essay entitled "Poetry and Politics in Chile." Among the poets represented in lively translations by Williams was Nicanor Parra, whose antipoems, full of profound trivialities, have been influential on a number of poets in nearly every Latin American nation:

> I've had it with God and the Devil
> How much is that pair of pants
>
> There are no girls left to rape
> The danger is in being sincere
> I'll do anything to make a buck
> Between the breast and the back is an abyss
>
> We deliver ham to your home
> Can you tell the time by flowers
>
> I dedicate myself to a slow yawn
> And the fuchsia looks like a ballerina

> (from "The Shuffled Deck,"
> *Poems and Antipoems*,
> New Directions, 1966)

Miller Williams, a fine poet himself, subsequently published *Chile: An Anthology of New Writing* (Kent State University Press, 1968), which incorporated his own translations of Chilean poetry, short stories translated by other contributors, and an interview by Williams with Parra (the interview having appeared originally in *Shenandoah*, Vol. 18, No. 1). Williams' many translations have been seen in numerous magazines, including the *Chicago Review* and *Prairie Schooner*, both of which have often offered translations of Latin American authors. It was in the *Prairie Schooner* (Vol. 39, No. 2), again for the summer of '65, that Miller Williams conributed to a special section entitled "Latin America and Spain: A Portfolio," which included articles and translations by various authors: "The Contemporary Latin American Theatre" by Carlos Solorzano; "Marginal Notes on the Twentieth-Century Spanish American Novel" by Roberto Esquenazi-Mayo; "Paraguay: A New Climate" by Bruce Cutler; poems by Vallejo translated by Clayton Eshleman; and other poems and essays in translation. Among Williams' contributions was a romantic poem he translated from the Spanish of Jorge Teillier, one of that Chilean poet's works which has long been a favorite of mine. Here is the last stanza of Teillier's "To A Boy In A Tree":

> The storekeeper goes out to close the shutters.
> The daughters of the farmer put the chicken to roost.
> Eyes of strange fish
> look menacingly out of the sky.
> You have to come down.
> Your dog comes jumping to meet you.
> Your island crumbles into the tide of night.

From my reading of Miller Williams' translations and his editorial work I gained a glorious sense of the Chilean tradition, with the result that ten years later I would complete a comparative dissertation involving two poets of Chile, Parra and Enrique Lihn (whose poem "Rooster" appeared in the same issue of the *Prairie Schooner* in a brilliant translation by Miller Williams), and two poets of the United States, William Carlos Williams and Robert Lowell.

Without being able to recall whether or not the *Motive* issue actually came first in the history of my knowledge of Parra, there was certainly another publication, *New World Writing* No. 14 (1958), where a translation by William Carlos Williams of one of Parra's antipoems, "Piano Solo," very early caught my eye. This 1958 collection also printed a special section of "New Writing from Latin America," edited by José Vásquez-Amaral. The selection included poems by Neruda, Silvina Ocampo, Parra, and a number of other outstanding authors. This and the Miller Williams' *Motive* selection for February 1965, as well as the *Prairie Schooner* issue for the summer of '65, antedate the August 1965 appearance of the heralded special Latin American issue from *Encounter* (reviewed elsewhere by Thomas Hoeksema), the *New World Writing* section even preceding the 1959 takeover by Castro, which some mark as the moment when North Americans recognized Latin America's political *and* artistic independence. There is no doubt that since 1959 a true explosion has taken place in the availability of translations of significant works from Latin America and the consequent awareness by United States readers of the originality and exuberance of such writing. To me, however, it is still 1965 that seems the watershed year, not 1959, since it was then that I myself first discovered Latin America and because then as ever it was the small magazines which had such a large hand in the growing attention that was brought to bear on the nature and measure of Latin American literature. For this reason I especially wish to credit here the major role of magazines, in an essay written, in a way, to celebrate the tenth anniversary of that fateful "summer of '65."

While teaching in Chile in 1966, having returned there on my own after the one-month exchange program had ended, I learned firsthand of the very active literary scene which was nurtured by such a magazine as *Orfeo* in Santiago. Listed in the back of this periodical containing original work by Lihn, Teillier, and many young and aspiring poets, as well as translations from languages as diverse as Swedish and Quechua, I found the names and addresses of the leading little magazines in Chile and other Latin American countries: *El pez y la serpiente* (Nicaragua); *Mediodía* (Argentina); *El corno emplumado* (Mexico); *Diagonal cero* (Argentina); *Pájaro cascabel* (Mexico); *Espiral* (Colombia); *Casas de las Américas* (Cuba); *Eco* (Colombia); *Trilce* (Chile); *Arúspice* (Chile); *Cauce* (Chile); *Arte y rebelión* (Argentina); and *Mester* (Mexico). Regrettably most of these magazines, including *Orfeo*, are now extinct, yet their impact continues, as will be seen by later references to several of these publications and the authors associated with them.

On returning from Chile in 1967, my wife and I stopped in Mexico City and, on visiting the University's bookstore, we ran onto copies of *Mundo Nuevo* (Paris), edited by Emir Rodríguez Monegal of Uruguay. This important publication went out of business in 1971 but the editor is presently associated with *Mundo Nuevo*'s English language equivalent, *Review* (Center for Inter-American Relations, an organization with offices in New York City). Subsequently I will have more to say on *Mundo Nuevo* and *Review*.

Settled in New Mexico, I subscribed to both *El corno emplumado* and *Mundo Nuevo*. It was especially through the former—a truly seminal publication—that I first became aware of poets whose works have since rocketed them into recognition as some of the brightest stars in the Latin American renascence: Miguel Barnet and Nicolás Guillén. of Cuba; Ernesto Cardenal of Nicaragua; Roque Dalton of El Salvador; and any number of poets from Chile, Argentina, and Mexico. The most striking thing about this extraordinary magazine was that it was abreast of the finest poetry throughout the world, not alone of Latin America. Edited by Sergio Mondragón and Margaret Randall, *El corno emplumado* went under too, once Margaret Randall moved to Cuba, where she now resides. Some of Ms. Randall's work is currently available from New Directions in a collection entitled *Part of the Solution: Portrait of a Revolutionary*. (See also Ernesto Cardenal's essay, "Shopping with Margaret Randall," in his *In Cuba*, New Directions, 1974, with the English version done by a top-notch translator, Donald Walsh.) Randall's best poetry has appeared in many publications, from *Road Apple Review* to *Poetry*, as well as in *El corno emplumado*. *Poetry* for January 1968 printed several selections from one of her characteristic pieces, a poem on Cuba entitled "So Many Rooms Has A House But One Roof":

> at the level of arches, columns
> framed in mahogany, pieces of sky
> a gull floats
> moves his wide wings towards poets
> we
> are sitting with cut glass, the colors
> of sea
> these blues and greens invade, belong
> to us
> as once belonged to dupont or
> (as i prefer to think)
> never belonged but built by him
> preparing for a change of colors he refused
> could not have held in hand
>
> or eye.

Even before my discovery of *Mundo Nuevo* and *El corno emplumado*, it was an acquaintance with Carlos Cortínez of Valdivia (Chile) which led to a number of my own translation projects, all owing to what became a lasting friendship with this energetic poet-critic. At the time that I first met Cortínez, in 1966, he was a regular contributor to *Trilce*, and in conjunction with the editor of that magazine, Omar Lara, Cortínez prepared a collection of important essays and poems entitled *Poesía chilena (1960-1965)*. In 1968 Cortínez traveled to Iowa and entered the International Writers' Workshop; the following year he guest-edited a special number of *Micromegas* (vol. 3, no. 3), a translation magazine in Iowa City founded by Frederic Will. This special number was devoted, quite naturally, to Chilean poetry, and as a friend I was invited to contribute, publishing there my first translations in a U.S. magazine, including, of course, a poem by Parra, but also a new one by Neruda which I had just seen in *Ercilla* (Santiago) and which I have yet to see collected anywhere else:

> Along Point Thunder I walked
> taking the salt in my face
> and from the sea, in my mouth,
> the hurricane of its heart:
> I saw it rage as far as the horizon,
> biting and spitting at the sky.
> In every gust it carried
> the armaments of war,

all the tears of the world
and a train loaded down with lions,
yet not even this was enough
as it demolished all it had made,
casting down on the rocks
a cold cold rain of statues.
O firmament of the reverse,
o boiling stars of water,
o tidal wave of rencor,
I said, looking long at the beauty
of all the unruly sea
in a pitched battle
against my nation
wracked by inexorable fear
and sinister designs of the foam.

(from "Data for the Tidal Wave of July 25")

Moving that same year of 1969 to Illinois, I became a contributor to *Road Apple Review* of Oshkosh, Wisconsin, edited by another friend, Douglas Flaherty. To make a long story longer, in 1971 I returned to Chile with the idea of putting together my own anthology of Chilean poetry, which *Road Apple Review* would offer the next year as a special number (vol. 4, no. 1). I mention all of this for several reasons. For one, I have not had these two special issues from *Micromegas* and *Road Apple* reviewed here (the *RAR* number having already been treated at length in *Review* 73, no. 9). Although both anthologies are part of the small magazine effort to develop an audience for Latin American literature, they are perhaps more interesting to me than to readers concerned with the larger picture, not just with the scene in Chile, and yet I would not want to slight the magazines which have furnished the space for showcasing what I consider some of the finest poetry in all Latin America. A further reason is that my awareness of other magazines, groups, and individual writers came about as a result of translating for *Micromegas* and *Road Apple Review*, and again I have them to thank for much of what I know of Latin American literature.

Let me say on behalf of my own anthology and that of Cortínez that finally the two collections are not very similar, since the Cortínez and my own print essentially different poets, with mine giving more space to most poets and collecting 65 poems by 22 poets as compared to only 27 poems by 20 poets in the *Micromegas* selection. Also, the emphasis in the *Road Apple Review* anthology is on a younger set of poets and includes usually only their most recent work, whereas Cortínez gives half his pages to four older poets, many of whose poems are available in translation elsewhere. As to the introductions to the two collections, I must admit to envy of Carlos's relaxed yet highly perceptive style:

Every anthology is capricious. Agreed. But the most capricious is the one that ignores the promise of its preface. Another is to honor it. . . . The authors chosen are in good health, except for a few of the illustrious dead. . . . Also left out, believe me, are pleiades of the forgotten-forgotten. For them, a moment of silent memory.

The fact that so many differing anthologies of Chilean poetry have appeared attests to the grand tradition of the land of Mistral, Huidobro, and Neruda.

At the very last minute another special Latin American issue arrived from *Micromegas* (vol. 6, no. 2), guest-edited by Carlee Lippman, who has done all the translations, except for a number credited to the team of Fred Will (editor of *Micromegas*, now at home in the Comparative Literature Dept. of the Univ. of Massachusetts, Amherst, Mass. 01002) and Fernando Arbelaez. The brief but cogent introduction by Lippman strikes this keynote for any authentic collection of Latin American poetry:

> Outwash waves of literary "ismos" have passed over Latin-America with almost the rapidity of her revolutionary leaders. Of more recent national consciousness than many fellow language-producing areas, she has had to go through her own ontogeny-recapitulates-phylogeny with unseemly haste, the unlikely result of which is a poetry taut and fermenting with creative desperation. . . . Desperation and felt solitude do indeed describe a broad swatch of Latin-American poetry.

The poems translated by Will and Arbelaez seem more preoccupied with apocalypse, which perhaps indicates those translators' basic taste for what Lippman refers to as the "desperation" side of Latin American poetry. Lippman's translations, on the other hand, emphasize the side of "solitude."

Ernesto Cardenal's "Apocalypse," an excerpt from which is presented by Will and Arbelaez, re-creates a contemporary Fall of Babylon with overtones of Revelations:

> and the angel said to me: those heads that you see on the Beast are
>   dictators
> and its horns are revolutionary leaders not yet dictators
> but who will be
> and they will fight against the Lamb and the Lamb will defeat them

The Colombian poet, Alvaro Mutis, also presents a type of apocalypse in "The Elements of Disaster," a prose poem in 12 sections. The "prophetic treasures" rise from the poet's contemplation of such items as coffins, coffee plantations, clouds, and muddy rivers. The style suggests the tropics, rich in "plants with soft trunks and leaves of silver down." The issue ends with a poem by Mutis "filled with the first signs of change."

Lippman's presentation of the theme of solitude encompasses poems by representative poets of Chile, Peru, Ecuador, Cuba, Nicaragua, Colombia, and Venezuela. Jorge Carrera Andrade of Ecuador seems to sum up this aspect of Latin American poetry in his "Solitude of Cities." The poet notes the effects of time on the solitary and despairs in the face of clocks:

> Everything has been invented,
> but there's nothing to deal with solitude.

In seeking some cure for solitude, Carrera Andrade and several other of these poets find that nature offers a certain solace:

> Peasants are less alone,
> being one with the earth.

> . . . The sanctity of small animals is a model.

Nature is also celebrated by Chile's Juvencio Valle à la Whitman and Neruda, while Peru's Carlos Germán Belli wishes to disappear "between the paws of very small animals." Cintio Vitier of Cuba finds that writing itself is a type of cure, that a pencil's "simple wood and noble carbon" make "loneliness fortunate." Joaquín Pasos of Nicaragua favors getting back "to the virginal tenderness of youth," but his sort of poetic lapse is extremely rare here, for the collection achieves a meaningful and even haunting struggle with desperation and solitude.

Alvaro Mutis makes an intriguing commentary on the inclination among Latin American poets for the "slow, minute retelling of strange accidents and memorable crimes," which may also be something of a cure for solitude. He goes on to describe the effect of this retelling as one of "dull silence that extends over their voices, like a gray carpet of boredom," but the result of these memories, he adds, has been "cause of an unforgettable vigil." In some ways this collection may sound "like a gray carpet of boredom" in its gathering of so many poems on solitude. On the contrary, the poets who have worked the fertile soil of this one theme have produced an amazing range of stylistic, imagistic, and philosophical flora and fauna of a New World variety. Rather than boring, their poems are certain to wake any drowsy Emperor, Imperialist, or Bolshevik. The selections and translations are stimulating, and Lippman, Will, and Arbelaez are to be commended on a superb job.

In 1971, just before my third trip to Chile, I discovered in *Mundo Nuevo*, for February of the same year, a selection of poems by seven poets from the north of Chile, members of *Grupo "Tebaida,"* their name taken from a magazine of the same title. Arriving in Santiago I immediately made arrangements to travel to Arica, a city near the Peruvian border and home base for *Tebaida*, with the object of collecting poems and meeting the magazine's editors, Alicia Galaz and Oliver Welden. After a week in Arica I was convinced that just with the fine work of *Grupo "Tebaida"* I had the nucleus for an exciting new anthology, so that out of the trip to Arica grew the special issue of *Road Apple Review*. At that time, the first year of Allende's government, *Tebaida* was the only remaining little magazine in Chile, and its existence had been fostered in part by Allende's socialist climate, yet *Tebaida* was dedicated to the revolution of beauty as much as it was to one of bread.

It is certainly difficult for a naive political observer like myself to account for Chile's combination of art and revolution, but as early as my first visit to the country in the summer of '65 I sensed that the nation, under President Eduardo Frei, was experiencing a new hope for justice and peaceful change. Many North American intellectuals seemed to consider Chile the last chance for a political solution to the continent's economic problems, as did many of the moderates among Latin American nations. It was during Frei's administration that Chile gained a controlling interest (51%) of her copper mines and that school and land reforms began. But the obstacles set up by conservatives of his own Social Democratic Party, plus those erected by leftists jealous that Frei was achieving without violence what they advocated through overthrow of the government, soon slowed the Frei effort to a frustrating standstill (with the leftists charging all along that Frei wasn't going fast enough!). Nonetheless, it appears to me that the stimulus for much of the literary-revolutionary activity, pro-and-con Frei, dates from the first years of Frei's administration: 1964 and 1965. (See Enrique Lihn's "Defeat," a poem expressing that poet's feelings after Allende lost to Frei in the presidential election of 1964.) By 1971 things were already so horribly polarized that even kin were no longer working together but belligerently against one another. Despite the overheated atmosphere, *Tebaida* continued as a sane magazine of quality art and passionate social concern.

One of the most astonishing facts about this magazine was that it thrived far from the capital and the intellectual nourishment of such a cultural center as Santiago—separated from it by almost 1,500 miles and the second worst desert in the world. And yet this has not been unusual in Chile, since both *Trilce* and *Arúspice*, two of the major little magazines in the country, were edited from the provinces, *Trilce* carrying on its lifespan of some 20 issues in the remote southern city of Valdivia. Just as New York is no longer the focal point of poetic activity in this country, so Chile's most significant movements in recent years have sprung up in less populated areas. There is certainly a lesson here for writers in the U.S. who would seek to make their art and display it despite their distance from the metropolis or their being isolated from established magazines.

Sometime in 1970 another important publication had come to my attention. In that year I saw the first issue of *Review* (1969), a magazine published by the Center for Inter-American Relations in New York City and intended originally as simply an annual compilation of book reviews on Latin American literature reprinted from newspapers and magazines. (For those interested in seeing this publication, check library holdings under Center for Inter-American Relations.) By the time *Road Apple Review* had issued my Chilean anthology in the spring of 1972, *Review* had grown to a quarterly magazine featuring not only book reviews but full-length articles on authors or single works, with whole issues being devoted to individual authors (Borges, Cortázar, Lezama Lima, etc.), works in translation, interviews (an especially valuable one by Patricio Lerzundi with Nicanor Parra in nos. 4-5), and useful news notes on events and publications of interest to readers of Latin American literature. The editor, Ronald Christ, a noted translator and critic of the work of Jorge Luis Borges, has been joined since 1971 by Emir Rodríguez Monegal in the capacity of contributing editor. With publication of the *Road Apple* anthology I sent a copy to *Review*, not really expecting such a modest production to be noticed by the editors, who were obviously going "Big Time." To my surprise and delight, editor Christ replied immediately to say that the anthology would be reviewed and that he was happy to know of its existence. Almost nine months later the review came out, along with five others of books from L.S.U. Press, E.P. Dutton, MacMillan, Black Orpheus, and Africana. Not only was *Road Apple Review*'s $1.00 offset issue treated as seriously as the $6.95 offering from E.P. Dutton, the Chilean anthology was given more space and a more favorable review. This was naturally gratifying to me personally but seemed to indicate as well that *Review* magazine was definitely more concerned with content than with cost, an attitude which is surely encouraging to any worker in the small press movement.

While in Washington, D.C. that same spring of 1972, preparing for a return trip to Chile on a Fulbright—an appointment I had to decline at the last moment—I came upon a copy of the first issue of still another magazine featuring Latin American writing: issue number one of *The Pan American Review* (winter 1970-71) from Edinburg, Texas, edited by one of the present contributors, Seth Wade. This first number features in part three selections of translated poems, one by poets from Chile, a second by poets from Mexico and Guatemala, and a third with poems from the Nahuatl, as well as an essay by Hugh Fox, the Latin Americanist, on an Argentinian graphics experimentalist, Edgardo Antonio Vigo. *The Pan American Review* has continued to feature translations of works by Latin American authors, has been beautifully designed, and the quality of the poetry is extremely high, in both original English and translated forms. In the first issue, which is the only number in my possession, Wade himself contributes several fine translations from Vicente Huidobro's *Crosswinds* and John Igo renders Miguel Angel Asturias' "The Indians Come Down From Mixco" with a marvelous sound. Here is the opening stanza of the latter:

The Indians come down from Mixco
Burdened with dark blue
And the city receives them
Into its frightened streets
With a fistful of lights
That like stars are doused
With the coming of dawn.

In addition to the work of these two Texas translators, the issue contains examples of those inspiring efforts of the Bly-Wright translating team. Here is a characteristic earthy and expansive passage from Neruda, a poet championed by Bly and Wright since at least as early as *The Fifties*:

> I walk through afternoons, I arrive
> full of mud and death,
> dragging along the earth and its roots,
> and its indistinct stomach in which corpses
> are sleeping with wheat,
> metals, and pushed-over elephants.

(from "Melancholy Inside Families")

Perhaps the only unfortunate thing about the inclusion of the Neruda is that the translations are reprinted from a 1967 Sixties Press book, *Pablo Neruda: Twenty Poems*. Too often in magazines and anthologies we are offered the same staple fare—somewhat the case with the special issue of *Nimrod*, also reviewed here. On the other hand, good men like Neruda and Cardenal deserve the widest distribution, and just as it is never quite an imposition to have a Bly-Wright version of Neruda, it is quite forgivable to find in *Nimrod* Ronald Christ's translation of Ernesto Cardenal's most famous poem, "Prayer for Marilyn Monroe." Sample, then, Christ's translation of Cardenal, a passage referring to Marilyn Monroe's search for God:

> The movie ended without the final kiss.
> She was found dead in her bed, her hand on the phone
> And the detectives couldn't find out who she was going to call.
> She was
> like someone who has dialed the only friendly voice
> and hears just a recorded voice telling her: WRONG NUMBER.
> Or like someone wounded by gangsters
> who reaches for a disconnected telephone.

The credit due Robert Bly for his introduction of Neruda and Vallejo to U.S. readers is great indeed. However, rather than trace Bly's contributions almost as far back as the time of H.R. Hays' pioneering *Anthology of Contemporary Latin American Poetry* (New Directions, 1947), I prefer to cite simply the first number of *The Seventies* (1972) in which Bly's discussions of the "Spanish Leaping" poetry of Machado, Neruda, Lorca, and Vallejo, along with his translations of Lorca and Vallejo, signal the continuing battle he is waging, with the arms of these allies, against what he takes to be hypocrisy and wrongheadedness in American poetry:

> American poetry faltered in the 40's and 50's: we can make a generalization: if the Americans do not have European poets to refresh

their sense of what association is, their work soon falls back to the boring associative tracks that so many followed through the *Kenyon Review* times and the dull political landscapes of the *Partisan Review.* The American poets are now turning to Lorca, Vallejo, and Neruda for help.

Whether Bly's theories are always right or not, he has certainly rendered an invaluable service to American readers by making them aware, in excellent translations, of the universal qualities of poetry in Spanish. At times it is perhaps difficult to take Bly seriously, but never those he translates so in earnest.

One magazine which has followed Bly's lead in including translations of Vallejo, in particular, is *American Poetry Review* (vol. 1, no. 1). The publication of selections from Vallejo's prose statements on poetry seems to me a real plus for this magazine. In what appear to be wonderfully natural translations, David Smith reveals to us the sound theory upon which Vallejo founded his moving poems and also the reason for his departure from the Rubén Darío modernist school:

> The new poetry based on words and metaphors is distinguished by its pedantic novelty and, as a result, by its complication and baroque style. The new poetry based on new feeling is, on the contrary, simple and human and at first sight one might take it for old or not notice if it is modern or not.

Again, it is typical of new magazines to resort to big names for the sake of borrowed prestige, but it is wholly justified when a work like this is even difficult to come by in the original.

To help me make this special focus on Latin American literature in translation as inclusive as possible, *Margins* advertised for pertinent materials, especially magazine issues featuring the work of Latin American authors. Only one magazine responded, however, and this was *Poema Convidado*, published by Backstage Books / P.O. Box 1105 / Bloomington, Indiana. Along with issue number four of *PC* the publishers submitted two books of poems in Portuguese by Teresinka Alves Pereira, *Torre de mitos* (1973) and *El amor de los narcisos* (1974), as well as *Anti-Poem For Christmas and Other Non-Christmas Poems* (1974), translated by Russell Tarby. Since I do not know Portuguese except by way of Spanish, I asked two persons knowledgeable in the field to do reviews of these items. A lack of time prevented them from accommodating me, but they did inform me that Ms. Pereira is an established critic and poet now living in this country. My own impression of these works is certainly based on no more than reactions to titles and the English translations, but I offer them nonetheless. The collection translated by Tarby presents little in English to attract a reader of truly contemporary taste, despite the apparent influence of Nicanor Parra. As for the titles of the other two books, *Tower of Myths* and *The Love of the Narcissists* (if I am translating accurately—the words seemingly Spanish rather than Portuguese, since *de los* usually appears as *dos*, at least in de Andrade), these strike me as dated and indicative of a rather traditional inclination. Enough said. What I think should be noted about modern Brazilian poetry in translation is that it is available in at least three important collections, which are Mario de Andrade's *Hallucinated Cities* (1968), a bilingual edition with English versions by Jack E. Tomlins published by Vanderbilt University Press, Giovanni Pontiero's *An Anthology of Brazilian Modernist Poetry* (1969), a text in Portuguese but with a fine introduction in English, published by Pergamon Press, and *An Anthology of Twentieth-Century Brazilian Poetry* (1972), edited by Elizabeth Bishop and Emanuel Brasil, published by Wesleyan University Press.

According to most commentators on Brazilian art of this century, the Week of Modern Art held in February of 1922 in Sao Paulo marks the beginning of Brazil's most significant literary event. Out of this celebration emerged two of Brazil's foremost artists, the composer Heitor Villa-Lobos and the poet Mario de Andrade. The latter published in July of that year his *Hallucinated Cities*, a work which could be profitably compared with Vicente Huidobro's publications of the same epoch and William Carlos Williams' *Kora in Hell* (1920). De Andrade's collection of poems bursts with energy, humor, Brazilian life, and is experimental in the best sense of the word:

> My Madness, be calm!
> Put on your raincoat of alsos!
> * * * *
> There is no terminal on the hill of ambitions.
> * * * *
> Sao Paulo—the great mouth with a thousand teeth;
> and amidst the trifid tongue the torrents
> of pus and more pus of distinction. . . .

All of this and much more is preceded by de Andrade's "Extremely Interesting Preface":

> Reader:
> Hallucinism has been launched.
> This preface—although interesting—useless.
> * * * *
> The Brazilian language is one of the richest and most sonorous.
> * * * *
> You will easily note that if grammar is sometimes scorned in my poetry, it does not suffer serious insults in this extremely interesting preface. Preface: skyrocket of my higher self. The poems: landscape of my deeper self.

Mario de Andrade is an equal among the best of the New World's poets who have created a localist literature under the universalizing influences of Surrealism, Dada, *modernismo*, and an awareness that to write modern poetry in the truest sense is simply to weep, sing, pray, bellow, scorn, suffer, and forgive.

As perhaps *the* international translation magazine in this country, *Mundus Artium* has a long and distinguished record for service to Latin American literature. Its latest addition (vol. 8, no. 1, 1975) offers a Central American selection which brings to a total of four the number of its special issues on Latin American writing, with the other three numbers reviewed elsewhere in this focus on L.A. literature in translation. An admirable feature of this latest issue, as well as of the earlier selections, is the fact that the editor has chosen to emphasize younger and less well-known poets of the six Central American countries of Guatemala, El Salvador, Honduras, Nicaragua, Costa Rica, and Panama. Conspicuously absent is Ernesto Cardenal, but as the editor, Rainer Schulte, rightly explains, Cardenal "has already been published in book form in English. Furthermore, his poetry is dominated by a rather strong social and political didacticism which would have made it difficult to include him within the frame of the present anthology." While I agree that Cardenal does not fit in with the writers here who "have written poems that can be understood and enjoyed without any historical or political orientation," I do find that my own taste runs toward poets who can give me a larger canvas and that the perfect image does not endure so well as the image within a full-bodied context. Setting aside that prejudice I can report, very briefly, since this issue arrived at the last minute, on a number of quite interesting poems in altogether superior translations.

Oscar Acosta of Honduras is represented by three poems translated by Harry Haskell, with the original, as ever in *MA* for poetry, on a facing page. Two of Acosta's pieces are similar in structure and theme, "Oblivion" and "Memories," where the poet defines these mental states by means of extended metaphors:

> Oblivion is a tunnel that slowly opens
> to the very heart of the universe.
> ... To an unknown country from which we can never return.
>
> * * *
>
> Memories are children that insist on surrounding us,
> insist we speak and narrate lost histories,
> insist we extract the heart from our chest
> like a red apple that we divide on the table
> which they share and devour patiently.

The translations flow smoothly and naturally, as do the originals.

Mauricio Marquina of El Salvador is represented by unpunctuated poems, in long run-on lines that remind me of Enrique Lihn, though without the Chilean's irony, urgency, and pointedness. A number of the other poets here have also written the prose poem, a mode Lihn has perfected in *Escrito en Cuba*. I wonder how well Marquina and the other Central Americans know the Chilean's work. (The younger Marquina, born in 1946—Lihn in 1929, published his first and only book to date in 1969 at an especially significant point in Lihn's production.) Marquina mostly lacks the Chilean's ability to create the sense of a person behind the narrative who is conscious of his own struggles and failures and who does not put them off on others or rationalize them in terms of some imagined superiority to the general system of hell:

> Some had been condemned for being innocent and they were in the majority; others, for having been naked during the religious services.

In this poem dealing with childhood, a favorite theme with Lihn as well, the voice is as talky as Lihn's but fails to achieve the latter's convincing conflict between the meaning the child would seek and that accepted by his fellows:

> By that time I had stopped believing in everything. Some in my underground generation continue to employ, since that night as their only weapon, irony against things. . . .

> (from "Childhood Dream")

Here, as elsewhere, the translation is somewhat stilted.

It is perhaps unfair to compare Lihn with Marquina, but surely it is more to the point to study Latin American poets in this way than to continue simply piling up more and more poems without attempting to understand how and why certain artists have developed a truly sophisticated level of achievement. *Mundus Artium* seems to me to furnish us with an opportunity for comparison as a way of appreciating the best that is coming out of Latin America today. After much proof of the high level of performance, the time has now come to evaluate more fully the peculiar contributions of a poet like Lihn. Prose fiction has already begun to receive this sort of attention, but poetry has yet to enjoy the same careful analysis.

Also of note in this issue of *MA* are Donald Walsh's translations of two poets whose styles are quite distinct—José Mejía González of Guatemala and Roberto Fernández Iglesias of Panama. Walsh handles both poets masterfully:

> Suddenly everything stops.
> Nothing is earthquake or outcry.
> She, the dancer, will spin in space
> with her watery gaze.
> With her wings of quicksilver,
> her dress of music,
> her earthquake house,
> the mysterious key of her blazing blood,
> her skirt of mirrors,
> her moaning ankles,

her geometry of wounded crystal
bleeding simple truths and distant music.

(from González's "Igneous Poems")

He felt strong
emaciatedly solid
until it happened:
that
    long
       instant
of the breaking off
of the first leaf
       that
          is still
falling

(Iglesias's "Untitled")

In addition to many curious and entertaining poems, the photos and art work in each issue of *Mundus Artium* always provide fascinating and original perspectives. One piece by Fernando Corel Duenas of Ecuador shows a hand growing from rippled earth or piles of fallen leaves, reaching to touch on the horizon an eye that is watching the outstretched fingers. A short story by Horacio Quiroga of Uruguay raises a question as to the fate of Rubén Darío's prose heritage in his native Central America, especially since no Central American short stories appear in either this issue or in the special prose fiction number of *MA* reviewed here consummately by Edward Aylward. In any event, Rainer Schulte is to be commended for another fine job of presenting contemporary Latin American literature in professional and sensitive translations.

In preparing this survey of magazines featuring Latin American literature in translation I have come across a number of special or related issues of magazines which are in the making. For one, Paul Foreman of Thorp Springs Press has announced that his magazine, *Hyperion*, will publish "a double issue of translations of world poetry from many cultures and many ages." Included will be work by both Spanish peninsular and Latin American poets. Although I have seen no official announcement, I have received word that the *Chicago Review* is planning a special Latin American issue for fall 1975. There will be non-fiction articles on poetry, poems, and graphics. Nothing is definite but it promises to be a substantial selection, with good representation from Brazil. Distinguished critic Ricardo Gullón is to introduce the issue. Robert Márquez of Hampshire College, who edited the special number of the *Massachusetts Review* discussed elsewhere in the present *Margins*, is inaugurating a regular magazine entitled *Caliban*, which will emphasize Third World literature and especially work from the Caribbean.

As a transition from magazines to single volumes of poems, I next want to discuss the work of a young Mexican poet, Carlos Isla, a group of whose poems have just appeared in Robert Bonazzi's *Survivors of the Invention* (Latitudes Press, 1974). The title for this anthology of eight poets is taken from a line by Isla, and the idea behind the collection is that it will be the first in an on-going series of anthologies of "not-often-published poets," although, as the editor admits, by now most, including Isla, have been seen in various little magazines and even in book form.

Isla seems to me a poet closer to the Simic-Strand-Matthews school than to his fellow poets in Latin America. However, this may be another example of a lack of understanding as to what *is* happening in Mexico at this moment, since all of Isla's poems in the Latitudes book appeared originally in Mexican periodicals. (Incidentally, Mark Strand edited and contributed a number of translations to Octavio Paz's *New Poetry of Mexico*, E.P. Dutton, 1970.) One of Isla's pieces coincides perfectly with the editor's note telling of the Mexican's interest in photography. In fact, most of Isla's poems share the imagist angle by way of the New York poets' focus on either fun or a type of Robbe-Grillet close-up of a view from a city window:

> At the foot of this page
> sun has licked the snow
> from most rooftops
> It's a July afternoon in Mexico
> except here
> moist solitudes have no smell
>
> At the foot of these letters
> I write decrepit pauses
>
> (from "Polaroid")

Isla's work, more than anything, reminds me of a type of writing Karl Elder has termed "poetic naturalism" (see *Margins* no. 12) in reference to an approach "which serves to draw the reader into the poem by either directly or indirectly addressing him." This is particularly true of Isla's "ABC":

> 1)
> From this page
> two eyes
> spy on you
> and perhaps
> a hidden microphone
>
> 2)
> I am deliberate
> as I write: Can you confess
> my motives to yourself?

3)
These findings depend
upon which side of the bed
you got up on

2)
The meaning of these few words has taken a holiday

1)
My typewriter
is an enchanted princess

These are intriguing pieces, but rather than "confess my motives" I can only say that ultimately I prefer my Latin American poems to give me more of a feeling for the psychological and moral terrain of the Latin experience, although this may be to disregard the role of art as a universal medium. At any rate, I leave Isla and move now to a consideration of two single volumes which to me are peculiarly "Latin American" in the most difficult and yet most revealing sense of that phrase.

In 1969 Lillabulero Press brought out a collection of 25 poems by Enrique Lihn, *This Endless Malice*, translated by William Witherup and Serge Echeverría. This bilingual edition presents the full range of Lihn's early work, though it does not cover his more recent and very significant development in *Escrito en Cuba* or in *La musiquilla de las pobres esferas*, which is understandable since these two 1969 volumes were appearing in Spanish simultaneously with the Lillabulero book. Nevertheless, this fine collection offers a sound basis for appreciating the very serious, religio-political quality of Enrique Lihn's sensibility. Modern in the realest purport of the word, Lihn's work deals with psychological states, political neuroses (he is a type of questioning communist), and love. Outside of Neruda, Lihn is one of the few poets in Latin America who has written convincingly on the subject of love.

Lihn's style is not only difficult to translate, it is often disappointing when seen to offer very profound observations in an essentially flat and repetitious vocabulary. This can be noted in the opening of his most famous poem, "The Dark Room":

> The mixture of air in the dark room, as if the bare ceiling threatened
>   a vague bloody drizzle.
> Of that liquor we inhaled, the dirty nose, symbol of innocence and
>   precocity
> to renew our struggle together secretly, but we did not know
>   we did not ignore what cause;
> a game of hands and feet, twice villainous, but equally sweet
> as the first loss of blood avenged with teeth and nails, or
>   for a girl
> sweet as the first flow of her blood.

The translation is faithful to the original in repeating "sweet" and "blood," which detracts somewhat from the perceptiveness of the observation. This has always seemed to me a problem in translation: should the translator "improve" on the poem?

In comparing the Witherup-Echeverría translation of "Rooster" with that by Miller Williams, referred to earlier, I find that Williams has injected more life into the English version, perhaps even more than the original owns, although this is a judgment no non-native speaker can ever comfortably reach. One effective change which Williams allows himself is to break up Lihn's long lines into more regular lengths. This alters, of course, the narrative tendency of the Chilean's style. Another liberty Williams takes is to simplify and compact phrases in order to supply the English with more punch than the Witherup and Echeverría version manages. The W-E translation is again faithful to the original arrangement:

> . . . His wives mean nothing to him nor the corn that will
>   make him kiss the dust in the afternoon.
> He limits himself to howling like a heretic in the fire
>   of his own feathers.
> And he is a gigantic horn
> that darkness blows as it falls into Hell.

The Williams' version not only creates sentences where there were none but effects a sound pattern not existing in the original yet in some ways comparable to Lihn's structure, which would in fact be almost impossible to duplicate ("hereje" and "hoguera" in the same line achieving a strange undertone in the poem, a type of soundless alliteration since the h's are silent):

> His wives count for nothing, nor the corn
> that in the evening he will kiss the dust for.
> He howls like a heretic in the bonfire of his feathers.
> He is a gigantic horn blowing the darkness to hell.

Above all, it is Williams' ability to use English imaginatively to match the imagery of Lihn that results in an exciting piece of poetry in translation. Colloquial phrasing ("count for nothing" and "blowing . . . to hell"), nice rhythmical units ("he will kiss the dust for"), and a combination of alliteration and accurate diction ("bonfire of his feathers" as compared with the plain and inexact "fire" of the W-E rendering), all aid in suggesting the true richness of Lihn's language. Yet having said so much, I feel that in a way Witherup and Echeverría have produced a work that is in reality closer to the unique, rambling rhythms of Lihn's original. Perhaps what I want are the positive qualities of both translations, though not even these will fully satisfy when it comes to such an illusive touch as Lihn has achieved.

Aside from its at-times pedestrian translation, the Witherup-Echeverría collection is one of the most important single volumes of a contemporary Chilean's work currently available, outside of the Donald Walsh version of Neruda's *Residence On Earth* (New Directions), the Ben Belitt *Five Decades: Poems 1925-1970* (Evergreen), also by Neruda, and the two New Directions volumes of Nicanor Parra's anti-poems translated by Miller Williams. For Lihn is without a doubt part of the grand Chilean tradition, and in a way that neither Parra nor Neruda is. Not only is Lihn a giant among giants in this long tradition, he is a master rarely equaled by poets of other Latin American nations. The exception, of course, is Ernesto Cardenal of Nicaragua.

[In 1979 the Institute of Latin American Studies at The University of Texas at Austin would publish my book, *Civilization and Barbarism: A Guide to the Teaching of Latin American Literature*. In addition to essays that survey Latin American writing in the major genres, this guide includes an annotated list of representative works from 21 Latin American countries and the West Indies. The following discussion of Ernesto Cardenal is taken from this later publication but is inserted here as a fuller account of the Nicaraguan's significant contribution to the making of the modern Latin American poem.

Cardenal's career represents a development from imagist and epigrammatist imitation to the creation of more epical poems based on American Indian and New World themes. His work thus encompasses both the Greek and Roman mode of witty epigrams and the American mode of native Indian legend and myth reconstructed on Pound and Williams' imagistic pattern for contemporary epic poetry. The influence of imagism remains a constant, as Cardenal unifies his longer, Indian-oriented poems around clear image clusters, as in "Recordings of the Sacred Pipe," where drum, ball, circle, and roundness (versus the square of Western civilization) are presented for purposes of a theme-and-variations treatment of the idea of peace and communication among men. Although certain of his early epigrams are concerned with American themes (as in nos. 13 and 18 from the "Epigrams," which introduce historical allusions, especially to Somoza, dictator of Nicaragua), many of Cardenal's poems in this classical mode treat of love and politics (nos. 8 and 41), of the transitoriness of life (no. 25), and of the relationship between poet and reader, lover and loved one, with the witty turn at the end adhered to after the classical manner (notably in the satire entitled "Somoza Unveils the Statue of Somoza in Somoza Stadium"). All of these poems are contained in *Apocalypse and Other Poems* (New Directions, 1977), edited by Robert Pring-Mill and Donald Walsh.

In addition to the many opportunities Cardenal's work offers for a consideration of classical modes and motifs, of imagist theory and practice (see especially "Above the Rain-Soaked Track," which owes much to Pound), and of the Latin American's use of Indian materials (based for example on sayings of Black Elk or the history of Mayan civilization—see his entire book on this theme, *Homage to the American Indian*), Cardenal also deals with modern civilization by means of character sketches of such figures as Marilyn Monroe or a meditation on the nature of love and life inspired by the death of his friend and fellow poet Thomas Merton (in "Coplas on the Death of Merton"). In "Apocalypse" Cardenal makes a visionary-allegorical statement on the contemporary world situation much in the way Allen Ginsberg does in "Wichita Vortex Sutra," with both poets utilizing contemporary allusions to point up their distress over inhumane conditions. Constant references to telephones, neon signs, and gasoline stations in Cardenal's works signal the substitution in our civilization of distance, advertising, and speed for true communication and understanding. The urge to reach retirement has taken the place of a desire to live, and Cardenal's poetry calls us back to a reconsideration of lost values. To do this the poet employs striking contrasts, as in his "Psalms," where he has made pseudo-religious statements about law and order to demonstrate our corruption of Christian values in the name of ungodly aims or gains.

Much of Cardenal's work will throw significant light on the writings of other important American poets, among them Charles Olson, Pound, and even Whitman. "Coplas on the Death of Merton" is in the elegy tradition, which includes Whitman's "When Lilacs Last in the Dooryard Bloom'd," for both poets use the occasion to meditate on the meaning of death and to prefer in the end life, since, as Cardenal writes, "to die is not to leave the world it is to plunge into it." On so many levels and in so many areas of his poetry Cardenal serves to reveal the power and vision, the understanding of classical tradition and of contemporary practice, as evidenced by the work of poets throughout Latin America.]

Published originally in Chile by Editorial Universitaria, Ernesto Cardenal's *Homage to the American Indian* is now available in translation (unfortunately not in a bilingual edition) from Johns Hopkins Press. Unlike so many pseudohomages to the Indian, this poem is not only a valid tribute, it is a modern work which tells us as much about our own contemporary failings as it does about the values of the Maya civilization:

> The word "Lord" was foreign to the tongue.
> And the word "wall." They did not wall in their cities.
> Their cities were of temples and they lived in the fields,
> among milpas and palm and papaya trees.
> The arch of their temples was a copy of their huts.
> The roads were only for processions.
> Religion was the only tie among them,
> but it was a religion freely taken
> and neither an oppression nor a burden on them.
> Their priests had no earthly power
> and their pyramids were built without forced labor.
> The peak of their civilization did not lead to an empire.
> And they had no colonies. They did not know the arrow.
>
> (from "Lost Cities")

In contrasting the culture of Mayapan with that of the Maya, Cardenal draws some derogatory analogies between twentieth-century North American and the unimaginative Mayapan lifestyles:

Dictatorship. The mediocre temple of Kukulkan
mediocre temples (copies)
Great stone façades, naked stone
coarsely carved
The columns aren't worth a shit
Monochrome pottery, monotonous
as at the beginning, as the Olmecs
or, as filling station billboards on a Texas highway

(from "Mayapan")

Although Cardenal's message comes through clearly enough in these translations, the versions are nonetheless uninspired in general, inaccurate at times,
and even positively insensitive at others. While the second excerpt is decided-
ly superior to the first, especially with the phrase "coarsely carved" as a rendering for "mal labrada," the significance of the first excerpt requires that it
be handled more carefully than the second. In the first line of the excerpt
from "Lost Cities" the reference, for example, is not to religion, since the
original reads "señor" not "Señor," and refers rather to the idea of no man
having a master nor of having to defer to another because of a class system.
The wordiness of the translating does not do justice to Cardenal's rhythmic
drive, nor does a construction like "The peak of their civilization did not lead
to an empire" serve in place of a simple word-for-word translation: "The apo-
gee of their civilization was not converted to an empire." "Turned into" is
another possibility for "se convirtió," but "The peak . . . did not lead to" is
far from the original and makes no real sense in English. My arguments may
be somewhat petty, but on the whole the translation does not suggest nearly
the ring of Cardenal's primitive-contemporary poem.

It is unfortunate that such an important work as this has been treated so
carelessly. It is hard to imagine how this happened in the hands of a press
like Johns Hopkins. On half again the number of pages—there is much wasted
white space—the press could have offered a bilingual edition, which makes me
wonder if the publishers feared comparison with the original. I sincerely hope
that another major press will soon bring out *Homage to the American Indian*
in a bilingual edition done by more dedicated translators.

By way of returning to the vital role played by small and large magazines
in spreading the word on Latin American writing, I will close with a final comment on the Johns Hopkins book. It is perhaps indicative of the need for passing through the magazine fires, before reaching a definitive manuscript, that
the only versions in the Johns Hopkins publication to appear previously were
a few sections printed in a New Directions Annual. Cardenal was done a distinct disservice by not having been made available to a number of little-large
magazine translators who, through a type of public competition, could have
proved their abilities to do justice to the Nicaraguan's talents. Only after judg-
ing the work of a variety of translators should Johns Hopkins have entrusted
such a labor to one who would have performed it with a proverbial but essen-

tial love for this text, which exhibits the highest qualities of Latin American civilization and art.

The Contemporary Poem as Cultural Bridge

Crossing the river at Laredo, Texas, and entering Nuevo Laredo, Mexico, or vice versa, involves the traveler in a displacement, a feeling of alienation, and yet this unnerving passage from one culture to another can serve to reintroduce a sense of strangeness and wonder that in turn reorients one more fully to his own origins. This same simultaneous disorientation and reawakening is equally the experience of contemporary poetry for those who would cross from one literature to another. Often we suspect we are being taken, as when a taxi driver picks us up and charges an exorbitant rate for an out-of-the-way ride. Just so, in choosing a book of "foreign" poems we are often suspicious, fearful of being left far from any real or imaginary landscape worth the time and expense. On the other hand, when we do encounter through literature the vital character of another nation, we come quickly to agree with the Chilean poet Gabriela Mistral that poetry is an international currency, recognized in every land as a legitimate and valued sign of deep understanding of, and profound feeling for, man and his search for self-identification and self-expression. For the poem does arrive, even in translation, bearing the stamp of common concerns: a need for vision, and the desire for aesthetic delight.

In an effort to suggest a number of meaningful bridges available to students interested in crossing either into the world of contemporary United States poetry or into that of the present-day Mexican poem, or both, a festival of readings by four United States and four Mexican poets was conceived at the University of the Americas for the second week of February, 1976. The idea of having an equal number of poets from each country was matched by the consideration that each pair of poets to read on four consecutive nights should represent in their work a similar approach to the poem. One night was to have been set aside for an all-women's reading, but as fate would have it, the Mexican counterpart was, at the last moment, unable to attend. Despite an imperfect arrangement in this regard, the pairings did come to include poets who typify in their work at least three of the major poetic modes in current United States and Mexican poetry: "poetic naturalism," the "deep image" or "tight nature poem," and the "poetry of place."

Before discussing these various modes or "cultural bridges," it is appropriate at this point to introduce the poets by name and to sketch out briefly their individual backgrounds. The first team, and I use the word advisedly, is

Reportaje de la pirámide no. 2 (winter 1976): unnumbered pages.

composed of Carlos Isla (Mexico City) and Robert Bonazzi (Austin, Texas), a pair of poets who have worked together prior to this meeting here at UDLA. In the spring of 1974 Bonazzi's Latitudes Press published a book entitled *Domingo*, a collection of poems written by three poets—Robert Bonazzi, Carlos Isla, and C.W. Truesdale. Patterned partly on *Renga* by Octavio Paz, Edoardo Sanguineti, and Charles Tomlinson, *Domingo* differs from the earlier publication in that the two Americans (Bonazzi and Truesdale) and the Mexican (Isla) do not identify who wrote which poems, whereas Paz (Mexican), Sanguineti (Italian), and Tomlinson (English) reveal their separate authorships by the fact that each writes in his own language. In *Domingo* the poems are unsigned and appear in both Spanish and English, thus concealing the linguistic origin of any one piece. This collaborative work amply illustrates a similarity of approach and preoccupation within the poetry of Bonazzi and Isla, for the vision and style throughout the poem's various sections are so consistent that they almost defy attribution to more than one author.

Among the many meeting grounds in the work of these two young poets I can mention first that both use "Latitudes" as the title for a publication based in the respective country of each—in the case of Isla his poetry magazine out of Mexico City and in Bonazzi's his press of that name referred to earlier. Both poets have also published widely in magazines of the other's nation: Isla in the *Minnesota Review, The goodly co., Pan American Review,* and in the anthology *Survivors of the Invention* ; Bonazzi in *El corno emplumado, El Heraldo, Excelsior,* and in Isla's *Latitudes.* In addition to poems, Bonazzi has published stories in *Tri-Quarterly, Seems, december,* and other magazines. His poems have been collected in *Living the Borrowed Life* (New Rivers Press) and *The New Breed: An Anthology of Texas Poets* (Prickly Pear Press). Isla has published two volumes of poems, *Gramática del Fuego* (Fed. Ed. Mexicana) and *Maquinaciones* (Ed. Joaquín Mortiz), the latter nominated for the prestigious national award, "Premio Villaurrutia." Through their sharing of mutual poetic interests has grown a deep personal friendship between these two American poets. It is just this sort of relationship which poetry fosters. My own experience has shown me repeatedly that the doors and hearts of differing peoples open with welcome when they share such love for the living poem.

Doug Flaherty (Oshkosh, Wisconsin) and Roberto Vallarino (Mexico City) form the second pair of poets, both of whom are proponents of what has been characterized by Robert Bly as the "deep image" poem. Even though Vallarino is a young poet at 20, he has nonetheless already found his way into *Plural*, the leading literary magazine in Mexico, and has discovered his own voice and what to say with it. Flaherty, at 36, is an established poet who has been developing his now mature style for more than ten years, publishing nation-wide in some of the best magazines of the United States: *The New Yorker, The Nation,* and *Poetry Northwest.* Both of these poets, despite their age difference, exhibit a strikingly similar subject matter and diction. Still, it is natural that Flaherty should have achieved far more in the literary world than Vallarino, given the former's years of experience. Thus, the Wisconsin poet is founder of *Road Apple Review*, a respected poetry magazine, and of

Road Runner Press, publisher of chapbooks of poetry by outstanding United States and world poets. Flaherty's own poetry has been included in such anthologies as *From the Belly of the Shark* (Random House) and *Poets of the Heartland, II* (Northern Illinois University Press). His chapbooks number upwards of seven, with a new collection due out any day. Vallarino, meanwhile, as winner of the "Diana Moreno Toscano" award for poetry for 1975 and recipient of a scholarship from the Centro Mexicano de Escritores (working there under the famed novelist Juan Rulfo), has not allowed his youth to keep him from making a name for himself early on among contemporary Mexican poets, and his poems are being seen regularly now in Isla's *Latitudes* and also in *Zaguán*.

The combination of Anick O'Meara (Dublin, Ireland) and Adolfo Castañón (Mexico City) does not provide any particular basis for stylistic or thematic comparison. Nevertheless, these two poets do have in common youth and the beginnings of literary careers that promise much for the future. Irish but now residing in the United States, O'Meara has published poetry as well as essays in her adopted homeland and has translated from the Spanish, having been a student in Spain for several years. Castañón has also published both poems and essays, in *Revista de la Universidad Autónoma de México, Plural,* and *Idea.* As an associate of the fine Mexican poets José Emilio Pacheco, who recommended the younger poets when he himself declined an invitation to participate, and Octavio Paz, Castañón is indeed well aware of the trends and directions of contemporary Mexican poetry.

The final pairing of poets brings together two writers of like minds though of very distinct styles. Ernesto Moreno Machuca (Puebla, Mexico) and Karl Kopp (Albuquerque, New Mexico) have both grounded their poems in a sense of place, celebrating the where and how of twentieth-century existence. A native of the state of Puebla [where the University of the Americas is located], Moreno Machuca has written numerous collections of poems, among them the two volumes entitled *Tesis para recibirse de Mexicano*, which specifically concern the towns and personages of both his native area and of other regions of Mexico. Winner of the "Premio Nezahualcoyotzin" for poetry, translated into Italian, and honored by his fellow countrymen and by foreign literary figures, Moreno Machuca has established himself as a poet of his people and of their mysterious, legendary land.

Like Pablo Neruda's work, which in its sense of place has become a part of every serious poetry reader's geographical and imagistic bearings, Moreno Machuca's poems have attempted to catalogue the qualities and characteristics of various locales throughout the Mexican state, their peculiar events, products, and prominent figures. Although the style is in no way experimental, the intent of the poet's work is very much that of the nationalistic writer who sees in his surroundings the stuff of a poetry to be sung primarily for the inhabitants themselves. The reach of such poetry, in spite of an eschewing of experimentation, is more than regional, for if nothing else it gives the non-native reader the sense of a life unique to one nation. Certainly Moreno Machuca's poems do not contain the level of complexity to be found in the work of such poets as Rubén Darío or Ramón López Velarde, whose poetry he greatly admires and to whom he has dedicated longish tributes. And while Moreno Machuca treats of provincial life, as does López Velarde, the former's work does not offer the kind of psychological or stylistic qualities influential on such a significant twentieth-century poet as Chile's Nicanor Parra, which is true of López Velarde's effect on the Chilean as well as on succeeding generations of Mexican poets. Nonetheless, Moreno Machuca does present us with a panorama of the life of Mexico, epic in its scope and inspiring in its respect for an inexhaustible source of poetic utterance.

Although Karl Kopp's poems are stylistically distant from Moreno Machuca's, whose work tends more toward traditional forms, they do share with the Mexican's a belief in place as a proper subject for the contemporary poet. As Kopp says in one poem, he writes principally to be heard; frequently he employs "rock rhythms." His poetry has appeared in publications throughout the United States and has been read by the poet at various universities. While he has led the nomadic life of a university professor, Kopp and his family have also spent a number of years in the Ozark mountains of Arkansas, a stay that inspired his third volume of poems, *Yarbrough Mountain* (Baleen Press), a remarkable collection that contains moving portraits of his Ozark neighbors.

In an essay published in the *South Dakota Review* (autumn 1975) and entitled "Regionalism: The New Common Sense," Karl Kopp has outlined his views on how place serves as a revitalizing force in contemporary poetry: ". . . To invest in a place, to decipher and to speak its many tongues . . . can lead to almost infinite depths/heights in the growth of oneself and one's work." Kopp offers a list of "what to know" about a place, from its flora and fauna, through its economy, to its hopes and fears. In his own work the poet has managed to include all the elements he catalogues in his essay. Often he presents these just as he finds them, lying about in newspaper articles, in letters, on or off the road, beneath his window, lighting up the room he happens to occupy just then, or in the conversations he overhears. Found poems in particular retain for the poet something of the moment he recognizes as significant for any time or place, and thus in the local he discovers the universal. This same realization is fundamental not only to the "poet of place" but to the practitioner of "poetic naturalism," which brings us back to the duo of Isla and Bonazzi.

Writing earlier on the work of Isla (in *Margins* 21/22, 1975), I noted that his poems did not strike me as typically Latin American but that they owed more to certain North American poets active at the present, especially Charles Simic and Mark Strand. Now that I have become more familiar with Isla's work I wonder why I did not see the similar strategies employed by both Isla and Nicanor Parra. According to one Mexican reader, Isla's work represents for him a poetry of "anti-structures." The parallel between such a characterization and certain attitudes expressed by Dada and Surrealism seems quite evident to me now and suggests an affinity between the Mexican's "anti-structures" and the Chilean's "anti-poems." However, Isla himself denies any direct knowledge of Parra's work at the time that he wrote the "anti-structure" pieces in *Maquinaciones* (1975). Still, there are similarities in their work that indicate a common point of view or sensibility. Isla's poems seem to derive in part from a British sense of humor, as do Parra's. Along this same line there is Octavio Paz's identification of Isla's patron saint for *Maquinaciones* as Buster Keaton, which is close to the comparison often drawn between Parra and Chaplin. That the Mexican has made imaginative use of found elements (see the Isla-Bonazzi-Truesdale section in *Domingo* based on a social security form), of advertising slogans, of colloquial expressions, of absurd juxtapositions for comic as well as for enlightening effects—this too underscores the fact that Isla is indeed very much a member of the new wave of Latin American poets. At the same time, such tendencies also link Isla with the United States movement, led by Simic and Strand, that Karl Elder has labeled "poetic naturalism."

The influence of American poets on the work of Carlos Isla may or may not be before the fact—i.e., publication of the poems collected in *Maquinaciones*. Yet many of these poems were in fact written in New York while Isla spent time there with the Texas poet Robert Bonazzi. Isla himself acknowledges that the poems are radical departures from his earlier, more typically Latin American pieces (lush with imagery and verbiage, in contrast to the stark, black-and-white poems of his 1975 volume). In working with Bonazzi, whose own poems also represent a tendency toward "poetic naturalism," Isla not only found a kindred spirit but in turn influenced his "gringo" friend. For example, Isla's poem "Sobremesa" ("After Dinner Talk") is echoed by Bonazzi's "Bagatelles." Below I give the original of each poem with its facing translation:

<table>
<tr><td>Llámeme Bonazzi o Isla</td><td>Whether I'm called Bonazzi
or Isla</td></tr>
<tr><td>
El sol será siempre
un loro de cabeza amarilla
que repite mis días
y deletrea mis noches
turnando sus ojos solamente</td><td>
The sun will ever be
a parrot with yellow head
that repeats my days
and spells my nights
only his eyes taking turns</td></tr>
<tr><td>
Si respondiera por otro nombre</td><td>
If I were to answer by another
name</td></tr>
<tr><td>
poema o estomagorevuelto
o queseyo
la realidad sería la misma . . .</td><td>
poem or upset stomach
or whatayacallit
reality would be the same . . .</td></tr>
</table>

*   *   *

<table>
<tr><td>Call me Isla
or Bonazzi
or I might be *tiempo*
where weather</td><td>Llámeme Isla
o Bonazzi
o yo podría ser el tiempo
donde el clima</td></tr>
</table>

& time	y *time*
are one word	son la misma palabra

At times employing each other's language, but more often sharing simply an urge to record what is happening to them at the present moment—environmentally and subconsciously, through dream-like and playful imagery—Isla and Bonazzi present the perfect example of "poetic naturalism" as well as of poets constructing contemporary poems that bridge a cultural gap, giving us in the language of each a vision of the modern world, in "anti-structures" that reflect an international state of affairs.

A final instance of poets of differing nations utilizing like styles and partaking of similar visions—though this has by no means been an exhaustive survey—is the case of Doug Flaherty and Roberto Vallarino, whose work typifies the contemporary trend toward what Flaherty himself calls the "tight, nature poem" or what is known as the poetry of the "deep image." In attaching either label to the work of Flaherty and Vallarino, the object is to emphasize the use made by both poets of an elemental imagery drawn from the natural world, of the lessons arising from basic observations of natural phenomena, and of the simplicity and integrity they discover in animal and vegetable life. These two poets are particularly attracted to the mystery in rocks, butterflies, and grasshoppers, such objects and creatures as exhibit in their acts or the facts of their existence the profoundest messages/songs the poet would hear and would reproduce in his own writing. The relationship between nature and the poet's kind of expression is a central concern, a stylistic consideration, and an emotional and philosophical basis for the work of the Mexican and the American. As Flaherty puts it, his poetry is an effort to enter "the guts of words," and vice versa, his words attempt to achieve a visceral identification with the physical world. Vallarino likewise finds that "en la lengua del hombre / nacían pájaros" ("on the tongue of man / birds are born"), that rocks are "gritos petrificados en su vuelo" ("shouts petrified in their flight"). The unity of the verbal and vegetal, the inanimate and imaginative is, once again, both an example of a common tendency among contemporary poets and an illustration of the proximity in spirit of culturally distant writers.

As the airline, bus, train, or taxi transports the poet from one nation to another, perhaps he or she brings nothing new, other than an awareness of the fact—for those who would hear or read the poems—that to know another literature is the surest arch over iron curtains or raging rivers, and that understanding such tendencies as "place in the poem," "poetic naturalism," or the "deep image" enables the listener or reader to feel at home wherever he goes, by page or by plane, and to find that the poetry talks everyman's language, speaking as it does of the same confusions and elevations as they ever exist in the vigorous minds of men. Certainly the learning of other tongues is an added dimension to our taste and intellect, but only by coming to recognize what borderless desires prompt the poet to expression can we be led to a renewed encounter with the meaning and value of the life around us, irregardless of the name we give it, which, as Isla says, varies from state to state, while its reality remains the same.

37

Introduction to *If Poetry Is To Be Written Right*

While in recent years it has become fashionable throughout Latin America to write so-called political poetry, the poet whose work is rooted in politics yet transcends the too-frequently narrow and propagandistic aims of dialectics is uncommon indeed. Just such a rare bird is Enrique Lihn, a Chilean nightingale who nests in the dark forest of Third World hopes, coups, and disillusions. His own metaphor for himself is that of the minstrel from the Middle Ages who survives as an anachronism in a 20th-century land which he recognizes stands in greater need of socialist programs than of metaphysical poems. It is, however, precisely out of this sense of "irrelevance" that Lihn has made some of the most insightful poetry in what the minstrel himself has labeled our "Age of Data."

Born in the Depression year of 1929, Enrique Lihn has long been acknowledged as one of the new major voices in Latin American poetry. His third book, *The Dark Room* (1963), was proclaimed by both Hispanic-American and British critics as a work of penetrating psychological reality, presented in a strikingly colloquial language mixed with dream and sexual imagery. Developing from the contributions of his predecessors, Huidobro, Neruda, and Nicanor Parra, Lihn has established himself in his own right as a political moralist who would preserve a traditional concern for the spiritual side of man, which requires as much sustenance as does his physical. While acutely aware of how his political vision of an improved state for "underdeveloped" peoples has placed him in an awkward position as a poet, Lihn has never backed off from discovering in himself and in those presumably dedicated to the political solution a deep failing, a falsity with which he struggles in earnest in his sinewy verse, creating through his frank confessions of failure, as well as through subtle satire of his comrades' hypocrisies, a poetic study richly revealing of the character of our modern poet-revolutionary.

A doubting Thomas in spirit, Enrique Lihn questions himself and his cause with an excruciating candor. Nevertheless, as his poems, short stories, and most recently his novel, *Batman in Chile*, vividly illustrate, Lihn is the master of a serious sense of humor. His novel presents a troubled, impotent, addicted Batman, who, in working for the CIA, is caught up in a Latin American political turmoil which confuses him to the point that he not only doubts himself but

Enrique Lihn, *If Poetry Is To Be Written Right*, trans. Dave Oliphant (Texas City: Texas Portfolio Press, 1977), pp. iii-v.

cannot tell which are the bad guys, which the good. He longs for Gotham City (translated tellingly by Lihn to Gothic City) where criminals were criminals, just as the poet himself harks back to the medieval world for a sense of moral certainty. The religious imagery which permeates the work of Lihn, while often ironic, is a clear indication of the abiding ethical quality of his writing. He wants to believe in himself and in others but finds it difficult, as we all do, each of us descended from the same doubt the disciple was heir to, and with good reason, considering the spurious nature of our motives.

In keeping with a tendency to suspect even his own best intentions, Lihn has continued to question the value of poetry and the notions of those who would practice the art. One of his characteristic themes is the nothingness of literature and the preciousness of the "peacocks" who would create it. In an essay entitled "Definition of a Poet" (1966), Lihn speaks of an attempt by young poets to impress the listener by making poems which are appropriate for singing or for doing tangos and boleros to. On the other hand, he finds a false obscurity another perennial attraction for those wishing to converse with friendly ghosts who, ultimately, have nothing to say in return. Yet despite his distrust of literature as a typical refuge for the petty bourgeois, Lihn consistently sides with Literature as "a good investment in history." Lihn's anti-poetic stance (inherited especially from his countryman, Nicanor Parra) makes his paradoxical repudiation/defense of poesy an extremely palatable position in our highly suspicious day. It is this dissonant blend in his poetry, of praise and criticism, which achieves an ironic tone, but which also brings to his championing of Literature a ring all the more timely and true.

The earlier poems of Enrique Lihn were made available in this country by Lillabulero Press, which printed in 1969 a selection of 25 poems, *This Endless Malice*, taken from his *The Dark Room* (*La pieza oscura*) and *Poetry in Passing*. In the present selection, drawn exclusively from collections published or written since 1963, it is particularly the tension between political awareness and poetical consciousness which results in a body of poems unique in the history of world literature. Arranged chronologically the poems represent five separate volumes: *Poetry in Passing* (*Poesía de paso*), 1966, for which Lihn won the coveted House of the Americas Award (Cuba); *Written in Cuba* (*Escrito en Cuba*), 1967, a long poem in perhaps the poet's freest and most original style; *Little Music of the Minor Spheres* (*Musiquilla de las pobres esferas*), 1968, a book which relentlessly pursues his urgent theme of the quixotic poet in the role of would-be political activist; *Album of Every Kind of Poem* (*Album de toda especie de poemas*), 1971, an unpublished collection, some of the pieces having appeared in such Chilean magazines as *Tebaida* and *Atenea*, a number also included in his *Some Poems* (*Algunos poemas*) published in Spain in 1972; and *Act of God* (*Por fuerza mayor*), Spain, 1975.

A resident of Chile throughout the Allende era, never imprisoned at the junta's takeover, so far as I know, the poet at this date is still making his home in his native land. As an astute critic, editor, and student of political history, Lihn remains an active force in the life of Chilean letters, whose grand tradition reaches back with Ercilla's *La Araucana* to before the publication of Cer-

39

vantes' *Don Quixote*. Knowing that Lihn survives is further proof of the staying power of Chile's literary heritage and its continuing hope for a humanitarian future, despite whatever present setback the poet and his people may be experiencing in a world where minstrelsy and data, soul and body, have yet to come to terms.

from *Civilization and Barbarism: A Guide to the Teaching of Latin American Literature*

The challenge of creating a New World poetry has been shared by poets of both Latin and Anglo America, and in recent times many poets of these two cultures have come to seek sources for an authentic American poetry in many of the same places. Charles Olson's interest in Mayan art and language (see his "Mayan Letters") may be paralleled with Miguel Angel Asturias' return to the legends of Guatemala in *Leyendas de Guatemala* and Ernesto Cardenal's homage to the Mayans in *Homenaje a los indios americanos*. All three of these writers have looked to Mayan civilization for what Olson refers to as "the rudiments of the first meanings." Earlier, of course, Walt Whitman had sought in America and in the American language the soul of a full new expression, and Pablo Neruda of Chile echoed this by cataloguing Latin American place names and everyday images or activities—from onions, oranges, and shards to underwear and mining—in an effort to discover in the near and familiar the spirit for a vital New World poetry. In Chile another poet, Nicanor Parra, has rediscovered the language of the street, finding, as Emerson suggested, in the "stinging rhetoric of a rattling oath in the mouths of truckmen and teamsters" something "vascular and alive . . . a shower of bullets." A useful starting point, then, in any study of Latin American poetry is to observe this need to unearth an authentic New World theme and technique, in terms of both its medium and its message, its artistry and its ideas.

Within such a broad concept of the American poem as this of a search for its own unique self, there figure prominently in Latin American poetry political, social, cultural, and esthetic ramifications. And although it may be true that the greatest achievements have come from three or four countries (namely, Chile, Peru, Mexico, and Brazil, with their modern masters in Neruda, Vallejo, Paz, and Mario de Andrade), it is equally true that almost every Latin American nation has produced an original poet worthy of study in his own right and in terms of this theme of prospecting for a uniquely American poem. Certainly an entire course could be devoted to the poetry of either Chile or Mexico, but for purposes of introducing representative works into any poetry or literature class, it is possible to find in the poems of El Salvador's Roque Dalton, of Colombia's Alvaro Mutis, of Hondura's Oscar Acosta, themes and techniques that run the political, social, and esthetic gamut of Latin Ameri-

Poetry section of *Civilization and Barbarism: A Guide to the Teaching of Latin American Literature* (Institute of Latin American Studies, The University of Texas at Austin, 1979), pp. 31-39.

can literature and reveal simultaneously the special metaphor and image-making powers of poets from those countries unblessed with size or by grand traditions in poetry yet favored nonetheless with talent and vision. As with any work of art, the ultimate test of its validity as a teaching tool does not depend entirely on its relation to an established literary tradition but rather on its communication of deep-seated human needs, which include hopes, fears, regrets, memories (good and bad), and discoveries full of wonder and revelation. And these same qualities are to be found in countless Latin American poems available in anthologies, collections, magazines, and chapbooks. The fact that most poems are short makes it possible to reproduce them easily and to fit them into a class discussion without the students having seen them beforehand. Thus, the advantages of teaching poems are innumerable, offering as they do the basic strategies of novels, a greater concentration than even the short story can manage, and national origins that include every region of Latin America.

Although Latin American poets have sought to create or recover their own peculiar voice, they have by no means been unaware of international trends in the art. The influence of the French Parnassians and Symbolists, the Dadaists, the Surrealists, and the English and American Imagists is an important consideration in discussing any Latin American poet, and this influence can be traced in the work of the major as well as the minor poet. (In almost every discussion of influence, reference is regularly made to T.S. Eliot, both by a well-known figure like Parra or a lesser-known poet like Ecuador's Jorge Enrique Adoum. See for instance Mario Benedetti's interview with Adoum in *Los poetas comunicantes*.) A figure like Pablo Neruda, of course, summarizes for us the international movements, with his own output spanning historically the eras of modernism, surrealism, minority consciousness, and deep image or leaping poetry, as well as encompassing the political, social, and cultural sympathies (especially those with the exploited, whether Indian, Black, or poor) which are common both to Latin American and Third World literatures. Perhaps the closest ties have been those felt by Latin American poets with Whitman, and this is due primarily to their urge, mentioned earlier, to create a truly American poetry.

Aside from direct references to Whitman in *Residence on Earth*, Neruda's poetry offers parallels to Whitman's with respect to themes and techniques that are basic to the philosophies of both these American giants. In "This Compost" Whitman explores the theme of earth, one equally close to Neruda, who approaches the subject in a similarly paradoxical manner in his "Entrance to Wood," one of the "Three Material Songs" from *Residence on Earth*. Both writers accept death as basic to earth and subsequently to life. Whitman reasons his way to acceptance, which is an older approach but probably in the end a more convincing one, whereas Neruda, essentially an anti-rationalist, a purely Theodore Roethke-type rooter with the worms, enters the wood with his fingers and speaks as if his very flesh has turned to fiber. Both poets can allude to the sexual nature of the experience as inherently a part of any relationship between man and earth—"This transparent green-wash of the sea of grass which is so amorous after me" (Whitman); "Pores, veins, circles of sweetness" (Neruda)—but the overriding concern in both poems is to accept what Neruda calls "opposition" and Whitman refers to as "such sweet things out of such corruptions." Whereas Whitman remains terrified to think that Earth "distills such exquisite winds out of such infused fetor," Neruda asks wood "to root me to your death." Without having to find these poets equals in either profundity or manner, it is possible to see their common concern for an understanding of life or a simple acceptance of the relationship between life and death, of a desire to place themselves in contact with the essential nature of existence. Dramatically Whitman's poem involves the reader on a more discursive level, whereas Neruda's attempts to immerse him in the sensual world of nature, as a means of vision ("let us make fire, silence, and sound, / burn, be silent, and bells"); by comparing them, it is possible ultimately to experience both poems more fully and to see not only the attraction Neruda felt for Whitman but also how finally the two poets' work differs fundamentally in form and content.

Other major Chilean and United States poets it is valuable to compare include William Carlos Williams, Nicanor Parra, and Vicente Huidobro (all three considered, in differing ways, "anti-poets"), as well as John Ashbery and Enrique Lihn (poets of another generation that has charged a prosaic and technological vocabulary with the heightening power of visionary poetry). Without necessarily pairing Peru's César Vallejo with any one modern poet, a study of his view of man as being divorced from a center of meaning in life can be paralleled with the Existentialist acceptance of this same state of things as a starting point for the task of making one's own meaning through choice and responsibility. Octavio Paz's almost mystical poems can be related not only to the ancient Aztec world but to Zen and its vision of a non-rational, non-egoistic immersion in things. A contrast between Neruda's sensual and Paz's more abstract contemplation of the physical world would produce a clearer understanding of these two poets' similar but essentially distinct trajectories, defining at the same time the possible influences on each of Incan and Aztec systems of thought, respectively, in Neruda's "Heights of Macchu Picchu" and in Paz's "Sunstone."

In seeking to take advantage of the work of a lesser-known figure like José Emilio Pacheco, who is overshadowed by his countryman Paz, it is important to find ways of introducing a single poem into a context more limited than those already suggested, where an historical survey is almost required before one can recognize the fuller implications of a comparative study. On a less ambitious scale, then, it is possible to present major aspects of Latin American literary thought and to give at the same time the younger writer a chance to show what he or she can do. Not only do the younger poets deserve such an opportunity but often they can open up young readers more immediately to discussion and to an interest in literature than can their rather more imposing elders. This may well be the case with Pacheco, especially when he is paired with the little-known United States poet Reed Whittemore, whose poem "The Tarantula" can be compared in various ways with the Mexican's "An Investigation of the Bat."

The poet's trick of making something beautiful, entertaining, and enlightening (literature) out of an ugly, disgusting, and insignificant creature (the bat or tarantula) can more than anything cause the reader to rethink his world, to see it as potentially charged with poetry anywhere he turns. This lesson transcends schools, traditions, and political parties, and is surely one of the most important a course in literature can hope to teach. The humor of Whittemore's lecture, matched by the wit of Pacheco's dissertation, will prompt an immediate response from almost any reader. Pacheco's poem pokes fun at the game of literary criticism, which will win most students over from the first: "Bats have no idea of their literary prestige." Whittemore, speaking through the tarantula, involves literature at a humorous but existential level:

> So I am ugly. Does that mean that you
> Should persecute me as you do? Read William Blake.
> Read William Wordsworth.
> Read Williams in general, I'd say. There was a book
> By a William Tarantula once, a work of some consequence
> In my world on the subject of beauty . . .

Both poets manage to touch significantly on basic ideas of love and misunderstanding, even as they are treating their unlikely subjects with imagination and humor. Both attempt to reinterpret what has been too easily rejected—another sure attraction for most students, who can readily identify with the outcast. Also, both poems illustrate the usefulness of an indirect approach to the nature of man, in these cases through their relating of the creature's or the poet's sensitive and probing questions to those fundamental to mankind. The indirection achieves in this regard both subtlety and surprise:

> Man confines [the bat] to evil and detests it because he shares
> the viscuous ugliness, the egoism, the
> human vampirism;
> it recalls our origins in caves . . .   (Pacheco)

> You carry
> This image about of me that is at once libelous
> And discouraging, all because you, who should know better,
> Find me ugly.   (Whittemore)

Finally, the style of both poems is conversational and quite expository in a way that makes it simpler for students to follow the argument. Furthermore, in the poems' appearance of being "true"—less fictive—through references to dictionary definitions and through explanations of allusive remarks, the effect is to engage the reader at a humorous yet highly readable and even educative level, while demonstrating at the same time how to make points clearly and meaningfully.

By finding parallels such as these, it is possible to suggest how close one literary approach may be to another, irregardless of the culture or the subject matter involved. At the same time, in order to present the peculiar qualities of one culture's literary tradition, it is useful to contrast our own with that of a different heritage. This is especially crucial in dealing with the political poetry of Latin America, where the demand for such is so great that even the best poets suffer from catering to the call for commitment, even though some have managed to create within this form a new kind of poem, far removed from anything known in the United States. Although it is valuable to compare Latin American and Chicano practices in this regard, it is more revealing to contrast the Latin and Anglo approach to the theme of injustice or cultural prejudice. Generally speaking, when we see the Latin American poet attacking imperialism from the outside we find it too much like propaganda and prefer instead the subtlety of such a poem as David Hilton's often anthologized "In Praise of BIC Pens," which tends to criticize our urge to conquer all of Asia—to eliminate the *other*—yet by means of a humorous, hard-hitting metaphor that captures our imaginations and wins us over, even cures our neuroses through its strongly alliterative lines:

> The common pen skips, leaves the page blank—
>
> But you, BIC pen, at nineteen cents, could
> trace truce terms on tank treads

Certainly Latin American poets like Enrique Lihn can also employ a combination of poetic and prosaic techniques to achieve a blend of metaphoric imagery and revolutionary fervor. When this is the case, as it is also with the poetry of Roque Dalton, we come to feel that Latin American poets can handle the essential elements of poetry even as they voice a political passion. In Dalton's "On Headaches," the clever analogy between aspirin and communism aids in his analysis of the nature of that political system, in his characterization of such vague concepts as capitalism and revolution, and finally in his attempt to illustrate the differences among the three. Roque Dalton's imagery and metaphors, as well as his allusion to paradise, all focus on the single idea of pain, exploring its relation to the communist state in a way that lends to stale propaganda a fresh lease on life, at least insofar as its literary impact is concerned:

> It is beautiful to be a communist,
> even though it may cause terrific headaches.
>
> And that's because a communist headache
> has historical weight, which is to say
> it isn't relieved by analgesic tablets
> but only by bringing Paradise on earth.
> That's the thing.
>
> Under capitalism our head aches
> and they tear it off.

In the struggle for Revolution the head is
a time bomb.

In constructing the socialist State
we plan on headaches
which doesn't make them scarcer, not at all.

Communism will be, among other things,
an aspirin the size of the sun.

Dalton has other short poems in his prize-winning volume, *Taberna y otros lugares*, that are also worthy of consideration, and although many of these are not available in translation, it is useful for the teacher who knows Spanish to translate one or more for the class or to ask that students who know the language might take a stab at it (even those in first semester Spanish), since the translation process will serve as the best possible introduction to the poetic work, revealing colloquial usage more dramatically and familiarizing the student with structural devices not so apparent when the English changes, simplifies, or substitutes forms or patterns peculiar to the original. Finally, translation serves to force the reader to interpret the meaning of the entire poem in order to render significantly each and every word accurately and poetically.

Since there are many schools of poetry to choose from—the physical, the metaphorical, the dream or surrealistic, the fantastic, the antipoetic—it is important to offer at least one example of each in order both to illustrate the range of approaches and to demonstrate that many Latin American poets are capable of more than one, as in the case of Vallejo with his sensual yet highly spiritual poems. In choosing works for translation by students it may be preferable to stay with less abstract, less surrealistic poems, though in order to appreciate the imaginative power of Latin American image-making it would be regrettable not to introduce such poets as Vicente Huidobro or Carlos Germán Belli, whose creationist or surrealist-inspired poems challenge the translator's ingenuity and stretch his vocabulary into areas he rarely suspects can exist, even in his own language. Pablo Neruda's odes offer especially brilliant examples of associative imagery, in which plants or objects are compared to the universe of animate life, as in the case of the artichoke, described as a "delicate heart" in "battle dress," or the watermelon, referred to as a "firmament of freshness," a "green whale of summer," a "warehouse of profundity." In the ode to the conger eel (*congrio*), the recipe for a fish soup becomes a metaphor for marriage and sexual intercourse, blending religion and sex after much the same manner as does John Donne. And although these odes are metaphysical, the language remains simple and earthy, the lines short and rhythmically reduced to the basic ingredients of clear and accumulative sound patterns that parallel the clarity of meaning they contain, as, again, in the "Ode to the Watermelon":

and one

would like
to bite you
sinking
into you
his face,
his hair,
his soul!

We see you
in thirst
as
mine or mountain
of splendid nourishment,
yet
you turn
between teeth and appetite
into merely
fresh light
dissolving
into a spring
that touched us
singing.

Another excellent example of Neruda's artistry is his "Ode to Scissors," where the poet relates this simple tool to many significant aspects of man's life: separation of the child and mother through a cutting of the umbilical cord, the cutting out of wedding and funeral clothing, flags in war, trimming hair and fingernails, and even the poem that might otherwise grow too long.

In addition to the numerous stylistic and theoretical schools, there are also the separably identifiable groups, such as the Indians—Aztec, Maya, or Quechua poets in translation—or the women poets, who, though they often fit into the same schools as the male poets, offer a special vision in terms of their point of view. Not wishing to suggest that the writing is essentially different insofar as basic poetic techniques are concerned, I do believe that it remains true that the woman poet's work presents a position the man may either overlook, steer clear of out of chauvinism, or simply be incapable of, given his make-up. Three women poets who represent in their work some of these "special" positions are Isabel Fraire of Mexico and Alicia Galaz and Cecilia Vicuña of Chile.

Although Isabel Fraire can be as abstract and metaphysical as her mentor Octavio Paz, her love poems are disarmingly sensual, as perhaps only a woman's can be when she gives herself wholly to the man, without the reservations so characteristic of the male who needs to remain in total control:

I am unable to move
unless surrounded by your gaze
your memory clothes me

the air that held your words
echoes in my ears
like an uproar of angels

my sleep-walking fingers
stumble on you
in every object

Alicia Galaz takes a position perhaps closer to that of women's liberation, complaining as she does of the woman's being relegated to a servant's role:

According to classification born a woman.
Eternal wife to pots, plates, sox,
brooms, kitchens, baby food and flour sifters . . .

High level plans condition my every move.
Over giving or not giving birth they
do all the talking . . .

And you there smiling, I'll rub you out of Paradise.

Like Chekhov's Dimitry Dimitrich in "Lady With a Pet Dog," man may make all the plans, but he cannot do without the "inferior race" for two days at a time. Cecilia Vicuña also voices this truth but in a more ironic, playful manner, as is typical of her refreshing, ingenuous poems:

it is for sure that there are a thousand more
                    beautiful waists,
but certain things are absolutely incomparable.
the sea-horses would have no latitude so warm
for swimming
the waves would be unable to navigate between my extremes
and would feel so lonely.
many flowers that have grown only
that i may lace them to my waist,
would prefer to wither away than
suffer any other fate.

In the teaching of Latin American poetry it is finally to the point to think of the same prominent categories into which the study of poetry is normally divided: period, form (sonnet, ode, elegy, epic, lyric), or theme (love, loss of innocence or initiation, wonder, and so on). Whether approached by region, school, sex, or politics, Latin American poetry offers examples of high-quality work comparable to the best written in any such category and can serve, first, as the basis for an understanding of the nature of every type of poetry being created today and, second, as a means of insight into the physical and spiritual

48

worlds of Latin America, from its flora and fauna to its political aspirations and existential solitude. Any theme or technique being taught can be illustrated effectively through Latin American poetry, at the same time that the characteristic culture of a region or the special impact of past, present, or foreign influence can be discovered by comparing Cuban, Mexican, Chilean, or any other *latino* poetry with that of England, France, Japan, or the United States. The availability of countless translations makes it virtually a trouble-free task to locate the right example for any assignment on the poem. The benefits of using Latin American poetry are assured by its quality, range, and unique cultural values. No course can fail to be enriched by the presence of a representative Latin American poet.

Review of *En el nombre del mundo*

Eduardo Zepeda-Henríquez, a Nicaraguan writer who has lived in Madrid since 1972, is the author of some seven earlier collections of poetry, an equal number of volumes of literary criticism, and two philosophical studies. He has also edited with a fellow Nicaraguan poet, Pablo Antonio Cuadra, a centenary anthology of Rubén Darío's work. Both Cuadra and Zepeda-Henríquez have been overshadowed by Darío and by the contemporary Nicaraguan master Ernesto Cardenal, and for good reason. Even though Zepeda-Henríquez composes with facility and at times with flashes of poetic insight and phraseology, he has no distinctive voice of his own and achieves no more than an essayistic approach to his subjects.

Typical of Zepeda-Henríquez's best work in the present volume, *En el nombre del mundo* (Madrid, 1980), are two poems: "Picasso-73," a piece that catalogues the various images and styles of Picasso, and "Cuenta regresiva," a poem that recites the effects of having returned to the everyday world following the act of literary creation. "Cuenta regresiva" ("Regressive Account") contrasts the two worlds of the quotidian and the creative, though the latter is merely implied. It is suggested that the act of writing allows the poet to create "el hombre que no ven los demás, / escribiendo al dictado de la realidad inefable" ("the man whom others never see, / taking dictation from ineffable reality"). Zepeda-Henríquez uses hyperbole to express the opposition he senses between the poem or song that helps him live and life itself, ascribing to the former

> un brillo más vivo que el de las explosiones de hidrógeno,
> y con más precisión que la bella sabiduría de las computadoras

> a brightness more alive than that of a hydrogen explosion,
> and with more precision than the lovely wisdom of accountants

The world meanwhile is characterized as a season of hatred, as filled with people with television faces ("con cara de televisión") that show the tatters of love ("con andrajos de amor"), and ultimately as

> almas y cuerpos en pena,
> cuerpos y almas de náufragos

Chasqui vol. 11, no. 1 (November 1981): 82-83.

souls and bodies in pain,
bodies and souls of the shipwrecked

The contrast is too black and white and even reminds one of Rod McKuen and other sentimental poets who oppose the machine and creativity. Two collections in this same press's series are even more closely aligned with sentimentalist verse and did not seem to me deserving of even the limited attention Zepeda-Henríquez's work merits. Yet like those other versifiers, Zepeda-Henríquez tends to see the creative act as largely an escape and the return from such as equivalent to bumping one's head or missing the curb. Zepeda-Henríquez's poetry in general seems rather opinionated and overly aphoristic in the sense that it offers pat responses to historical conditions and situations.

One curious aspect of the poet's work in the longer poems is its use of the *vosotros* form in place of the more common *ustedes*. Although I am told that this is peculiar to Nicaragua, one is still hard put to locate in Zepeda-Henríquez's poems much trace of a Latin American feeling rather than what I take to be a more peninsular influence on this transplanted Nicaraguan. In "Collage" he catalogues the contents of daily newspapers of New York, Paris, London, and Rome, concluding with a reference to Nicaragua and the fact that the world's newspapers make no mention of Managua, with the poet's description of that city suggesting either an earthquake cleanup or destruction in it from civil war. The reference remains for me quite unclear and is yet the only direct link with the poet's home, other than poems devoted to Yoyontzin, to the Indian maiden Ixquic, and to a mythical Nicaraguan figure in the long poem "El testimonio de Agatón Tinoco," a work that holds little interest as poetry, even though those familiar with the speaker, Agatón Tinoco, may well find it appealing. To me the writing is simply unconvincing as poetry, either in sound or sense.

Zepeda-Henríquez appears more at home as an academic, and this is reflected by "Picasso-73." Here the poet is quite in his element as an essayist, reporting on the impact of Picasso's art:

> la explosión demográfica de su pintura,
> . . . sus trasplantes de corazón su pájaro de fuego
> su existencialismo su teoría
> de la relatividad sus pantalones de niño
> y su mano aniñada, cuando otros tienen las manos muertas.

> the demographic explosion of his painting,
> . . . his transplants his firebird
> his existentialism his theory
> of relativity his boy's short pants
> and his childish hand, when others have dead hands.

Zepeda-Henríquez's own poetry lacks the kind of integration and synthesis he observes in Picasso's art:

El mar de su cerebro se sosegaba
buscando la integración del análisis y el amor,
del amor y la síntesis.
Conoció la rebeldía en las aristas de las cosas;
amó a la mujer por sus conos, sus esferas y sus cilindros;
amó, en sus viajes espaciales, la perfección del ángulo recto
y ese juego del espacio con dado de cristal
con el dado de la vida dentro de un dado
dentro de otro dado de la vida dentro de otro.

The sea of his mind was calmed
seeking the union of analysis and love,
of love and synthesis.
He knew rebellion in the grains of things;
loved woman for her cones, spheres and cylinders;
loved, on his spacial trips, the right angle's perfection
and that space game with a crystal die
with the die of life within a die
within another die of life within another.

Even though the Nicaraguan has come to Picasso much later than e.e. cummings, whose section III of "Portraits" in *Xli Poems* characterized the painter some fifty years before, Zepeda-Henríquez does compare favorably in that he observes several of the same qualities cummings included in his poem, which is nonetheless more original both as poetry and as "criticism":

(out of the
black unbunged
Something gushes vaguely a squeak of planes
or

between squeals of
Nothing grabbed with circular shrieking tightness
solid screams whisper.)
Lumberman of The Distinct

your brain's
axe only chops hugest inherent
Trees of Ego,from
whose living and biggest

bodies lopped
of every
prettiness

you hew form truly

In "Cuenta regresiva" Zepeda-Henríquez refers in passing to having experienced a "baptism of things," which of course is precisely what Picasso's angular art does for its subjects. It is any actual immersion in objects, personalities, or occasions that the Nicaraguan has failed to enact in his own poems, with the exception of his treatment of Picasso and his art. As a critic, Zepeda-Henríquez obviously knows of what true art is made, yet he has not in this book managed to create it by means of his own imagery or voice but only through repeating—accurately to be sure—Picasso's well-known achievements.

Toward a Texas Renaissance

With the passing of the big three in Texas letters—Dobie, Bedichek, and Webb (a sort of literary equivalent to the King, Goodnight, and XIT ranches, and identifiable in many respects with that rural way of life)—not much has been heard from the Lone Star State. A few novelists like Larry McMurtry and William Humphrey have staked out their claims and been made into movies. As for a concerted effort, however, aimed at reviving the serious achievements of DB&W, little has been undertaken in that direction. McMurtry has clearly made the most significant contribution toward an understanding of the modern Texas writer's relation to his region's history, at the same time that he has attempted to record and comment upon the contemporary situation in which such a writer finds himself. But neither the novel nor the essay is the genre to look to for an authentic link with the past or a penetrating account of the present. It is from the poet that we must ultimately seek the meaning of where we have been, the problems with how we are, and a prophecy as to what the future can hold, once we have learned from his songs our true inheritance and from his recitals of our backsliding ways the challenge of the here and now.

Unfortunately, there is still today the stigma of any such regional tag as "Texas poet." We would be universal, not down-home. This despite the fact that most all our celebrated poetry has grown from a clearly definable region, that of Williams, Sandburg, Lowell, Olson, Jeffers. Frost himself said he would first be an individual, then a native of a given ground, and only last a universal poet. For many in our own day the difficulty is not so much learning to know a specific region or to identify with it, rather it is a matter of retaining a regional feel or developing it once we have been uprooted. So many poets today earn their living as teachers (which may or may not be a handicap, depending on the individual) that it is common to find these recorders of a region's heartbeat transplanted where they never quite belong, and unable, once their profession calls, to carry on as poets of any one place. Forced by the academic system to leave the state where they received their roots—their education, their fundamental memories, their basic inspiration—they often either dry up or adopt themes and manners untrue to their poetic nature. Thus far I have been speaking mainly about my own predicament, although a few other poets here may share my experience and point of view. But since only around a fourth of the poets in this anthology are in "exile," the concerns of most are not nec-

Introduction to *The New Breed: An Anthology of Texas Poets* (Prickly Pear Press, 1973), pp. 10-17.

essarily my own. Even to these, however, being a Texas poet is, as Carolyn Maisel has written, "a matter of survival in the most difficult sense." And yet this same poet is "convinced that for reasons we all know but find hard to explain . . . Texas is one of the most fertile artistic environments in America," if only because of this necessity to survive in alien surroundings. For those who find none of this reason enough for a collection of Texas poets, it may appear that I have simply wanted to make an anthology, which is true. Still, it has long been a dream of mine to awaken in Texas poets a sense of the heritage they share and to encourage in the state's magazines and their audiences a greater receptivity to a new variety of regional writing.

One result of having lived in another section of the nation has been the advantage of a certain objectivity with regard to the question of regional literature. For many poets, rejected by those readers for whom their poems were originally meant, there is a warm reception awaiting their work outside their native state. This, though an encouraging fact, does not excuse a region's disregard for the writings of her native sons who render such a vital service. It is the age-old "no man's a prophet in his own land." To some even being granted asylum elsewhere is no bargain, for, as John Steinbeck writes in *Travels With Charley*, "A Texan outside of Texas is a foreigner." Nevertheless, I for one have found that Midwest audiences do not look upon me as a curiosity but listen with the same enthusiasm with which they hear their own poets. This is the consequence, I believe, of a respect on the part of such listeners for the regional poet and all he represents. It may just be the nature of a Texas poet's condition that he be ever a singer in a strange land, even when he never leaves his native soil. Of the poets collected here who are now living coast to coast, some return often, others infrequently, to the towns and cities of Texas, drawn back as by a loadstone. Some never felt at home in an atmosphere they basically considered hostile to poetry. Others long to land a job in one of the many urban centers they grew up in or moved to from smaller communities in search of even a meager intellectual climate. Regardless of which attitude it may be, it is evident from the poems in this collection that Texas has had a deep effect upon her poets. And in return, her poets have responded with a poetry which both does her honor and calls her to account for serious shortcomings.

Dave Hickey, a short story writer who apparently, like many others, gave up the art when he found both regional and national publications unreceptive to his Texas stories, once made an observation about the state that seemed so obvious after he had pointed it out, but that struck me as worthy of a Texas poet's constant awareness. He wrote in *Riata* (spring 1965), the University of Texas student literary magazine, "it is hard to be a texan, for texas from a given point is always extending." He illustrates this by noting how every area of the state becomes in a sense part of the region on which it borders, though is more than any of these (Louisiana, New Mexico, Oklahoma, Mexico) by virtue of being something of them all. This may seem merely another basis for a joke on the Texas size complex. But I think that, more than just a geographical consideration, it tells us that Texas is indeed rich in a variety of cultures (the plains, Faulkner's South, the Rocky Mountain plateau, and the Spanish and Indian influence of Mexico), and that unlike Illinois, for example, where the state is essentially the same from one end to another, to be from East Texas is nothing like being from El Paso, although something of all the sections is present in each. So that if, as Steinbeck asserts, "Texas is a state of mind," it is a complex one. This anthology demonstrates such complexity, for these poets have indeed cultivated it. Here a reader will find all the state's contrasting landscapes, with the images and ideas those suggest. The reader will also discover a vast array of styles and forms, from concrete poetry to traditional and experimental sonnets, from narrative and surrealist to lyric and imagist poems, not to mention representation from the prominent minority groups of the region, since every poet is in himself, by definition, a minority group of one.

Unlike the Texas anthologies of the past, this present volume is far-reaching in its implications; certainly it is not the usual cactus and cowshit collection associated with the Southwest. Its themes, its techniques are those which may be found in the work of the nation's leading contemporary poets, published in such prestigious magazines as *Poetry, The New Yorker, The North American Review.* And in fact a number of these Texas poets have appeared in those same periodicals. More importantly, such young poets as Charles Behlen and Leon Stokesbury have contributed to many of the smaller magazines. The same holds true for James Hoggard, Seth Wade, and Del Marie Rogers, and this is significant, for as Richard Kostelanetz points out in *Margins* 8 (Milwaukee), "All new directions in serious writing first appeared in small-circulation journals; so have all the American modernism's major writers." On the other hand, poets here have by no means turned their backs on their own unique heritage. Even though they may give the lie to any characterization of Texas writing as simply concerned with sand and ranch life, these poets remain faithful to a literary tradition which draws on the Spanish contribution to the region, the stoic character of its people accustomed to the land's undependable ways, and through the closeness of earth and sky to a sense of man's nearness to a larger scheme of things. Far from the famous braggadocio associated with Texans, it is this latter aspect of the poet-state relationship which has inspired a poetry well aware of man's smallness in the presence of natural and cultural wonders. Connected to this is the poets' feeling of both shame and humility before the large inheritance they have come into. It is especially the Spanish contribution to their culture that causes them pain when they consider the disrespect shown this background, at the same time that they are fully cognizant of their great good fortune at having been handed this opulence by the mysterious migration of peoples. The fact, then, that Texas spreads out wagonwheel fashion to touch on so many and distinctive features of the Southwest, as those of its religions, languages, histories, and arts, may make it difficult to be a Texan, but it also offers, particularly to the poet, the makings of a true enrichment. And it is to this possibility that the Texas poet now aspires.

Although no poet of the past has achieved a composite of these various natural and cultural elements, it is my firm belief that many of the poets here have at the very least begun this valuable process of amalgamation. In the case of a few, in particular Peter Wild, this process has already resulted in highly imaginative poems which combine a western tall-tale brand of surrealism with both social criticism and folk wisdom. Several of the poets, such as Robert Bonazzi and Stan Rice, exhibit a sophisticated understanding of trends in poetry of other nations. What many of these poets are doing lives up to the spirit of DB&W's instructions: to "have a genius for soaking in and oozing out"; to preserve "a tenderer regard for the whole of the animate world"; and not to be so utopian as to isolate themselves from what others have done. And if the poets here are "the new breed," this implies that there has been an older line from which these descendants have taken their pedigree, either in imitation or reaction or both. To overlook the earlier poets of the region, or those who are still quite active in the development of a regional literature, would be more than an oversight, it would be a true sin of omission, a lack of gratitude for their contribution, and a self-defeating blow. For not to know from whence one has evolved is to understand little about where one is going. I want immediately to acknowledge my own indebtedness to John Graves' *Goodbye To A River*, a sourcebook for many Texas poets, to the Texas poems of Thomas Whitbread and William D. Barney, R.G. Vliet's "Clem Maverick," a poem on Dobie, "Acrostic," by Tom Sutherland, and William Burford's "South, Southwest." The work of these men, and that of many others, among them Howard McCord, Judson Crews, Vassar Miller, and Archibald Henderson, has shaped a generation of younger writers by showing how a Texan may find in his region the form and content of fine contemporary poetry. These are the giants upon whose shoulders we hope to have climbed. If we see beyond them, it redounds upon so many pioneers for having furnished us the wherewithal.

Any anthology is limited by time, space, and the editor's own peculiar taste. *The New Breed* is no exception. For this reason there are poets of this generation who have been excluded, unknown, or simply impossible to contact. Some are, in my mind and in those of many other readers, already strongly identified with another region. Three of these, who are certainly otherwise deserving of inclusion here, are Betty Adcock (widely published as a North Carolina poet), Lewis MacAdams (known as a New York poet and closely associated with that "school" through its magazines and anthologies), and Paul Foreman (editor of *Hyperion* in California). Two poets in this present collection, Stan Rice and Robert Bonazzi, have been publishing from California and New York, but both have been closely connected with Texas letters—Rice through his "On the Murder of Martin Luther King" (in *Quickly Aging Here*), with its study of the sources of a Texan's racism, and Bonazzi by reason of his outstanding magazine *Latitudes*, which he edited for several years in Houston. Poets like Franklin Haar, John Igo, and Nefthalí de León work in modes which do not exactly fit into this particular collection. Nonetheless, they and many others are out there doing their part, and this anthology in no way means to discount their contribution. On the contrary, it is the aim of this collection to encourage more rather than less diversity, at the same time that it calls for a unified effort for the good of a regional consciousness. Another anthology would serve well as a corrective to the limitations of this one and would thereby further demonstrate the wide range of Texas poetry.

And what, then, is a "Texas poet"? Perhaps it is, as Steinbeck suggests, a state of mind, but the extreme case of such. Perhaps no such "animal" has yet been bred, with more crossbreeding required before we can arrive at the genuine article. And if this is so, then hopefully this anthology may prove a necessary step toward that creation. For to "breed" a Texas poet, as I envision him or her, would mean that the process of amalgamation had reached a level at which the term "Texas poet" would be synonymous with an awareness of, and respect for, the various challenging and inspiring strains of a line known not for pureness but for its blending of such strains in a way that does credit to each separately and to all in combination. This is what any region's poetry, I believe, must aim for, and in doing so will both define its bounds and transcend them.

In the last analysis, of course, it is the poetry we look to for answers to questions of time and place. People, regions, and good poetry go together: a truism. But there can be no truth in this statement unless the interdependence of the three components is taken seriously. Always the poetry faithful to the best in man lives with and evaluates where and how he is, has been, and wishes to be, and I trust that this is true of the poems in this collection. What strikes me most about the anthology as a whole is, indeed, its indebtedness to the past and its hope for the future. A young poet like Charles Behlen, dedicated to the art of poetry with all his intellectual and emotional energy (which is great even after painting houses for a living), bodes well for the years ahead. All of the poets here are paying their respects to the past, and in looking both backwards and forwards lend evidence of Texas' maturing literature. As a sign of this dual perspective, the anthology has fallen, simply through the fate of an alphabetical arrangement, into that same healthy pattern: the first poem, peering out the back of the bus at an older order, and the last, contemplating those yet to come. In betweeen these windows and doors to the past and future, the poems here focus, finally, on what it means to be in the 1970s full of song and concern.

Introduction to the Texas Section of
Southwest: A Contemporary Anthology

As much as size, the variety—of landscapes, cultures, hopes and regrets encompassed by the state—has undermined the conscious and unconscious lives of Texas writers. Most every literary artist who has sought to evoke or probe the nature of the place—its people, its heritage, its language (all in the plural)—has met with overwhelming demands, made on him or her by diffusiveness (in terms both of territory and of the grandiose treatment required), as well as by the necessity of creating with no audience or with a hostile one at best. There has always been a tendency among the natives of the state to distrust and belittle anything homegrown, except for beef and barrels of crude. This is even reflected in a drawing from the early fifties meant to encourage investment in the state's insurance companies, which pictured a cow with her head in Texas, grazing, while New Yorkers milked the tits.

The result of this situation is that many a Texas writer has settled elsewhere, or for a limited view of subject and style in hopes of achieving even the off-and-on respectable label of "regionalist." In addition to the reluctance of many Texas writers to produce "rooted" material, a haughty challenge is inherent in the heart of Texas itself—that *it*, by God, will take more from an artist than it will ever grant. Recently, despite the odds, Texas writers have begun to return, in spirit and in person, to a well which seemed eternally dry, and have found even to their own surprise a thirst-quenching source left long untapped. The new writing derives basically from an acceptance of limitations, of the small gains for inordinate pains, from a desire to plumb the depths rather than just to scratch the surface with cliched drill bits, and from a dedication to making do on what is seen at last as suitably native: the stubby subject that is yet durable as a common post oak; the cedar chopper's furry, rusting, sweet-scented stake which, as he would say, may be crooked as a dog's hind leg but can stand a hundred years.

Likened throughout its history to hell, by both the visitor and the settler, Texas, with famed heat and monotonous plains, has been looked upon as not even fit for the devil himself. This attitude, along with the typical western image and its wearying burden, has deprived her artists of the ability to come to grips with the truly diverse and deeply fertile character of the region. For the land has proved a magnet of torment attracting peoples as distinct as Scotch-Irish, Mexican, Comanche, Italian, Black, German, Swede, and Jew—and would

Southwest: A Contemporary Anthology, eds. Karl and Jane Kopp, and Bert Lanier Stafford III (Red Earth Press, 1977), pp. 71-73.

seem to call for no less than a Dante, a Milton, or a Whitman to tally it. But it may be that Texas will produce, instead, a throng of minor voices of every race raised not in praise of any one vision but as an expression of thanks for each and especially for the very least.

In the make-or-break Texas crucible the new writer faces the same fearful yet inspiring prospects on the literary score as his forebears knew on that of oil patch or cactus range. The healthiest signs are that native writers are taking Texas seriously, are also seeing the humor in many sides of the state taken too soberly in the past. As to any place offering the artist a ready-made pattern for theme and form, it remains true as ever that these the artist must make for himself, inventing in a sense even the place itself. To answer her haughtiest challenges, even knowing that in the end the writing may turn out to be a mere tight-fisted testament to a place which has ever insisted on the impossible from its inhabitants (while somehow in return promising and supplying a measure heaped as real as it is rare), offers an undertaking unequalled in potential at present by any other region of the nation.

Traveling from Fort Worth in the north (Amon Carter's comeuppance reply to dandified Dallas), through Waco (home of the Baptists and of Brann the iconoclast), Austin (city whose industry is "non-polluting" paper—Capital and seat of the sprawling University system), San Antonio (welcome mat for the Chicano-Mexican migration), swinging near but missing sight & sound of kill-dee & Gulf at Corpus Christi, passing on to the orange groves of Harlingen and finally arriving at palm-treed Brownsville on the border, the changing sameness, the dry and then humid heat, altered styles of year-long lightweight dress, drawling modes of address, all seem too much for any one author to handle. If he knows those areas lying beyond this narrow strip down the middle of the state, he will feel even more humbled, or rather pulled apart on this procrustean bed, incapacitated in the face of what will strike him as great stretches of the imagination, a beckoning like Scylla & Charybdis on either side threatening to wreck even an enlarged sense of place on the vast reaches of piney woods to the east (where men have lost their ways and never come out alive) or the brush country endless and exhausting to the west.

Looking to the skies near Kingsville, one takes in the long wavering lines of geese written against the billowing clouds above alternating marsh & prickly pear, but how to get them down, how to imitate such alexandrines escaping the coastal page, with that same sweep & grandeur of their going? In fields extending flat to the horizon, bundled hay lies like pungent, compact quatrains the Texas poet can barely dream of penning before the image of mesquite or oil slick breaks in upon his romantic reveries. Just as he has registered his impressions, so many prize-winning herefords of words, the blatant city lights & accents put them down as out of date, cornball, tied too closely to a tradition no town boy in his right mind could ever accept. Yet he must feel that to record alone the hotrod racket of metropolitan streets is to remain too silent upon the ingenuous twang of his country cousin's rockabilly guitar. Listening to the Mexican-looking, native-born Texas at the chain store register making change in two languages at once, the writer wants to blend his images, his words, his rhythms, but wouldn't that be copying what is natural to the Chicano, cutting in, riding around on a fad? How does one man find it in himself to incorporate such diversity? Where in himself can he honestly discover the right to so much land, so many tongues, at a time when corporate holdings present such a singularly evil aspect?

Indeed, it is this very paradoxical and unsettling state of things that comprises the stuff of his richest writing. And we are back to variety and the question of whether one writer can contain it all, whether he should even worry when he has managed but a meager hold on a minor part of the whole. Today there is no one figure we look to in Texas as laureate or leader, and why should we, when the landscape demands more than a single voice can ever hope to sing, urges its artists to try their hands at every available form, denying none, just as the land would have not a thorn nor a devil's claw less in its array of satanic plants. What is needed, then, and what we are beginning to get, is a harkening (here & back) to the many stories and poems, old and new, those of the folk and those of the refined, an encouraging of each in what it would say of a place we can only know once it has been sounded by those who love its ways, those begrudging fields that yield less than we foolishly want, yet more than any man or woman will ever need to make it on.

Faced by the vastness of the task, Texas writers may in the long run come to create a smaller art, one more in keeping with their sense of the worth of each man's contribution in a land where the mythical individualist is seen at last as not so heroic in himself as he is in relation to the grander scheme of true regional representation. The Texas writers of our day indicate they are on that road by their modest carriage and the genuine message they are learning to bear.

Texas Poetry
A Beginning with William Barney

For readers trained in world literature and in the major writers of North America, familiarity with any poetry outside the mainstreams of classroom consideration tends only to come, if at all, early or late in our reading careers. The more's the pity, since not always at those times are we so able to judge properly or to accept so readily the value of regional writing. Perhaps the first poets or poems sighted on our limited horizon are those of the region where we are born or reared, but with our education either lacking or quickly taken in hand by those aware of more far-reaching contemporary currents, the regionalist pales in importance as a lower mountain does before the higher, more imposing peaks that rise above. Indeed, we often reach those distant heights by the foothills of the regionalist's work, yet little thanks he has for his efforts, much less for the worth of his own unassuming prospects. After years of studying "foreign" giants, often in search of what has all along been cultivated in our own backyards, it is only out of curiosity that we return to consider the long-since adjudged "minor" figures of a native landscape. With a shock of recognition we may well see in these local artists not only poets worthy of critical acclaim on their own account but poems of a tradition other than the one we have fallen into feeling exclusive, as well as of a thought and technique quite deserving of our notice and equal in some ways to those of more prominent authors.

Just such a case is this of William D. Barney, the accumulation of whose work as a Texas poet has taken place quietly until today it forms a body of poems unique to Southwest letters and in certain respects original even beyond any regional tag. Born in 1916 in Tulsa, Oklahoma, William Barney has, since 1928, made his home in Fort Worth, Texas. Author of two published volumes, *Kneel From The Stone* (1952) and *Permitted Proof* (1955), both from Kaleidograph Press (Dallas), Barney is presently a retired postal worker, though still a very active poet, as poems from the 60s and 70s brought together here in the present volume so amply and remarkably demonstrate.

While it is perhaps his latest work which merits special attention, in order to understand from whence he has come and to appreciate better where his previous work has carried him, *The Killdeer Crying* gathers poems from the earlier collections which are characterized essentially by their employment of traditional techniques, techniques the poet has continued to utilize even more

Introduction to *The Killdeer Crying: Selected Poems of William Barney* (Prickly Pear Press, 1977), pp. 11-19.

effectively in recent years. The question of whether a poet's predilection for standard metres, rhyme, and conventional stanza patterns may act as a hindrance to his fullest expression is one which must be treated in any consideration of such a "traditional" poet, for it is a central point in regard to Barney's achievement, his at-times old-fashioned sound and sense, yet often the source of his very decided triumphs. Even as a self-confessed admirer of Frost, Barney has managed nevertheless to create a poetry of his own, peculiar to his own region and to his own inexhaustible though meticulous use of vocabularies drawn from fields as remote as mathematics and ornithology. In general, Barney's poetry does not call attention to the poet, does not bring judgments against any group or type, nor does it complain or disparage. Even though it is largely impersonal, it yet leaves the reader with the impression of a man behind the poems of great humility, one who is high-minded (in the best sense of that phrase), imaginative, thoughtful, and ever sensitive to language and to the world about him. Above all, William Barney's poetry is one of praise.

Despite the strength of his mind and the delicate music of its expression, Barney and his work have for the most part gone unknown or ignored by Texas readers. To suggest that his poetry has not been noticed at all, however, is to overstate the case, for both of Barney's collections from the 1950s won Texas Institute of Letters Awards and the title poem of the present volume won the Robert Frost Award of the Poetry Society of America. His work has also been taken into account by such critics and anthologists as Frederick Eckman, Martin L. Shockley, and Betsy Colquitt. While *The Killdeer Crying* is the fullest selection of his work to-date and will hopefully showcase the poet as he truly deserves, the comments and contributions of earlier critics and editors have encouraged the making of this third collection of William Barney's warm but engaging poems.

In *Poetry* (Chicago, volume 89), Frederick Eckman reviewed Barney's *Permitted Proof* (1955) along with works by Robert Creeley, Robert Duncan, Paul Blackburn, and Lawrence Ferlinghetti, all the latter, as Eckman points out, writing under the influence of William Carlos Williams. While Eckman sees Barney's book as less daring than, say, Creeley's, he does state that the Texan is not conservative, though formal in expression, and that more than the other writers reviewed, Barney has "in his work a good deal more of affirmation, of an ultimate (if hard-won) faith in the human condition." The critic admires particularly Barney's handling of animal poems, his Bach-like lines in "Bach as a Propagation of Cells," and his strong narrative bent. Although Eckman believes that Barney's poetry "deserves a wider audience," he does not feel that the poet is so highly successful when he comes to local western themes, as in his "Canticle for a Cutting Horse."

Taking quite the opposite view from Eckman, with respect to this very same poem, Martin Shockley in his edition of a *Southwest Writers Anthology* (Steck, 1967) remarks on the poet's deftness in following the canticle form. He explains how praise for the mount develops, first, from pleasure in her sheer movement, next to delight in the relation between animal and spirit, then to a rejoicing in the glory of the subject itself, on then to a treatment of the animal as a symbol for the mind, and finally to simple celebration of the cutting horse as "her image, nothing shall rightly encompass." Within these five stanzas the phrases, word combinations, and concepts are wonderfully worked out. The pointed phrase, "A blend of desire and dissent," presents the piece's central paradox: the horse's urge to perform well but at the same time to be free of the force that demands a performance. Instead of a poet's own subjective desire, weakening the poem by that very fact, Barney's canticle provides an objective portrait on a more universal level—thus denying any local limitations his subject matter might otherwise suggest. The whole poem is, however, rich in suggestiveness, as the uncommon analogies and the natural allusions combine to form a right relationship between the imaginative and the real:

> Like a spider she weaves the kinetic web of enclosure,
> she throws her great breast as a shuttle.
> . . . A talisman in her tawniness
> for any who praise the pursuit
> of the quick metaphor, the well-cinched word . . .
>
> Leave her to the high mesas,
> to the open llano, her proper stage: let her dance
> her tango of intricate measures . . .

In addition to the notice of Barney's work taken by these two critics, the anthologist and editor of *Descant*, Betsy Colquitt, has included the poet in her fine collection, *A Part of Space: Ten Texas Writers* (T.C.U. Press, 1969). The selection of a dozen poems from work done during the 50s and 60s serves as an important introduction to this little-known Texas poet. Among her choices Colquitt includes two poems from Barney's 1955 volume, and it is his earlier work which I now wish to discuss with a view to its significant place in the poet's development over a span of more than thirty years.

Beginning with *Kneel From The Stone* (1952), Barney exhibits many of the linguistic and thematic preoccupations which mark the entire range of his work, though, as in most first books, there are single poems that point to a learning process which will only later result in the sure touch. The influence of Frost is quite evident, though this is not derivative in a dependent way. Perhaps an even more important influence has been Audubon (Barney has even written an unpublished verse play on the life of the naturalist), and the poem "On a Detail from Audubon" contains a stanza that illustrates concisely the poet's awareness of the need for both manliness and control in the best of writing:

> A soft stroke lames
> the line, depraves.
> The fierce detail
> enhances, saves.

It is another instance of the success accorded poets of the contemporary persuasion who make use of a historical figure like Audubon that simply because they versify from letters, journals, or government documents it is thought they have created "modern poetry," especially when they adapt an Audubon to their own special views of history or art. I am thinking specifically of William Heyen's recent use of Audubon in *Noise in the Trees* (1974). Though normally I much admire this poet, I tend to agree with one critic who comments that "the advantage of setting the facts in verse isn't always apparent." Working much earlier within a strict rhyme scheme and metre, William Barney reveals the firm and exact art of Audubon. As in the best of Yeats's rhymed poems, the meaning is strengthened by Barney's crafted stanzas. Unlike Heyen's account of Audubon's career, which simply versifies the facts in a prosy, journalistic fashion, Barney's poem is stark, wastes no words with self-consciousness, nor with cutesy introductions to a poet's philosophical plight:

> The hand that snared
> the cobalt wing,
> that froze the blue
> thief plundering
>
> caught also—look—
> the vine's hard claw
> of tendril writhing
> at the bird's craw

The directness, the clarity of color and interaction, and the shrewd observation of the artist's design are all done with the greatest respect for the object in view. Its reality is presented and the poet receives, or should, our total attention for this reason alone and not for any "poetic" rendering of what someone else has written. The writing here is Barney's, and the subject is fortunate in having it so.

Even more to this point of objectivity is the last poem in the 1952 collection, "Bracero," which is a first-rate narrative and close in this sense to R.G. Vliet's better-known "Clem Maverick," as well as in its presentation of a Texas subject matter. The style is somewhat dated, but the viewpoint is convincing. Told partly in the words of the bracero himself, the story is moving at the level of its portrayal of the love of a man for his wife and children, for whom in his lowly position he is incapable of doing much of anything. The tragedy is not of the kingly sort but will serve. The bracero's attempt to give his wife a false satisfaction is gripping, and the language sustains the irony throughout. The drama derives from the father's desire to keep certain facts from his wife: that the son is dead and that the daughter has prostituted herself, both owing largely to the father's having crossed his family over the border in search of a better life. But again, it is Barney's craft that makes of a typical tale a memorable one:

> The lies came quickly to his lips; he fashioned

> them with ease.
> Yet his soul was not in his voice, and Suerta
> would not listen.
> She would have but truth, she would
> press his heart like the yellow grapefruit
> and drain the last bitter drop.

There are many poems of power and pleasure in Barney's two collections from the 1950s, but it is in the later poems to be found in Colquitt's selection, *A Part of Space*, that one observes how the poet has come into his own as a master of language and its objective use. Of the poems from the 60s included in the Colquitt book, all are worthy of comment, though I shall limit my discussion to four pieces which most clearly represent Barney as a model Texas poet: "The Calculus," "A Matter of Nerve," "The Day They Moved the Post Office," and "On Greer Island a Copperhead Lies Slain."

An indication of how Barney has slowly developed certain consistent themes may be seen by comparing "The Calculus" with a 1975 poem, "A Stone for Stumbling," where the poet writes of "The Man from Split City" that

> He'd a solid-geometry mind, he supposed;
> liked to see things fleshed out in space
> (otherwise they'd be figments, skinny abstractions,
> and you couldn't tell shape from shadow).

As earlier "The Calculus" suggests, Barney finds mathematics a fascinating subject, perhaps because it reveals our need to live with "mid-fact, half-lie." The poet notes that in calculus "what is given never is defined," as if to say that we always posit the unreal. In doing so he seems to feel that we should not "dissolve / the fabric of what's real, or rip the seam, / unhinge the valve." The poem teases us with its playful treatment of a serious theme: trying to tell "shape from shadow." In what is probably a pre-Borges vein, the Texas poet ponders the relationship between subject and object in any calculus problem:

> In dry despair I sit and think how I
> should think, or not;
> yet do I think, or am I by and by
> but something thought?

This stanza illustrates the metrics and rhyme scheme of the entire poem, but from first to last the reader can hardly hear the poet at work. Just as the language is natural, so is the thought, even while it turns upon itself, inside out, and leaves us every way but loose.

A similar poem is "A Matter of Nerve," where the poet once again plays with the problem of who is doing what to whom. Here the subject is apparently a western one, with the use of a barbed-wire fence as antagonist (or protagonist?). The situation is this: the "he" of the poem is caught between gate post and wire:

> And so he stood in equipoise:
> there wasn't any slack
> to let away the post, and none
> to slip the held hand back.

After several stanzas of trying to figure out a "mathematical" solution, the narrator affirms:

> It came down to a matter of nerve:
> whether something could assert
> the necessary injury
> it took to quit the hurt.

Barney assumes, rightly I think, that there is no easy way out—and of course the metaphor and paradox loom larger than the mere western image the poet employs.

In much of Barney's work, despite a certain serious intent, there is almost always a touch of humor very tender and human. An example is "The Day They Moved the Post Office," in which we find the objections registered to the move by a town drunk. The poem re-creates the speech of the character but more movingly suggests the way it is with his life:

> 'There's a boon knot between me and this place.
> Didn't I stand for counting?' . . .

> We thought for certain now he'd make it clear
> how it could make a difference to a sot
> where the post office was, where it was not,
> and who'd have written.

While many of Barney's ideas for poems come from his long association with the postal service and from his bird-watching activities, there is nothing limited in his scope, for these two subjects alone have supplied the poet with a far-ranging variety of observations and insights. This is the result principally of the poet's ability to settle into his surroundings. As a recent poem has it:

> The only need is to adapt your roots
> to where you are, gather up what feeds
> your kind (once you know it) and let bloom.

The final poem from the Colquitt collection I wish to comment on is the beautifully-structured piece on the death of a copperhead snake. While many of the lines involve inversions, the effect fully makes up for this disapproved-of practice. The diction is exquisite in its realization of the aesthetic qualities of the creature, as well as in its re-creation of the observer's reaction to the living reptile:

> This jack of diamonds dull and smooth,
> this copper-coopered smouldering band,
> thicket can never again soothe
> him sleeping in sleek ampersand.
> The spice of peril shall be gone
> from fallen log, from flaggy stone.

> What easy thing now shall we say
> for sentiment, a small rebate
> to salve with pardon? Rather pray
> for your enemy in his strait.
> This Ichabod has left us poorer.
> Where will we turn for simple terror?

Both Emily Dickinson and John Greenleaf Whittier would have found much to admire in the Texan's poem. (The reference to Ichabod, incidentally, is to Whittier's poem of that title and to I Samuel IV:21—"The glory has departed.")

Fortunately, while these highly-developed poems date from the early 60s, Barney has not let up, his production continuing, his eye as observant as ever. Among his most recent work collected here is the marvelous "Episode with Tomato." The ease of the language (almost a Chaucerian simplicity, yet modern), the naturalness of the rhyming, the down-to-earth subject matter, and the conclusion that makes us pause in assent and sadness—all of this is characteristic of the best poetry of William Barney. And it is much, not only in a state almost entirely unknown for poetry but in a nation where poetic fads come and go as quickly as the frivolous fashions, where yet the authentic poet, to quote a popular Texas song, "seldom is heard."

What makes of William Barney a Texas poet of whom we may be especially proud is the penetrating manner in which he has come to treat of the state's flora and fauna, as well as of her people—in poems on Mr. Bloomer, the town drunk (with that most telling and complex aside: "and who'd have written"), on the negro with a new car, the bracero, and the women who learn to live with the weather and with their men. In observing natural and human lives Barney has a special awareness of the knot and the flaw ("A Crooked Feast" and "Thaw"), an ability to see in these the beauties passed over by the impatient and undiscriminating eye. In writing of his friend and fellow-poet, the late Arthur Sampley touched on these same qualities he personally felt were most striking in Barney's work. In a letter dated June 21, 1975, Sampley wrote that William Barney "has his own way of seeing things and his own taut, figurative way of recording what he sees. His nature poems catch the fleeting, unexpected glimpse, the surprise of beauty in the commonplace or in the grotesque." To experience Barney's poems on both the tangible and technical levels is to appreciate, then, their fullest range and import, for it is through an integration of these two worlds that the poet has achieved a body of work truly rich in sympathy and earthly intelligence.

One last note I feel is necessary, and this is in reference to the press which supported Barney and other older Texas poets of his stature, among them Arthur Sampley, who died in Denton in the fall of 1975. Kaleidograph Press began printing books of poems in 1931 and ended publication sometime about 1960. More should be known of this important imprint and the significant contributions it made to Texas letters. Knowing more of Kaleidograph's history may one day provide an incentive for the emergence of other such presses in support of Texas poetry, that the beginnings made by Barney and others may not be lost on this or succeeding generations.

Small Presses in Texas

During the late 'thirties, my parents had their own printing business in Fort Worth—a small, low-overhead operation they ran themselves. Mother and dad produced work of high quality and made a fair living, yet in doing so they became competition for the larger printers who could not do the same fine work for the little it cost my folks. The result was that the larger shops, through a power play, cut my parents off from all sources of paper and effectively drove them out of business.

This Depression tale has come to me long after the fact, but I find it fairly typical of the plight today of those who would make livable incomes by managing their own concerns. Certainly it is the case with small presses, especially those which seek to produce works of literary value even when they are unable or disinclined to compete with nationally-based publishers. Like most groups, small press people are often chauvinists when it comes to their role in life. Though small in terms of financial wherewithal and the size of their pressruns, they are dedicated to creative quality and to the contribution their publications make to a living literature. Operating out of bedrooms, with money skimped from precarious incomes at temporary jobs, many small press editors work for others in whose art they believe, expecting little or no return, except the pleasure of seeing writing kept alive. Government grants help, but expenses far exceed monetary gains, and this is to say nothing of the endless hours of labor (phone calls, typing, layouts, proofing, collating) which are never accounted for in the total costs of production. More copies are given away than are ever sold. And if a book sells for $5.00, often the outlay per copy comes to more than $6.00. Bookstores take 40 percent of the cover price, which leaves the press with a return of only 50 percent of the actual unit cost, if not less. No banker can believe such businesses exist, and the Internal Revenue Service will check for a year or more to ascertain whether a one-man press with a debt of $8,000 is in fact a nonprofit enterprise. Yet small press publishers consider their craft well worth the sacrifices. They argue that the value of the service they render can never be put in dollars and cents, even though loan officers and scholars with tenure security continue to disagree. Small press people believe that ultimately the audit will show that almost single-handedly they have saved literature from going broke.

In the face of almost prohibitive odds, the small press movement has come into its own in the last decade, arriving recently on the Texas scene with amaz-

The Texas Observer (4 November 1977): 3-5.

ing energy and tenacity. There are various types of small presses established in the state; the smallest—and most numerous—are those devoted to the publication of poetry. There are two principal reasons for the concentration on verse: (1) more people write poetry than work in any other literary genre, and (2) poems are the form of literature cheapest to set in type and print. Prose writers have far fewer outlets than do poets—again, largely because of space and cost limitations. However, with the return to Texas of native publishers, who often left in reaction to the dearth of interest in contemporary prose fiction, even the situation for short story writers has improved greatly.

Still, the most active and determined small presses remain those devoted to poetry. A helpful recent development has been the formation in Austin of Texas Circuit, a small press distribution cooperative organized almost entirely by editors and writers interested in the printing and dissemination of the state's "new-found" poetry talent. Believing that Texas poets deserve a wider audience, Texas Circuit was founded to promote the distribution (through bookstores, to libraries, and at poetry readings and statewide book fairs) of both new and older writers who have appeared suddenly, have returned from "exile," or have been here all along.

The increase in the number of Texas poets producing work of a caliber meriting both regional and national recognition has prompted the appearance in the state of more than a dozen small presses. These include Chawed Rawzin (Lubbock, edited by Charles Behlen); Cedar Rock (New Braunfels, edited by David Yates); Trilobite (Denton, edited by Richard Sale); Place of Herons (Granger, edited by James Cody); Lucille (Austin, edited by Stephen Harrigan); Thorp Springs (Austin, edited by Paul Foreman); Cold Mountain (Austin, edited by Ryan Petty); Texas Portfolio (Texas City, edited by Dwight Fullingim); Noumenon (Austin, edited by Loris Essary); Texas Center for Writers (Dallas, edited by James P. White); Energy BlackSouth (Houston, edited by Ahmos Zu-Bolton); Caracol (San Antonio, edited by Alfredo and Susana de la Torre); Snake, Rattle & Roll (Austin, edited by Michael Prochoroff); Endeavors in Humanities (El Paso, edited by Daniel Conway); Latitudes (Austin, edited by Robert Bonazzi); Liberated Trash (Austin, edited by Mark Christal); Wings (Houston, edited by Joanie Whitebird), which is the newest Texas press yet has already printed chapbooks by Vassar Miller (*Small Change*) and Susan Bright (*Julia*), and will soon bring out collections by Michael Ventura and Joanie Whitebird; and my own press, Prickly Pear (Fort Worth).

Since bookstores rarely deal in publications lacking New York trade names and central distribution systems, small presses must beg for space on retail shelves and plead with book review editors to allow even a short column for notices. Once a small press publication has received good reviews, it is extremely discouraging for the publisher to hear from booksellers that they are still uninterested in stocking the book. Small presses have persisted nonetheless, and now with Texas Circuit providing a systematic distribution program, the growing audience for small press publications should find contemporary Texas literature more readily available.

Another significant development is the recent addition by *The Texas Quar-*

terly of its first book review section, which will be open to small press publications. (A related undertaking by the *Quarterly* is a projected series of books of original and translated poetry to be published under the *TQ* imprint.)

Quartet (College Station, edited by Richard Hauer Costa) has long provided space for reviews of new Texas writing, while the *Southwest Review* in Dallas has done next to nothing for small presses (although J. Frank Dobie once described the magazine's policy as one of "asserting Southwest literature"; were the grand old man still here I feel certain he would agree that the most important developments in Texas letters are taking place on the small press front).

Among Texas' small press magazines that have themselves added review space, five are particularly noteworthy for the attention they have paid to the state's poets: *Wood Ibis*, from Jim Cody's important Place of Herons Press, which has also published some half dozen chapbooks by nature-oriented poets; *The Gar*, something of a Third World magazine in the *Nation* format, which has printed poems, reviews, and long assessments of Texas and African poets; *Cedar Rock*, which prints both full-length essays on poets and excerpts from small press books as reviews; *The Pawn Review*, edited by Michael Anderson in Dallas, which offers review space almost exclusively to Texas small press publications; and *Texas Portfolio*, which has carried reviews and articles on national and regional artists. In addition, Texas Center for Writers Press, with its *Texas Books in Review*, has instituted an annual compilation of Texas press publications, as well as running lengthy reviews. Also, the Texas Association of Creative Writing Teachers' *Newsletter* regularly publishes solid reviews of small press publications. A new outlet for reviews, *Book News* in Dallas (published by *The Texas Arts Journal*, a slick, pretentious magazine which prefers the cast-off, second-rate work of big-name, out-of-state writers) initially ran critiques of small press chapbooks but has reportedly dropped them out of a mistaken belief that they have no real audience.

The proliferation of small press publications in Texas is due at least as much to the quality of the output as it is to the quantity. Two large anthologies of Texas poetry that have appeared within the past four years bear witness to the new level of artistic achievement: my own *The New Breed* (1973) and Paul Foreman and Joanie Whitebird's *Travois* (1976). Both collections include the work of Texas poets who have attracted national attention—Vassar Miller, Leon Stokesbury, Stan Rice, Robert Bonazzi, and William Burford among them. Walt McDonald is represented in both anthologies by poems which last year won him the Texas Institute of Letters award for poetry. In response to the increasingly distinguished work showing up in the state's small press publications, *Texas Monthly* and *The Dallas Morning News* have given review space to such books as Lucille Press's *Giants* and *From Hell to Breakfast* and Thorp Springs Press's *Travois* and *Beyond the Rivers*. Reviews of *The Killdeer Crying: Selected Poems of William Barney* (Prickly Pear Press) are scheduled for winter issues of *The Texas Quarterly, Western American Literature,* and *Choice.*

Along with the interest taken by general circulation publications in the work of Texas' small presses has come increased support for their activities from the National Endowment for the Arts, the Coordinating Council for Little Magazines, and the Texas Commission on the Arts and Humanities. Not only has the number of presses applying for funding tripled in the last year, but the average size of grants received has gone from about $3,000 to over $5,000. Latitudes Press has been awarded a $6,000 NEA grant to produce five books. Place of Herons and Cold Mountain have, between them, received $5,000 in NEA money, while *Lucille, Caracol, Cedar Rock, Tejidos,* and *Espejos de la mujer* have been given some $4,500 by the CCLM. The Texas Commission expects at least a 2 percent rise in small press grants, perhaps even more. (Commission awards are actually book purchase arrangements: the press selected sells a set number of copies to the Commission for Texas library distribution, and then pays for postage, packaging, and book seals. The result is that the press is assured of sales that can bring in an income as great as 50 percent of the total cost of a book's publication; usually, however, the income realized amounts to only about a fourth of the final production bill.)

To give an idea of the range of work produced by small presses in Texas, I will describe briefly some of the books they have published in the last five years. I begin with Prickly Pear Press of Fort Worth because it is probably the oldest publisher of the poetry chapbook (a standard small press publication—inexpensive, offset, stapled, usually about 40 pages, with a pressrun of 200 to 250 copies). Jim Jacobs and I founded Prickly Pear in late 1972, when I was living in Illinois and functioning as a long-distance editor and publisher of Texas verse. The first poet we printed was Jon Bracker, a long-time advocate of Texas poetry from the period of the early 'sixties when he edited *Penny Poems,* first from Amarillo and later in Wichita Falls. Since the Bracker collection we have published Joseph Colin Murphey's *A Return to the Landscape* and, most recently, William Barney's *The Killdeer Crying: Selected Poems.* Winner of the Robert Frost Award for poetry in 1961, Barney is Texas' first important poet and his *Selected Poems* was Prickly Pear's first hardcover publication. In all, the press has printed a 200-page anthology of Texas poets, a collection of Texas student poetry, and four individual volumes by Texans.

Austin's *Lucille,* begun in 1973 by Stephen Harrigan (currently the Texas Institute of Letters Paisano Fellow), has published nine issues and the two books mentioned earlier. In 1975 a special issue of *Lucille* was devoted to children's poetry. Eager to publish poetry of the most inventive sort, *Lucille* has featured the work of Texans John Ramington, winner of the Oliker award for poetry from *American Review,* and Thomas Whitbread, author of *Four Infinitives* (Harper & Row).

Perhaps the oldest small press still active in the state is Robert Bonazzi's Latitudes, which began as a magazine in Houston in 1966. Bonazzi moved Latitudes to Austin after some five years in New York City and now runs it as a press operation specializing in experimental prose and poetry. He has printed nine editions in both cloth and paper; three more books are scheduled for publication this fall. Several of his books have been reviewed nationally and all are handled by Serendipity, the prestigious California small press distributor. *The Library Journal* has cited Latitudes as one of the most important publishers of experimental work being written today.

A small press particularly noted for its beautifully designed poetry editions is Trilobite, founded by Richard Sale in Denton in 1973. In addition to publishing three collections by Texas poets—*Hog Killin' Time* by Bruce Davis, *Five Faces* by J.M. Linebarger, and *Eyesigns* by James Hoggard—Trilobite has also produced a book of plays by Robert Lockwood, *Transformations*.

Two of the most ambitious figures in small press publishing have been James P. White (Texas Center for Writers Press in Dallas) and Dwight Fullingim (Texas Portfolio in Texas City). White's large-run edition of *The Bicentennial Collection of Texas Short Stories* (1974) was the first of a series of books presenting both experimental and traditional writing; the series has also included a volume devoted to the work of Texas women writers. A new series of single-author works is in the offing, as is a second anthology of prose and poetry. Fullingim has, since early 1976, been producing two magazines, *Texas Portfolio* (published by B. Weberlein) and *Poetry *Texas* (published by the College of the Mainland in Texas City). Each magazine has its own chapbook series. To date *TP* and *P*T* have issued a dozen chapbooks, including two collections of translations by Texans. Fullingim's edition of Naomi Shihab's *Tattooed Feet* has gone through an unprecedented second printing, thus becoming a small press bestseller. (Shihab's second volume of verse is due out later this fall.) The energy of both of these editors is unmatched by anyone in Texas letters.

A final pair of presses which seem to me on a par with those already mentioned are Paul Foreman's Thorp Springs Press in Austin and David Yates' New Braunfels-based *Cedar Rock*, a tabloid magazine that finances an active chapbook series. Foreman is a native Texan who began publishing in Berkeley, California, but from the beginning he has actively supported writing in his home state, first through his magazine *Hyperion* and currently through another venture entitled *Tawté* (Texas artists writers and thinkers in exile), which premièred in June 1974 under the coeditorship of Foreman and James Cody. Thorp Springs has published an impressive anthology of Texas poets, *Travois*, as well as a number of single volumes by Texans and a book of translations of Paraguayan poetry, part of a Latin American series undertaken by North Texan Charles Carlisle.

Yates' *Cedar Rock* represents a highly original approach to the cost and distribution problems facing small presses. By publishing his magazine on inexpensive newsprint, Yates has been able to print an unusually large number of poems, add a chapbook series, include lengthy regular columns by talented commentators (most notably, R.S. Gwynn), and run reviews, ads, and news-notes—all for a per-issue price of 90 cents to a rapidly expanding readership. An especially successful issue of *Cedar Rock*, edited by Naomi Shihab, was comprised of poems from students of the Poetry-in-the-Schools program.

While Texas' larger and older small presses have much to be proud of, many of the younger and scruffier ones deserve a good word for the way they conduct their business and the readerships they choose to serve. Wings in Houston is unique in that it is the only Texas small press paying royalties to authors

(5 percent on all books sold). Wings is also unusual in that it prints on an 1890 hand-operated press, restored and lately motorized; almost all the other small presses in Texas, too poor to afford more than a typewriter and a chapbook stapler, must job out their printing to commercial presses. Caracol basically serves the needs of Chicano poets, Energy BlackSouth those of Black poets, Frieda Werden's Texan Woman Press those of women poets, Jim Cody's Place of Herons those of any race or creed, so long as their poetry lies close to the land, while Loris Essary's Noumenon Press (publisher of *Interstate* magazine) provides periodical and chapbook outlets for poets leaning toward the dada and concretist schools. The most encouraging development is that all the small presses, new and old, regardless of their special interests, are pulling together to promote the contemporary Texas poet. The ingenuity, persistence, and dedication of Texas' small press publishers have contributed to a growing movement that is clearly here to stay. This can only be a healthy sign for Texas letters, for as Richard Kostelanetz has pointed out in his influential book on the trials and tribulations of small press people, *The End of Intelligent Writing*, America owes the publication of many of its most important literary works to the nation's small presses.

Who's Afraid of the Big Bad Poem?

Certainly Whitman wasn't, nor was William Carlos Williams, and neither are
most of the poets of the 1970s. According to James Dickey, who went over
like a lead balloon on saying so before a gathering of Latin American scholars,
Pablo Neruda was the last of the great bad poets. The idea was not original
with Dickey (nor meant the way it was taken), yet serious as the claim has
been in some quarters, it seems unlikely to stand the test of time, since the
"bad" line of Whitman and Neruda appears due for a long and international
respect. Even before the nineteenth century, there were other great poets who
feared no evil from writing poems the New Critics would never approve. Thanks
to Whitman, Williams, and Neruda, today's crop of poets is not intimidated in
the least by the prospect of falling short of perfection. (This observation is intended only slightly as a tongue-in-cheek criticism of the contemporary poem,
for despite certain reservations about the promiscuous poetics of some of our
generation, by and large I feel that we should not be cowed by a vision of the
perfect poem.) The fact is that the recent outpouring (and publishing) of poetry by names hardly recognizable and rarely identifiable with any one school
is the result of a healthy view established by those three American giants who
found the writing of poems a concomitant to our residence here on earth. The
books, anthologies, and saddle-stitched collections received of late by the *Texas
Quarterly* testify to an exciting array of writing that might be attributed to a
disregard for high art but which, considering its quality, seems more the product of less fear and greater love for the genuine act of making poems.

Granted, a distinction must be made immediately between the "bad" work
of a great writer and the best performance of a poetaster. What may be justified as innovation in one author (Gertrude Stein noted how the new may be
ugly when first attempted) can be simply mediocrity in those who adopt the
posture but fail to render any service of substance. There is a Whitmanesque
looseness which is deceptively informal or, stated another way, is subtly so.
Thus, it may be that looseness for its own sake has no place in poetry as
such. While the poet may properly require a period for loosening up his lines
and for learning a feel for his lives, there may be little to justify his serving an
apprenticeship in public. Nonetheless, if the poet does choose to publish at
an early stage, critical judgment may aid him in this whole loosening-up process by considering if a work is significantly "bad" or is not yet beyond what
Pound called writing poorly out of ignorance and inexperience. Ultimately,

The Texas Quarterly, vol. 20, no. 4 (winter 1977): 190-99.

I think, it should be clear that the recent explosion of poetry publishing has at least carried forward one aspect of Whitman's vision of poetry-America: "the tremendous audacity of its crowds and groupings and the push of its perspective spreads with crampless and flowing breadth and showers its prolific and splendid extravagance."

Representing the broadest cross section of regions, races, and styles, within the limits of this omnibus review, *The Face of Poetry* collects the work (and full-page photographs) of 101 poets, from coast to coast. Perhaps because the photographer and principal editor, LaVerne Harrell Clark, is a resident of the Southwest (Tucson), there is a fair concentration of poets from the area of New Mexico and Arizona (a dozen at least), but all deserve to be included, even those who may be less prominent than many others excluded from this selection subtitled the work of "Two Significant Decades—the 60s & the 70s." While there is only one poem per poet, the choices are generally excellent and quite representative, though not the usual pieces which we associate with figures like William Stafford and Richard Eberhart. Speaking of the photographs of the poets, Eberhart states in his foreword to the anthology that these are not the posed, impersonal portraits we often know poets by but rather are "offhand, informal depictions" which "increase a reader's interest by doing what LaVerne Clark does so well in this focus on the chance moment, a special moment of being." Likewise, the poems themselves are frequently "offhand, informal depictions."

If contemporary poets fear anything, it is to be too formal. The conversational tone is, of course, cultivate. The dangers of this studied naturalness are evident in Stephen Dunn's contribution, though he does have better work to offer elsewhere:

> My poems are approximately true.
> The games I play and how I play them
> are the arrows you should follow: they'll take you
> to the enormous body of a child. It is not
> that simple. At parties I have been known to remove
> from the bookshelf the kind of book
> that goes best with my beard.

Here even the poet's self-criticism is overly cute and self-conscious. A better effort deriving from the "song of myself" tradition is Dan Gerber's "A Fine Excess," which pays direct homage to Whitman and recalls Neruda in its great leaps in sea and space. The title of the poem also suggests an appreciation for the epical, even though the speaker admits "I never learn from experience." Gerber's main point is that the excessive in poetry is a fine thing. In his case, the poetry seems to support his position, though in other instances in the anthology the freedoms taken are somewhat annoying, as in Charles Simic's "Further Adventures of Charles Simic"—a clever analogy involving the question of his being afraid of death, which ends with the line: "His tongue will slash his throat." Fortunately, however, much of the work here is extremely moving and rings true even when it is apparent that the poets are "playing" with, for example, an ethnic theme. Robert J. Conley's "Self-Portrait: Microcosm, or, Song of Mixed Blood" builds a sad commentary on the loss of "the ancient forms" when a half-breed can only hunt "with the channel selector." Leroy Quintana's "Untitled" touches on a similar paradise lost, that of his grandfather's world, where the poet was first taught the four directions:

> He spoke their names as if they were
> one of only a handful of things
> a man needed to know

My favorite photograph is that of a friend, Karl Kopp, whose poem, "The Hanging Man," contains characteristic lines from this most hard-looking, soft-hearted of men:

> till one cow blunders close
> horned like a bull
> Look I don't want trouble
> Git

> when from the barn a sudden cry
> (I'd thought it empty
> but a calf of course
> not two weeks old so Denver told me)
> this its mother with bulk and horn
> to brave the man-thing
> (and now I see she trembles)

> It's okay
> I have my own young son to guard
> to love so hard it sometimes shakes me too

This excerpt forms part of Kopp's recently released collection, *Yarbrough Mountain* (Baleen Press), a book which re-creates the life of Arkansas mountaineers with whom Kopp lived as friend and neighbor.

A really lovely photo and a beautiful "last song / i'll ever sing" are those of Joy Harjo. On the other hand, Maxine Kumin's head-erect, olympic-posture pose goes well with her rather uptight poem, "Body and Soul: A Meditation." Appropriately, a number of the pieces feature autobiographical snapshots we can match up with the facing photographs, as in Richard Shelton's case, where he writes,

> you won't have to look close
> to see what I am
> or what I want to become
> or that I'm not becoming it

Another enigmatic poem that makes one look to the photo to try and discover what the poet is getting at is Miguel González-Gerth's "Tragicomic Conceit":

> Behold here a man at once rapt and afraid:
> Though he is the betrayer, he looks the betrayed.

Since the book is designed as much to showcase the faces as it is to present the poems, it is difficult to do the anthology justice without reproducing both. But for those wishing to see *their* favorite contemporaries caught by a fine camera artist, as well to enjoy many good recent poems, this collection will serve as a valuable reference for the faces of poets whose work is known and admired already and for the work of those whose poems will move readers to want to view the face that goes with them, or vice versa.

Another but more limited anthology—restricted to the poets of a single state—is *Travois, An Anthology of Texas Poetry*. Despite this regional restriction, there is no hint here of parochialism or of narrowness of approach, attitude, or subject matter. What struck me from the first about this collection was the great energy it implies. For one thing, there are 156 poets represented (the same number of pages but with many more poems), and there are still others who could have been included (Leon Stokesbury, for one). The sense of a ground swell in Texas writing is clearly evinced by this anthology. As co-editors Paul Foreman and Joanie Whitebird so aptly phrase it in their brief introduction, this collection of Texas poetry gathers like "a summer storm out of the gulf." So overwhelming is the amount of poetry and so electrifying is it in so many different ways that it seems pointless even to discuss the weaker efforts among a "front" that has moved upon the arid Texas poetry scene (of a few years back) with remarkable power, excitement, and the refreshing aroma of our own native soils and seasons. To continue with the editors' analogy, a reviewer can only say that the forecast, for those interested in the present Texas poetry/weather conditions, is one of scattered showers—some of the poems hit, others will pass over with hardly a shadow to cool the emotions or to stimulate them with thunderous words. I certainly have my favorites, but every reader will find his as well. On recommending the book to a creative-writing class, I found my own students surprising me by their critical reactions to poems I had not fully appreciated. For the record I would like to say that I find Ryan Bernard's "The Second Coming (of the Flaming Wino)" a particularly intriguing piece, one to which the anthology introduced me. Among those poems I had seen elsewhere and encountered again in *Travois* with renewed pleasure, let me mention Walt McDonald's "The Hammer," a fine poem from his *Caliban in Blue*, and also Charles Behlen's "Keen Brake." Other pieces I did not know include Robert Bonazzi's "How I Became A Poet," Richard Sale's "Stilts and Other Vehicles," poems by Les Standiford, Sandra Lynn, Naomi Shihab, and too many others to catalog. The book is an absolute must for those concerned for the present and future of Texas poetry.

Naomi Shihab is probably the leading female light on the Texas poetry scene today. Born in 1952 in St. Louis, she has been a resident of Texas since 1967, working for the past several years as a Writer-in-the-Schools with the Texas Commission on the Arts and Humanities. Her poetry is characterized by its attention to everyday sights, sounds, and routines. The opening piece from her *Tattooed Feet*, in editor Dwight Fullingim's *Texas Portfolio* chapbook series (published by B. Weberlein), sets the tone and almost religious attitude of her poetry's "Pilgrimage" to the holy land of the near and diminutive:

> If we have destinations
> they are small,
> they can be walked to . . .

This statement grows out of an interest in "tightly wound cabbage rolls" and "hair braided / so it won't come loose," though the connection between imagery and statement is itself fairly loose. For Shihab this looseness does not seem to matter, since, as she states elsewhere in comparing her poetry with sunlight,

> It is coming through
> touching plants
> scars on the old wood floor
> in a new light way
> I have everything
> to say
> I could begin
> anywhere

Her theory is that art "is very small, / lives in miniature caves in the hillside / and comes out for crumbs." Her poems are essentially small, start from anywhere, but generally end by winning us over. In one line she can capture what little our repetitive lives come to, surprising us with how rich that smallness really is. Not that she attempts to make anything special out of what she merely presents with simple but subtle music. As she says in speaking of her grandmother's tattooed feet,

> They have enough to do without my
> making them more than they are.

In "Little Blanco River," Shihab even entreats the small to remain that way:

> no one makes a state part out of you
> you're not deep enough
>
> little blanco river
> don't ever get too big

If these poems verge on the sentimental in their encouraging of the slight and the underdog, this is very difficult to fault, principally because the expression of such views is fresh and engaging. At times the philosophy does become somewhat overexposed:

> there was nothing obscure about melons
> nothing involved about yams
>
> if she were to have anything to do with the world
> these would be her translators

More often than not, however, there is just the right amount of imagery and statement. One of the best examples of this combination is to be found in "Night Shift," a poem not included in the present collection but also published by the *Texas Portfolio—Poetry*Texas* people. I quote from this piece as an example of one of Shihab's finest to date:

> At 2:00 a.m. the world is populated
> by a mysterious breed.
> Pale-skinned, the creatures shake, sweep, & dust.
> . . .
>
> Children live for years
> without knowing they exist.
> . . .
>
> So many nights I have stripped away
> the cigarette butts & peanut shells
> with a new deliberation.
> . . .
>
> I polish the counter,
> fill each tin canister with sugar & tea,
> stack the tickets on their neat metal spear.
>
> And I know, wherever I appear to be in the world,
> I will always be here first.
> This dark task is tattooed on my heart,
> pure & necessary.
> I will do it over & over
> as long as it needs to be done.

In contrast to Shihab's simplicity, Alison Touster's use of vocabulary in *The First Movement* has the effect of overkill. A poem with great possibilities subject-wise, "The Cock Fight," never comes to life because the poet is too intent on employing a diction that cuts off any sense of immediacy:

We sit outside the small house:
Sturdy, incongruous beside the tall corn

We wait, ourselves somewhat incongruous in the light

This kind of writing does strike me as bad, simply because it is so wordy and so concerned with setting an internal mood that actually seems to matter very little in the poem, nor does it allow the scene to come into focus on its own, repeats instead a word (*incongruous*) which is more proper in prose fiction, if even there. It may be unfair to characterize an entire book by one poem, yet the rest of this collection is marred by just this type of vocabulary: "avuncular," "curvature," "radical territory," "gradual disownment." There is *bad* writing, as the Black poet would remind us, and then there is simply bad writing, unredeemed by any sort of stimulating, daring, or antipoetic but authentic qualities. What Touster's poems lack is a context for the technical vocabulary, some ironic playing off of poetic and unpoetic, some sensual atmosphere able to absorb the jargon and make of it an integral part of the composition. Until she provides such a context, the words will remain flat and inert, which are other words for bad writing.

Four Bk Mk Poets is a collection by women writers ranging in age from the early twenties to the early seventies. This represents a theme and technique reaching back to Emily Dickinson (in the work of Virginia Scott Miner) and forward to Denise Levertov (in that of Jari Dykstra), while the poetry of Joan Yeagley and Heather Wilde speaks for the now generation in its concern for politics and therapeutics. However, even though this book tends to include a wide variety of styles and subjects, there are few poems here that exhibit a rightness of form or expression. Miner's work sounds convincing as structured thought, but in its urge to imitate Dickinson it too often mistakes form for substance. The verses click off nicely but finally far too neatly.

What we have in this volume is complete fearlessness of bad writing. The attitude seems to be not to sweat the bad, just to get to the good and let the rest take care of itself. There is almost no desire to discourage the inept phrase or to cut the gab, rather to let it lie where it happens to fall and to rush on to the catchy analogy, as in Yeagley's title piece from her section of poems: "bureaucracies of crawdads backing into holes." There are good lines at times, but this seems accidental or incidental to the larger effort, which is taken up with piling on pointless, unrelated observations or "meaningful" pronouncements. Yeagley handles descriptions of dances and body movements well, but in the same poem will lapse into a heavy-handed statement of a trite idea. "The Stripper" has many fine touches yet concludes with a stanza which all but cancels everything that has gone before: "Tell me, did Eve / Have such tiny feet / And how did she pass / In the Ordinary world?" Ultimately, Virginia Scott Miner's "old-fashioned" poems outshine her sister poets' Erica Jong-inspired liberated-relevant outcries. She calmly renders a version of life in towns where

It's not hypocrisy, we like to think,
only impossibility
of saying, "I am I," and having
others reply in kind.

Here is the fine first stanza of Miner's "Frames":

It's a small town where a Latin teacher
almost got fired by the American Legion
because she took *The Nation* and listened
to a Communist speaker on the courthouse lawn.
It's a go-to-church, skip-the-liquor,
Woman's Club kind of place—yet kind,
filled with great O's of goodness
if you stay inside its frame.

It has been observed that expensive gifts come in small packages. Shihab's poems often attest to this truth. Susan Bright's *Container* is truly a small package—one of three minipublications received from Noumenon Press—a six-page chapbook composed of three-line haiku-like pieces, all separated by the repeated word CONTAINER typed in capitals. Read as individual pieces, the tercets are often arresting in and of themselves:

shape of wooden shoe
body of peasant
bend of work

brown paper bag
held open
for the cat

Seen as parts of a larger theme, which appears to be a fear of space and an attraction for shapes and movements which may be slight gestures, fragments, flaws, knots, crusts, or again, small containers, such as jugs, pots or spoons, these three-line sections present a vast index of tiny attentions to be opposed to the grandiose and distant:

i sleep
with my back to the stars
they frighten me

Elsewhere the poet reiterates this fear: "i turn / away from / the stars." Bright discovers instead galaxies in the everyday. Her small packages are indeed rich in returning us home:

cling to the roof,

do not blow off
the surface

If I read her right, there are some fine loaded puns in this little three-line stanza. For those interested, Bright's latest volume is *Julia*, a larger, beautifully-printed collection (from Wings Press in Houston), though perhaps no bigger in spirit than her smaller *Container*.

Another six-page Noumenon chapbook is Tamara O'Brien's *Affairs*, a work that moves helter-skelter for me, and unlike Bright's collection never quite focuses on much I can feel or identify with. At the end of the title poem, however, the poet manages to evoke a scene I can visualize and to which I am attracted by its "clear" double meanings. At this point the poetry achieves a greater depth—the metaphor, significantly, one of swimming in a pool—and this contrasts dramatically for me with the shallow and overly sound-oriented aspects of the earlier sections of the piece. Other readers may well find O'Brien's rapid-fire writing more successful and appealing than I do.

Carl D. Clark's *Desire, Chasing a Cow* is the other Noumenon chapbook submitted for review, and like the Bright and O'Brien collections it too is a six-page publication. Like Bright's poem, Clark's appears made up of isolated observations which somehow interrelate. With Clark's work, however, it is more difficult to discover a pattern, partly because the cummings-like breakdown of words into unsyllabic divisions too often interferes with the sense and yet seldom if ever adds a visual dimension to the meaning that the poem would, I assume, wish to convey. Like O'Brien's work, Clark's rushes headlong, ending mostly in traffic jams and tie-ups:

goi
    n
gona
  he
    ad

Clark alludes characteristically to the chase as "here just a second to say / and no sooner done than / claptrap." There is a definite connection between title and content, for the chase is constantly "goi / n / gona / he / ad," but other than the pure pleasure of breaking up the lines and words into random arrangements, and from time to time offering a curious line in relief ("A / roar to buy my eye"), the work puzzles as to where the poet has headed, taken me, or whether there was any "desire" to arrive or to catch the never-imaged cow. For many, curiosity kills the "cow," and in poetry the purely curious may rarely prove long-lived. Given Clark's concretist-dadaist aesthetics, of course, I am guessing that he couldn't fear less. Experiment is often looked down on as no end in itself. But someone should be carrying it on, with all of Whitman's exuberance. Who knows where it will lead. I would hope that Clark continues to chase the cow, even if he himself has yet to catch a glimpse of its tail. Sooner or later he may bring the meat to our tables.

As I have tried here to understand myself, there seems a clear though not easily definable distinction between bad writing—that is, the faulty or mediocre performance—and writing which may fall short of perfection but which, in attempting a more difficult, complex or challenging task, reaches far beyond the merely good poem—meaning the piece that is competent, carefully crafted, and neatly complete. What I miss in much so-called good poetry is the poet's willingness to go in over his head, even to force relationships which leave him vulnerable to charges of going too far, of creating outrageous oxymorons. In the small, well-wrought poem, the poet tends to remain satisfied with fitting the pieces so tightly no objection can enter in, though no life either. Emily Dickinson and Blake's short poems are obvious exceptions, for they manage to leave their pieces open-ended and porous with possibilities for interpretation. Likewise, in W.D. Snodgrass's "Heart's Needle," section three of the poem moves us through simple-sounding rhymed stanzas, yet there is nothing easy about the thinking. The analogies are far-reaching as they force us to struggle with political, familial, and poetical implications which involve both a real war and the universal dilemma of giving up for someone else's good, of surrendering pride to allow at least for living, if not for our vision of an ideal life:

> It's better the poor soldiers live
> In someone else's hands
> Than drop where helpless powers fall
> On crops and barns, on towns where all
> Will burn. And no man stands.

Walter McDonald's *Caliban in Blue* (winner of the 1976 Texas Institute of Letters Award for poetry) is a collection based principally on the author's experiences in and his ponderings of the war in Vietnam. For this fact alone the book has had and will continue to enjoy a wide appeal. McDonald's sensitive responses, his insightful observations, and his craftsmanship in shaping his experiences into meaningful statements will long elicit our admiration.

All of McDonald's poems are short (no more than two pages at the most), for the poet is well able to re-create important moments within very few lines, as in "Flight Orders":

> It
> has come, the
>   pledge
> of all uniforms,
>   the
> flat spin no
>   jet
> can rudder out
>   of,
> suction down with

no
operative ejection seat.
War.

The cumulative effect is of a survey of a historical period. This perhaps is the aim of the imagist or objectivist poet who studies an era through small pieces of large events. The epic poet since Pound has chosen essentially this approach. And most modern readers prefer the shorter poem. Often they will pronounce the long poem a failure but will point to individual, imagistic sections as worthy of being excerpted. Thus, while we fear the bad *big* poem, we can accept the sparkling bits and pieces that make it up.

McDonald avoids the epic issue by not attempting a long poem, and the result is that each separate war poem succeeds, though taken together they do not go very far in providing a really penetrating assessment or representation of the war experience. There is lacking here a sense of the universal applicability of the trials and temptations, the enthusiasms and regrets that rise above the subject's inherent message that war is terrible. Somehow the poems remain at a *Catch-22* level (McDonald is a serious student and scholar of this novel), and while the absurdity and sadness of the political struggle is revealed through a many-sided human involvement, the overall intent of the collection is too limited to sentiment and literary allusion.

Compared with Snodgrass's "Heart's Needle" or even with D.C. Berry's lesser *Saigon Cemetery* (Michael Casey's *Obscenities* has never meant much to me, as I find it overly self-conscious in its playing to contemporary taste), *Caliban in Blue* is too prone to stand outside the events. (It seems to me that to make a nice imagistic poem on a war theme belies the nature of the experience. Stephen Crane only appears to write neat short pieces on combat, for underneath is an irony that reveals the essential horror or indifference of the war machine. Certainly McDonald at times achieves a similar irony, but it is too clinically removed from poetry's necessary allegorical reflections on any such intense moment that tests man's always conflicting attitudes and qualities—his very soul, as it were.) Perhaps to become less objective, less impersonal, is both a risk and a departure from Pound and Eliot's tenets, but somehow it strikes me as worth the gamble and the sacrilege. Our magazines may be partly to blame for discouraging the bigger, "badder" poem, yet some themes surely call for larger, more fragile canvases. Plainly the large and the experimental open themselves up to the greater likelihood of falling apart, but one reason for the abundance of poets today in an age with a decreasing number of significant figures (in our own country, at least) is perhaps just this increasing satisfaction with the small "perfect" poem.

While I admire McDonald and Shihab's achievements, I do believe that it is time we quit wading so close to the shore and sailed out farther, as Whitman suggested, recklessly steering for the deepest waters, even if it means sacrificing the ship and all. Nothing ventured, nothing gained, as the adage goes. Or to return to my original metaphor, some critics cry wolf so often that perhaps we *should* ignore their fears of the less than perfect poem.

Texas Poetry & the Hi-Tech Race

My favorite fable is Aesop's tale of the tortoise and the hare, where the slower, steadier creature catches and passes his faster but frivolous fellow. In reading lately of the technological race I find that there are a number of turtles in Third World countries which are about to beat the United States to the gold carrot of commercial enterprise. This turn of events could well affect our literature adversely, since nations powerful economically tend to enjoy the leisure necessary to create and support the arts. If this financial situation is crucial to artistic creativity, it may be that Texas, despite the rest of the nation's decline, could well achieve greater stability in terms of its economy and as a result perhaps reach to higher levels of creative quality, for it is clear that the state is on the verge of becoming a giant in more than size. Yet literature is no respecter of riches and can thrive in such poor countries as Chile, Paraguay, or modern Greece. And when it comes to great art, Milton, Bach, and Brahms were actually behind their times yet have outdistanced the field of those running for an ageless appeal. While much of modern art has rushed to originality, only to find it a distracting patch of greenery along the tedious path to true artistry, the more patient and dedicated artists have tended to appear old-fashioned or preoccupied with following a tradition which is neither thrilling nor record-breaking over the short haul. But once the decades have been clocked, it is seen that it was the turtles who crept across to claim the trophies of admiration and a continuing and growing audience. And even though this has yet to happen for the turtles of Texas poetry, I foresee that the case will indeed be just as I have described it for some of the poems of William Burford, William Barney, and Joseph Colin Murphey—three among an even larger number of Texas figures writing significant work during the past thirty years.

For these turtle-poets to receive their well-deserved recognition, however, it is still necessary that their poems be read with a clear sense of the unique contribution they have made to Texas letters at a time when more trivial writing has captured the attention of a college-educated readership. The attraction of the distant and fashionable blinds us to the near and familiar which are too often precisely from what we so wish to escape. In choosing to flee the famil-

A talk delivered at Cooke County College in Gainesville, Texas, on Awards Day, spring 1978. Quoted passages are found in the following publications: *Chicago Review* (winter 1975-76) for the translation of Ritsos's "Harvest of Space"; William Burford's *A Beginning* (Norton, 1966); William Barney's *The Killdeer Crying: Selected Poems* (Prickly Pear Press, 1977); and Joseph Colin Murphey's *A Return to the Landscape* (Prickly Pear Press, 1979).

iar, however, we abandon our best means of understanding ourselves, as well as our basis for comparison and contrast of other cultures, attitudes, and literary practices. As a result, we lack a point of departure and, as Joe Murphey has phrased it, a landscape for return. As have these three Texas poets, their readers must learn first to take pride in where they are. Not a false pride that one place is bigger or better than another, but a realization that any place, and especially where we are, is the surest source of meaningful experience and the most significant provider of a fund of words and scenes able to contain and express our deepest discoveries. And unlike oil wells or technological advances, it is doubtful that a place will ever be drained dry or become obsolete in terms of literary inspiration. A prime example is the modern renaissance of Greek literature in the hands of such poets as George Seferis and Yannos Ritsos, the latter especially basing his work on contemporary scenes from Greek streets to achieve a timeless moment in a time-worn nation. Consider, for example, his "Harvest of Space":

> Tall plane-trees, muscular torsos of coolness.
> The shade is not intended to hide anything.
> Brave light, brave shade—
> useless daring—to counter what?—
> simplicity breathes in the air.
>
> People sit beneath the trees,
> they dine on small wooden tables, they talk,
> they do not suspect the magnitude covering them, the magnitude
> that regulates their innocent gestures. Toward evening
> someone sang (drunk perhaps). The plane-trees
> moved in a silent procession toward the horizon.
> The area emptied. The waiter, with his white apron,
> appeared for a moment at a distance, in the crimson dusk,
> holding in priestly fashion the tray with the empty glasses.

Here the everyday is the source for a renascence of the religious nature of a simple scene faithfully and feelingly rendered. And should one think that description of an outdoor cafe scene is a limited subject, this poem by Ritsos seems proof against such an assertion. On the other hand, if such scenes cannot produce in every poet or for every generation a new theme and technique, Evolution continues to furnish new plants, animals, and man-made objects set against an essentially unchanging backdrop. As William Barney points out—ornithologist-poet that he is—the cattle egret has made its way to Texas in recent times from Africa and now provides him and other "naturalist" writers with yet another exotic image in their own back yards. Like the geologist who retraces the rich layers of fluvial deposits to discover the force that keeps wheels on the road and wings in the air, the poet can search through the arts of antiquity, its flora and fauna, for a deep reserve of poetic power and inspiration. Just as technology finds new uses for the past, so the poet can turn to his advantage the ageless images forgotten yet still intact and awaiting him to touch them back to life with the magic of his imaginative art.

One exciting fact about Texas poetry is that, unlike that of the Greeks, it does not need to attempt merely to recapture the glories of a past tradition but is faced rather with the challenge of creating for the first time a body of poems worthy the name. So that in a sense the problem of reworking materials on which Homer and Plato stamped their unmistakable genius does not confront the Texas poet. Certainly he or she must contend with an overworked western image, but this has little to do with a tradition in poetry. No form aside from the ballad is strongly associated with the western mode, so we are free to seek new forms or to find in tried and true ones a proper vessel for our own homegrown philosophy or vision. Also, little in poetry has come of the western theme or landscape, especially as it relates to the cowboy convention, so that here too we have a fertile field for interpretation, reinterpretation, or even, if we choose, for total disregard.

For the most part the three poets whose work I wish to consider here have only incidentally been attracted to the typically western motif of range life. If a cowboy appears in one of their poems he bears little resemblance to those of movie or folklore fame, versions so familiar to all the world. More common in their poems are smalltown or city people, figures who inhabit the populous regions of the state and have almost nothing to do with ranching as a way of life. William Burford, who is the youngest of the three (though ironically he taught Joseph Colin Murphey, his teacher's elder by a dozen years), has perhaps most fully ignored the Texas images as we know them—that of the rough-and-ready past and that of the now jet-age blend of country-western guitar and NASA sophisticated hardware or Texas Instruments software. (He has, however, written two of what may be his finest pieces—"South, Southwest" and "Going to School"—using metapors drawn from the cattle industry and from physics.) Burford has principally taken as his province the mind as such, in Texas, in England, in France, or in legend. By tracing back to its beginnings the mind's desire for happiness, the poet calls for "the new heroes" to "bring this [happiness] in their hands." The idea that man must make his life himself, and essentially in the mind, eliminates in one way a concern for place. In "The Days of Love," a poem for and of his wife, the poet observes how far we remain from what or whom we love, even when that place or person should lie beside us. Burford would have us realize that each mind is inevitably separate, sadly but perhaps rightly so. Speaking of the physical man he writes:

> In this same mortal place
> That stones can break—
> How thin is the division
> Which holds the one life here,
> And the other, there beyond touch.
> . . . .
> Each thing must teach us
> That we are elsewhere,
> Not to be held.

When he does come to reproduce a familiar Texas scene, as in "South, Southwest," which treats of the Capitol in Austin, Burford finds it an image for our lost past and our even greater loss of any present satisfaction with lives that are marked by the "savage clasp" in love and the "snatch" of "shiny rings that make [our] eyes wide." As he says candidly, "We are animals." Despite his despairing tone here, Burford generally concludes, as he does in "South, Southwest," with a hopeful image, in this case of the Capitol by night when the lighted building appears like a pile of white salt, a symbol of the past at which "our spirits lick." Even when Burford does turn to such a familiar Texas scene, he renews it through a powerful symbolism tied to his deep concern for contemporary man's loss of attachments and meaningful experiences, as well as to his (the poet's) need to discover a simple image that will limn for the mind a type of replacement for what we are missing. Another example of this urge to suggest a lasting source of nourishment, along the lines of his salt lick image, is found in section III of his subtly rhymed poem "Twenty-year-old Poet":

What comfort, then, can a man find?
Good friend, let us walk a while
Together. It is night. The fog is in.
The sea air is chill. There is no sign of life.

From far down the street
Shone a light like a star,
But the rays were cold
And did not reach
To warm the heart.
In all that world
The only thing heard
Was our own echoing feet

Approaching the place
Where the paving stone
Broke off in empty space—
The Museum loomed up
In whose cavernous rooms
Christ's body lies
For the dissecting knives.
And the stumps of the trees

Confronted us,
Monstrous teeth
Breaking through from beneath.
We reached the canal
Where the black water ran
And the barge at the bank
Lay huge and still

As the funeral bier.

"Here we must part, and not fear.
"Clasp hands. Pledge eyes."
And he gave me manly blessing.
Then he turned. But I
Stood and watched on that bank
The living coal of his pipe
Glow through the engulfing night.

Although William Barney has not gone so far afield as Burford in order to find likely images for his highly-wrought stanzas, neither has he depended on what is most typical about the Texas landscape or what at least has been taken as characteristic of its western image. Instead, Barney has looked closely at the knots and scars of the familiar, discovering in them galaxies of meaning beyond their typical Texas associations. Beginning with a scene on a popular pier, the poet notices what nebulae the weathering process has created, and simply by seeing these "unspectacular" gnarls and grains in the planking he opens up the reader to a new sense of time, space, and, as he says, to "patterns not meant to be understood" but which we joy in discovering because of his discriminating eye and his careful way with words and formal design. Here is the entire piece, entitled "A Crooked Feast":

Out on that narrow fishing pier
he'd walk gingerly on the planks,
not because of some dizzying fear,
rather because wherever he stepped
nebulae spread in amazing ranks.

Weathering did it. A two-by-six
paled into shining strand, sunswept,
except for a giant cicatrix
here and there in the vacant grain
(in the nothingness gnarls of pain).

He knew a flaw only marked the place
where a branch or knuckled burl
had interrupted the wooden space:
cut cross-wise, it showed a swirl.
So would the earth, if you cut it right.

He sensed it came of over-sight,
from paying heed to things awry,
patterns not meant to be understood.
It was some crookedness in his eye
feasting on knots instead of wood.

When Barney has chosen western subjects, such as the cutting horse and a barbed wire fence, he has used them as a means for exploring, in these cases, the nature of symbol, the process and end of writing, and the realization that freedom only comes through the choosing of pain. The poet's ability to involve a wide range of topics and images within the western context is a mark of his truly creative imagination and his understanding of the function of poetry as a form of meditation upon the deeper meaning of even the most commonplace scenes or objects. In "Canticle for a Cutting Horse," Barney not only employs a sophisticated stanza pattern based on the canticle form but moves through some half dozen stages of thought. A more recent poem, "The Cranes at Muleshoe," turns an annual Panhandle scene into an apocalyptic allegory:

> With no more skill than men
> can they arrange a right society,
> resolve their noisy dithering in space.
> A simple symmetry eludes them:
> too many compasses must be divined,
> and the vague, skittish auspice will not form,
> the pattern riddles, escapes the tribal mind.

Like Brahms waiting until he was 44 to write his first symphony, taking his time to learn his trade, Barney has slowly but surely developed a theme and technique which will endure beyond what Chaucer, in his critique of those who "can not love ful half yeer in a place," calls a constant need for "newefangelnesse."

Joseph Colin Murphey belongs with Barney and Burford not merely because he is of their same generation, but also because his poetry represents a slow development toward formal and thematic achievements vital to the creation of a lasting Texas literature. In fact, Murphey's development has been longer and perhaps fuller than those of his fellow poets, in that he has moved from a traditional line—as in "Ode to the Statue That Found a Trade" or "Requiem for a Long Dying"—to the contemporary prose-like rhythms of his portrait poems, such as "Beauty Is Kin Deep" or "The Short Happy Bloom of Lurline Scruggs." And even though in this sense as well as formally all three poets are ultimately quite dissimilar, they do share an intense and accurate perception of the contemporary world, especially those manifestations of it in Texas which have been overlooked or misunderstood.

In a late poem like "Crop Duster Disaster," Murphey has caught for all time the sad glory of the cowboy image modernized yet still as untrue as it has ever been, as any such romanticized self-image will be, even as it mesmerizes those who worship its "hard core death defying smile." What Murphey has done in a number of such poems is to reinterpret the heritage we have all lived with uncomfortably but with a certain awe. And though his reinterpretation reveals the reality behind the mask, it is done with such sympathy that we are moved by the scene even as we acknowledge its essential irreality.

In "A Meeting of Saints," Murphey has revisited the revivals to which his and many later generations have continued to owe their religious upbringing and their grudging sense of a spiritual world. If many of us feel we have left behind such superstition, Murphey reminds us of an undeniable emptiness to which his "dumpy, red-faced" aunt's revivalism still speaks volumes. For despite the down-to-earth world to which his aunt returns after the service is over, during it

> she would rise arms extended
> and on small tippy toes
> dance all around the pulpit
> like a toy bear on wheels.

> At the same time, while
> she shouted and sang, "Hallelujah!"
> a tall, long-faced man
> in a gray-hung scarecrow suit
> would jump flat-footed: Boing!

> boing! silently over benches
> in great inverted U's lightly;
> and an old lost Jewish rabbi
> with a long beard would stand
> translated, "speaking other tongues."

> How my aunt bloomed then
> beneath her bonnet like a ripe peach!
> Was this the woman who made such
> miraculous pies and whose kiss
> was apple-sweet?

> All the next week I watched
> how serious and slow she hoed
> her patch of corn, how heavy
> the dancing feet went down
> the long, hot rows of her days.

In the poet's remembered world of aunts, dare-devil fliers, and men who drink coffee at the Texan Cafe (in "Yippee Yi O Ti Yay"), there is a renewal of spirit much like that of the revival era, when the disbeliever is suddenly lifted unwillingly into a realm of regeneration and greater sympathy, even with those he had laughed at or rejected as cracked or touched in the head, those he held below him.

Like Barney and Burford, Murphey returns us to what is seemingly insignificant but fulfillingly vital in our regional experience. And all three have done so by focusing on where they are, whether at the Capitol grounds in Burford's case, walking a fishing pier in Barney's, or observing in Murphey's a pilot at

Duffers having his coffee. The result has been a penetrating through to the real, a tapping of the poetic reservoir with its allowance of associations never to be depleted in our own generation or in those to come. When every form of fuel has burned itself out, like the cocksure hare running himself headlong to lesser attractions off the familiar path, these Texas turtles will still be crossing the finish line with their carefully thought-out regional but universal poems that celebrate, reinterpret, and advance the cause of Texas letters. I thank them every time I read their work, as should those truly interested in the real thing—the turtle poet who will lumber past the technological rabbit that has lost track of where he started for, why the getting there requires patience and pride along the way, and all that it means to stick with the little one receives from any time or place.

Review of *River City Rising*

Among several new magazines to appear in Austin, *River City Rising* stands as an entirely original blend of poetry, line drawings, photographs of people involved in human rights gatherings (including the one found on the bluish-gray cover), journal entries by a dancer, thoughts of an elderly woman from her rest home, a disturbingly informative interview with a Mexican-American farmworker, and an invitation to translators, writers, and subscribers to participate in the forthcoming quarterly issues of this magazine edited by Michael Fernandes and Mimi Taylor and to be published each solstice and equinox.

Most of the pages are taken up with illustrated poems by eleven male and female poets. Coeditor Taylor's two poems are impressive in terms of their strong thematic development (one on death and the other on birth) and their fine metaphorical structures. In "Mercy Laughs on Sundays" Taylor depicts the life of a slowly dying youth. Similes of "tiny fists drawn hard / As pine cone" and of a mother's "spinning top of a boy wearing / Down like sidewalk chalk" present the pathos of the situation where the youth struggles against a death his doctors have already foretold. In the face of such prophecy the boy "swelled like a cantaloupe in the newness / Of living" and "put death away like a precious / Plate—that fragile circle of your childhood." Similarly in her "Paper Mother" Taylor uses metaphor to suggest the fragility of birth: "I sat with ants in my spine until that child / Bloomed between her legs—round like a new fig / Blue as a fresh bruise." In a fairly objective, narrative style, Taylor unfolds layer after layer of metaphor to reveal the inner lives of her subjects. Both poems, however, verge on bathos, so that while Taylor's work is worth watching for, it can be hoped that her treatment will mature rather than settle for a too popular surface meaning, a too easy playing with such issues as doctors' "insensitive" prognoses or the unwed mother's passing out "adoption talk like cigars" and the boy being considered one day a bastard by all those emerging "through the same soft burrow."

Other poets with appealing contributions include Craig Underwood, whose "Swish Swish" contrasts his being accepted for shooting baskets in a state tournament with his being rejected for protesting segregation in Birmingham in '63; Calvin Doucet, whose "Postcard for Steve" presents in prose-poem fashion scenes from "Texas villages near the Colorado and Brazos"; Arnold Williams, with two vignettes from the life of "Crazy Henry," a town character from Earth, Texas, who collects nails ("no telling how many flats / he saved the

Texas Circuit Newsletter, vol. 1, nos. 6/7/8 (Sept.-Nov. 1978): 6-7.

people of Earth," though on suggesting this the speaker is laughed at by those knowing Henry "didn't have the sense / for that"); Susan Bright, whose "Silver" contains a "plastic / rabbit which I have always been able to locate at a moment's / notice as if. Someone were to say to me, alright! You've had / twenty years the test is over. Where is it!"; and Albert Huffstickler, whose "Secrets" builds on the analogy of a tree trunk being like his mother: "limbs twisted by drought, bent by the wind, / and its green top thrust out into the canyon / as though it would take flight"—a poem nicely illustrated by Paul Pfeiffer.

In general the poems offer a wide variety of approaches, though most lean toward the prosy, especially editor Michael Fernandes's philosophical musings on vision and understanding. Some pieces are wordy (Anderson's) and some are terse to the point of meaninglessness (Armentrout's). Each poet does establish an individual voice and will be heard by those readers listening for a certain type of imaged speech. In keeping with the overall idea of the magazine, a majority of the poems concern themselves with "that which is liberating, instructive, expansive...."

Occupying the center section of the magazine is an eight-page interview with Julio Coreño, a farmworker from Mercedes, Texas, who is active in the Texas Farmworkers Union and who, though uneducated and a speaker only of Spanish, is a highly articulate man. His interviewers, Enrique López and David Morris, have asked questions which in fact help Coreño address himself to a related issue: education and exploitation. Coreño touches on this theme throughout the interview, discussing education as something that does not guarantee an end to exploitation: "If I go to school and nevertheless there is still exploitation for hundreds and hundreds who are out in the fields, then what good does it do for me to go to school?" By Coreño's own account he never went to school (arriving in Texas from Mexico when he was fifteen; he is now forty-eight) because his parents were too poor: "I've never seen a school from the inside, just from the outside, from the sidewalk." Like his fellow workers, Coreño grew up in the fields, where whole families must work to earn a bare existence, where mothers must take their babies, "with their bottles, in the sun, in the wind, exposed to poisons from the work, to insecticides." Planes spraying have even flown so low as to strike workers because there is no law protecting the workers from insecticides or poisons used in the fields.

Coreño, for all his lack of education, uses language colorfully and logically. Speaking of the way workers are treated like machines, Coreño concludes that men are replaced as casually as tractors. As to government benefits, Coreño points out that these are like a "locked chest," and

> If nobody opens the chest to take out what's locked up inside, it'll stay locked up there, no one gets it out. The people are the key to that chest, which is the government. As long as the people don't push for benefits for themselves, for the communities, for the poor people, the government gives nothing. They just want to keep things coming in, coming in.

Coreño's most telling indictment is reserved for the educated. While he assures us that he's not against education ("Education is good," he says), he is against "the exploitation that comes about because of the education people have. Those who get an education then exploit the ones below them." Comparing workers with plants, Coreño advises that each kind of seed needs "a certain amount of soil to sprout." Given the wealth of Hidalgo County, the second richest agricultural county in the nation, it does not seem that Coreño is asking for too much: minimum wage, laws to protect against insecticides, and protection from those who live off the labor of farmworkers while gaining an education they will use against those earning low incomes, which in turn keep them in an exploited condition.

It is good to have a magazine combining social concerns with poetry (something *The Texas Observer* used to do), though to say so may argue against my earlier objections to Mimi Taylor's treatment of social issues in her poems. The whole question of artistic handling of content in poetry is a thorny one and certainly promises no simple answer in the near future, if ever. Essentially the poem and the interview are worlds apart in focus and intent (the one transforming facts and the other trying to get them straight), so that it is useful to have both between two covers, the one perhaps complementing the other. In the end, however, there should not be a confusion of the two forms, as is at times the case here. (Blake, of course, achieves dramatic social criticism in "The Chimney Sweeper" and "The Little Black Boy," owing largely to his effective and convincing manipulation of a child's point of view.) At any rate, *River City Rising* raises some valuable issues to be debated in both fields, the social and the aesthetic. Those interested in following the development of what is billed as a bilingual publication (though not so in this first number) should be on the lookout for the second issue of a magazine (scheduled for the winter solstice) that has already made its place as an attractively designed and distinctively edited addition to small press publishing in Texas.

Olson in Texas

Paul Christensen's *Charles Olson Call Him Ishmael* is one of the most valuable of several works on the poet to appear during the past three years and signals a long-needed reckoning with the figure that one commentator claims everyone in the world "who cares for poems has learned from." Though such may come as a surprise to those who think we have been totally out of touch with post-World War II poetics, Olson's influence reached even to Texas as long as twenty years ago. How deep or lasting an effect he has had or may have is yet to be determined, but certainly any Texas writer who is interested in renewing his or her acquaintance with Olson's theories and practices will want to take Paul Christensen as a guide.

In the first place, this is a book that offers in very readable prose an extended definition of projective verse. It also reveals something of a paradox at the root of Olson's "composition by field"; that is, by employing an imagist technique (close attention to observable facts, or what Louis Zukofsky called "contemporary particulars"), the projectivist seeks to expand consciousness and to create a new mythology based on the minutiae of everyday sights and sounds or those of a history close at hand. In his attempt at a "more comprehensive study of the underlying unities which the poems, essays, letters, and other works subtly, teasingly suggest," Christensen traces this process of moving from immediate observation to mythmaking throughout Olson's entire productive career, as well as through the work of his students and colleagues at Black Mountain College. (While the discussion of his followers is a very useful aspect of the book, I personally would prefer more analysis of Olson's own poetry.) Most significantly, Christensen's study is a survey of the modern urge to write a successful long poem, with Olson's *The Maximus Poems* deservedly considered an indispensable American example of this "projected" form.

Reading Christensen's account of Olson's career has meant for me an opportunity not only to review the critic's solid contribution to scholarship but to recall my own introduction to a tradition begun by Whitman, furthered by William Carlos Williams, and carried on ably by Olson—the effort to discover the makings of poetry where we are. In 1960 a visiting professor at The University of Texas at Austin, Frederick Eckman, came to our Whitman course that spring with a mysterious, unopened package which, on his unwrapping it, proved to contain a copy of Donald Allen's *The New American Poetry, 1945-1960*. Eckman proceeded to read to us from comments by the poets in-

The Pawn Review, vol. 4, no. 1 (winter 1980-81): 86-90.

cluded, as a way of demonstrating for our purposes the homage (perhaps only lip service in some cases) those "new" poets were paying to Whitman. Many of the statements also illustrated a common respect for Williams and his struggle to establish an American idiom. Following these excerpts came a reading from Charles Olson's essay, "Projective Verse," where he refers to Robert Creeley's idea that form is merely an extension of content. Eckman pointed out that this too provided us with proof of Whitman's continuing influence. With regard to the idea of using the familiar as a basis for composition, Christensen summarizes this whole line of thinking when he quotes Creeley, who has said that he learned from Crane, Williams, Zukofsky, and Poe "an explicit possibility in the speech that I was given to use . . . the condition of being American not something chauvinistically national but the intimate fact of one life in one place at one time."

During that same year (1960), *Quagga*, a small poetry magazine, began its brief life in Austin, with Eckman, I suspect, serving as an advisor to the several editors, among them James Smith, Paul Schmidt, and Glenn Whitehead. *Quagga* number one featured a lively collection of poetry, as well as an essay by Eckman, whose prose sounds to me now like both Williams and Olson as it addresses itself to one of those poets' favorite subjects—creative man: "It is not a matter of merely coining metaphors—this anyone can do. It involves *liberating the imagination*, by whatever means. BY WHATEVER MEANS." Even the typography has the look of Olson's projective writing, as Christensen would note, and the ideas of minimizing metaphor and expanding the imagination are central to Olson's creation of a "new poetics" where, to quote Christensen, "direct perception" replaces "'a series of reference points' in which individual objects are merely described in terms of other objects." Moreover, Eckman's poems remind me of what Christensen, in his fine survey of Creeley's books, finds characteristic of the latter: his "theme of the despairing husband." In "Love Lies A-Bleeding" Eckman treats similarly of a contending husband and wife, in this case over who takes out the trash, a struggle presented in the tight lines and colloquial language so peculiar to Creeley's work.

Creeley's first book from Scribner's, *For Love—Poems 1950-1960*, appeared in 1962 and made available the complete range of his poetry. Two of the pieces in that early collection, "The Women" and "The Paradox," were first published in 1960 in the second issue of *Quagga*, probably owing once again to Eckman's presence in Texas. Unfortunately, after these first two issues of the magazine (which were superb yet cheaply produced—typical of the kind of out-of-the-way publications Olson long supported), *Quagga* grew overly institutionalized, with even bigger names appearing (Cummings, Wilbur et al), and even though the format and printing was improved, the quality of the poems fell off considerably. The influence of Eckman on *Quagga* seems to have been crucial, so that with his departure in late 1960 (following the publication of *Quagga* number two) the impact of the Whitman, Williams, Olson, and Creeley line *through* Eckman dissipated, and one of the first truly up-to-date poetry magazines in Texas slipped into the quagmire of academicism, with its final issues offering lifeless translations, poems replete with classical allusions, and the usual trite metaphor-making. All of this parallels Christensen's very helpful analysis of Letters 5 through 7 of *The Maxiumus Poems*, which attack Vincent Ferrini for putting out *Four Winds* in Gloucester and yet making it "merely another literary magazine that could be printed anywhere in the country. It is not born and bred of the things of Gloucester. . . ." As in all of Christensen's interpretations of letters from *The Maximus Poems*, his discussion of the Ferrini pieces is insightful and underscores Olson's basic tenet at work: "The complaints against Ferrini's journal spring from the conviction that only immediate experience is a subject for art." *Quagga* in its first two numbers was devoted to poets like Eckman and Creeley, as well as to the work of such local poets as Del Marie Rogers and Stephen Gosnell, the latter's contribution being reprinted in *New Campus Writing*. Olson encouraged a sense of the local along with a deep awareness of tradition, and Christensen's informative overview of Olson's readings in philosophy and in Pound's poetry and criticism—the critic presenting much tedious thinking in a light and lucid manner—provides vital background material for an understanding of the poet's methods in observing the immediate with an eye to its consciousness-expanding capabilities. It was Olson's concern for immediacy that visited Austin in 1960 and left us for the most part when Eckman took his leave.

The tradition in which Olson worked was a radical one in the sense that it rejected ready-made or egocentric perceptions. Like the Objectivists (Williams in the 'thirties, Zukofsky, Oppen), Olson believed, as Christensen states, that

> Objects exist in a network of wholly different laws from those of human society. The more any individual willingly confronts this reality to learn what "secrets objects share," the more he may discern that such laws do in fact govern his own existence in more basic ways than do human norms and edicts. When that person shifts his attention from traditionally humanistic concerns to what lies around him as nature, he may discover that human conduct is often ignorant or in violation of natural laws that would enhance his existence and make life more meaningful.

The last of these comments is close in spirit to Shakespeare, and well it should be, since it was Shakespeare to whom Melville had gone for his vision of the Ahab tragedy of man closing himself off from or seeking control over nature. According to Christensen, it was Melville's call for openness to the environment that Olson in turn advocated as a means of attaining greater receptivity to our surroundings, a fuller relationship with them, and through this relationship, a higher "condition of self-awareness." As may be seen from even a sketchy outline of Christensen's book, the critic has fully indicated the unity of Olson's thinking, from its beginnings in *Call Me Ishmael*, through *The Maximus Poems*, and even, as a result of his teachings, into the work of such students and followers as Creeley, Duncan, Dorn, and Eckman.

Olson in Texas was, then, an early fact, thanks to Frederick Eckman. And thanks to Paul Christensen of Texas A & M University, Olson is back—by way of a praiseworthy publication from the University of Texas Press. Anyone interested in poetry will want to pick up a copy of Christensen's guide to Olson, for above all this book returns the reader to the poet's texts, which should be the purpose of any critical work. And for those concerned to recover a sense of where they are and to learn how this awareness may serve in the making of vigorous poems, *Charles Olson   Call Him Ishmael* is a sure place to begin.

Reviews of Books by Two Texas Poets

One—if not the most important—event in recent Texas small-press history has been the rise of *Cedar Rock* with its concomitant chapbook series from Cedar Rock Press. Editor David Yates has not only established a nationally recognized magazine outside the metropolitan areas of the state but has given to columnists, poets, fiction writers, and correspondents throughout Texas and the nation an opportunity to engage in a wide range of literary expression, unrestricted to any one school or region. Although most of the columnists are in Texas (all, in fact, with the exception of Judson Jerome), contributors of poetry and fiction are located from coast to coast. The mark of every issue of the magazine is its catholicity of representation—from prison poetry to a homemaker's dishpan verse, from prose poems to one of R.S. Gwynn's brilliant columns in Popelike rhymed couplets! The editor's taste leans heavily toward natural lines that express a lively attachment to the things and occasions of contemporary life. This same general view of the magazine's contents holds largely true for the poems found in the press's chapbook series (with again the exception of a hardback edition of Judson Jerome's collected poems). Of the half dozen titles published under the Cedar Rock imprint, the most outstanding are *Riding for the Dome* by Yates himself (his second chapbook—the first, *Making Bread*, is also from CR Press) and *One Thing Leads to Another* by Walter McDonald, his second of three published volumes.

Designed by Dwight Fullingim along the lines of his own earlier chapbook series from *Texas Portfolio*, these are attractive publications, with the cover art of Yates's volume remaining its only real disappointment, and that apparently not Fullingim's but the poet's idea, since the former always prefers a photograph of his authors, as in the very striking example on the front cover of the McDonald chapbook. As with the tasteful choice of format, the poetry included in both collections is appealing, and it is representative of each poet's strongest work to date. While the poems belong together as a group, they are limited neither in form nor in subject. Indeed, both chapbooks signal the coming of age of two essentially unlike, though authentically regional, stylists.

David Yates's work contains the necessary ingredients to make of him a popular poet in the tradition of Carl Sandburg and Vachel Lindsay. His poetry is lighthearted and meant to be read aloud to an audience, which Yates does often and always with success. And yet there is subtance to the poetry; it holds up well on the page. A perfect example of the poet's ability to combine

The Pawn Review, vol. 4, no. 1 (winter 1980-81): 90-97.

humor and artistry is "Sex," with its almost hilarious opening lines:

> I think about it
> everytime I'm in Mentone, Texas,
> way out there in
> lonely Loving County

There is a vital use of old material (a "making it new") in Yates's handling of Texas' unpredictable and extremist weather. The analogy between human sexuality and the atmospheric conditions over the Permian Basin is true at once to West Texas life and to the universal response of love making. Although the ending is somewhat unrelated to the carefully worked out conceit, it is typical of Yates's tendency to settle for a fairly tame conclusion after the rather wild, attention-getting start. The point of many of his poems is ultimately on the side of sentiment or is left open, perhaps as a way either of minimizing, in his playfully unassuming manner, what has gone before or of emphasizing the ongoing nature of his subject matter. One reason the cover design of the book falls short of the volume's high level of writing is that its amateurish drawing of a hooded skeleton at the wheel is so uncharacteristic of the poet's basic point of view. Yates is all for life, not death, and even when his poems come to endings less vivid or memorable than one could wish, what is presented along the way does evoke and celebrate everyday incidents, dramatizing them through a durable, imaginative diction.

Thematic concerns in Yates's second volume vary just enough to maintain the reader's enthusiasm from poem to poem, despite a certain repetition of such topics as the poet on poetry, the longing for escape or for a return to the good old days, and the century's lack of human communication. To summarize Yates's themes in this way, however, does not do justice to his undeniable rightness of tone in poem after poem. We are won over by the speakers' urgency and their intense desire to have their say. Above all, Yates should be recognized and is to be commended for his creation of a cast of unforgettable characters who may talk of the same obsession—mostly of how to escape our wasteland of indifference—yet who do so in winning lines that hold us breathless up to the end (perhaps another reason a Yates closure eases off a bit compared to the rest of the piece). Uncle Reno, Uncle Stafford, Dickey and Aunt Dickey, Daddy and Mom—all these and more are popular figures with whom any reader cannot help but identify fully. Whether tender or absurd, their declarations are destined to move and delight us each time we return to Yates's beautifully modulated narratives. Here is a favorite with many readers already:

> Dickey hollered to us all—
> but to no one in particular—
> that he was no longer for sale,
> that he was nobody's real estate any longer,
> that he was tired of chasing
> stray cows and breaking wild horses,

that he was on his way to Dallas,
where he'd be the Lone Ranger
and not have to answer
to nobody:
not his sisters or his mother
or Daddy or Aunt Dickey
or the big-assed ranch foreman
or the earth the sky the rain
not anything, not anybody!

All this declared, of course, before he passes out in the middle of the street from an all-night binge.

Structurally Yates's work is also varied just enough to satisfy our need for the formal aspect of any poem worth its salt. In "Watching the Super Bowl in Uncle Reno's Home in Dallas," the poet alternates the man and woman's voices to a wonderful ironic effect as each speaker concentrates on his and her immediate object. (McDonald has tried this sort of alternation in "My Neighbor Who Kept Pigeons" but fails to bring it off nearly so well.) The man in Yates's poem wants his football team to win, while the woman wishes the man would pay attention to her. By turns the situation is funny and touching, the writing pulling us both ways at once. Here the ending functions artfully as it drives home the final phrase, "don't take a chance," which bears significantly on the hopes and fears of both figures involved. The poet shifts points of view deftly, both here and in the finely wrought conversation of "Snickersnee." In the latter Yates mixes colloquial language with allusions to a dictionary meaning and to a battle in snow during the First World War, creating simultaneously in his measured quatrains a realistic bit of table talk and a thrilling moment of surrealistic revenge. References to the wind cutting to the bone, to what kind of feed is best for old horses, and to carving the turkey—all are blended into a metaphorical episode where "senile" Uncle Stafford gets back at the family for ignoring his explanation of the word "snickersnee":

I see him rise from the table until he
hovers above us, brandishing a saber.

He shakes that saber at Daddy and stabs out
an eye. He plunges deep into the heart
of Uncle Reno and severs Aunt Dickey's
head. He slashes Mom in her left side.

But they never stop. They keep on. Dad, with
one eye gone, asks Reno what's the best
fertilizer. Reno wipes blood from his chest
and says horse manure. Aunt Dickey, her head

on the floor, chews another potato,

and Mom, her whole side bleeding, says Reverend
Draper's preaching tonight and shouldn't we go?

The unobtrusive and only occasional rhymes add irony to the formal structur-
ing of an outrageous scene. In at least two other poems Yates employs rhyming in an equally effective and subtle manner. Generally the look of his poems
and the way they read so clearly and flow so naturally disguise the fact that
the poetry is internally and externally shaped and tuned by a fine eye and ear.
Again, the pure sound of the poet's work makes it a sure hit with any audience,
while on the page it rewards the closest reading and rereading.

Walter McDonald has also staked out for himself a poetic territory for cultivation and harvest, in his case the unlikely area of Lubbock and the Llano
Estacado. In *One Thing Leads to Another* (1978), the poet may have gathered
his finest group of poems, even though he has two other strong collections to
his credit: *Caliban in Blue* (1976) and *Anything, Anything* (1980). Both Yates
and McDonald share with a number of other contemporary Texas poets the
production of important bodies of work that are impressive in volume alone.
McDonald has himself gone from being an occasional poet to one as nearly prolific as Emily Dickinson in 1862, the year she wrote 366 poems—McDonald
having written more than 100 during 1977 or thereabouts. At times poets are
criticized for writing too much, as when the individual pieces cannot justify
themselves, and McDonald's work may be open to such a charge. Yet this collection from Cedar Rock Press suffers only partially from the effects of an obsessive writing habit. It may be that most of these poems came prior to his *an-
nus mirabilis*, for some appeared in magazines several years earlier. Another
point in this chapbook's favor is its length—only twenty-seven pages of poetry.
The selection is divided into five sections and each offers a mere handful of
poems, though most stand on their own. All work well within the sections and
some are as good as McDonald's best. The poet may have poems equal to many
of these and better than several, yet as a whole this collection introduces
strengths not present in the poet's first book and performances surpassed
rarely, if at all, in his third volume.

For the first time a McDonald collection contains a section of poems devoted exclusively to the poet's native region, though he has since written numerous poems on West Texas life—where it seldom rains, where trees are at a
premium, and where most people stop for "good" after finally giving up on
finding El Dorado. McDonald sees his people as adaptable, a quality he obviously admires and celebrates in poems that treat of those who arrived, looked
around at the godforsaken place, "Said hell" and "help me hitch up the plow."
The crop yield is as grim as the life that brought it forth:

> plants with bones
> for stalks survive the wind
> and grow red fists of flowers.

McDonald has recorded with a natural objectivity the violence that has also grown from such a tightfisted existence. An increasing number of the poems refer to his people's essentially unsettled ways, which seem the result of the region's severe strain on their emotional systems. Some adapt but others take to getting back by knifing the priceless trees in a strangely perverse revenge.

Paul Christensen has referred to a Texas poet's rites of passage as a typical theme, and in McDonald's work one can easily find a representative instance. Yet a poem like "The Year She Turned Sixteen" is not simply characteristic of a Texas upbringing but speaks of that age when the young awake in a "glory" of sex:

> Her eyes sheened
> Gloria would come late to homeroom
> clothed in cologne.
> Glory, someone would groan,
> with all rows moaning Glory
> Glory.

(This opening stanza *might* be seen as a Texas version of Herrick's "Upon Julia's Clothes.") Later in life McDonald comes to experience this same awakening in the lives of his own sons who cannot believe he once tracked down the magic of love like a Jack and the Beanstalk bringing back the goose who could lay the golden egg. And then in "With Cindy at Vallecito" he describes his daughter's excitement at fishing and beating her brothers by snagging the biggest catch. The need to find magic at all ages is beautifully rendered in the best of McDonald's work, where one poem after another leads us to a discovery of those memorable, if painful, moments of youth.

Recently, however, in *Anything, Anything*, the poems have grown more sinister. Two of the finest poems in the earlier volume, as well as many which carry through with similar interests (retelling of biblical stories, regional sketches, and family relationships), are found again in this third collection and represent a continuation more than an advance. This is certainly no small accomplishment, given the high quality of McDonald's previous work. But by and large it is the sinister nature of this new book that makes it what it is—a further commentary on the desperate lives of the region. If this is intended as a metaphor for contemporary life, it is even more disturbing than if it merely speaks of the desperation of a wasteland in the American West. Three poems at the heart of the book sum up the situation: "Signs and Warnings," "At the Human Development Center," and "The Girl in the Mackinaw and Panties."

As in the earlier book, tortured cats serve as a symbol for the cruelty of those who somehow hold a deepseated resentment. (Curiously, and perhaps revealingly, a book entitled *Kitty Torture* was published in Austin some year and a half ago and was extremely popular in certain quarters.) Cats that are decapitated and dropped on the speaker's porch (in "Signs and Warnings") or that have been beaten in the head and are mercifully (?) shot with a B-B gun by the man who finds them (in "Overheard")—these suggest a perversity inherent in the region, or again, throughout our entire contemporary world. In his description of the Human Development Center the poet remarks that

                              Nothing
            about this place seems like a hospital.
            They must not think they're sick.
            Only unlucky. That, they can understand.
            Here what they get is luck: methadone,
            valium, the address of AA, whatever
            it takes to get them by, sometimes
            no more than fifteen minutes of crying
            in a room with someone who doesn't
            beat them.

McDonald has descended into this hell and returned to report of its suffering with oppressingly ironic overtones. The message is almost too painful to bear, yet the poet must be praised for the truth of his vision. Here it seems undeniable that the reference is to man's inhumanity to man, in or out of Texas. And though I must admit that my own squeamishness in these matters (James Cody having called my own poetry "timid beyond belief") may prevent me from finding the new writing in *Anything, Anything* superior to McDonald's earlier achievements, clearly it is strong medicine.

   Another hang-up I have is with the use of the pronoun "you" in place of the narrative "I" or a third-person pronoun, which I find presumptuous and typical of the Iowa Writers Workshop approach. Still, I can see how McDonald has made good use of this device in his poem on picking up a hitchhiker, the better perhaps to distance himself from the embarrassed narrator who finds himself caught up in another person's fearful flight. The poem is a telling one and epitomizes the sinister nature of McDonald's recent work. Written in three-line stanzas, the poem is carefully crafted—with line breaks, similes, and conversational excerpts all controlled for the final effect of the poet's subtle suggestion that there is some unseen figure or force threatening the girl's very existence. Here, however, the menace is not the same as that hinted at in "Especially at Night" or "On the Farm," where death and the unknown flash their malignant "signs and warnings." For "The Girl in the Mackinaw and Panties" is probably just showing her boyfriend or husband she won't take any further abuse. In some ways melodramatic, the poem is masterfully done, with internal rhymes calculated to underscore the uncomfortable feeling experienced by driver and rider alike, their situation at once laughable and unnerving:

                        You open the pickup
            door and she climbs in,

            her panties showing. Hi there,
            you say, shifting up as you go.
            You live around this way?

Just take me the other side of Slaton,
she says, her words hard as her knees.
You try steering your eyes off her

bare legs to keep from killing
you both. Lose something
in a poker game? You try

to joke. Listen is all she says,
shut up and drive. She keeps
looking back. Faster, she says.

Between these two important poets there may lie a world of difference in terms of their points of view, though both share similar techniques and both have written on similar themes. But more significant is the fact that together they have brought to Texas (as natives of the state) a vital new writing with its roots in the region and its branches extending beyond to all readers who would appreciate the genuine article. If the one can chill us with versions of our deepest fears and darkest deeds, the other will warm us with his deeply human portraits of aging men and love-starved women. Both deserve a sensitive readership, for each in his way has created poems to which all can respond, just as McDonald's son does on looking through his binoculars at the moon, "a round orange tunnel / in the east," in "At the Football Stadium" from *Anything, Anything*:

Silent, under the savage crowd noise,
beneath the lenses and his fists
he mouthed an O.

from Texas Poetry in Translation

And why Texas? Why translate the poetry of a region little thought of within, much less beyond, its borders, a region only known abroad for oil, cattle, and the Kennedy assassination? With Latin American readers aware for the most part of few poets other than those of the Pound-Williams-Eliot-Stevens era and those of the Beat Generation, it would make far more sense to students of contemporary United States poetry to translate the New York poets or those belonging to the easily identifiable Iowa Workshop school. Certainly there are regions and stylistic movements that have produced more popular and perhaps more significant work than that done by Texas poets, yet every region's writing has something to recommend it, irrespective of the level of sophistication achieved or the opinion in which it is held by those in literary vogue at the moment. In this regard, my coeditor, Luis Ramos-García, has pointed out aspects of Texas poetry which he believes will make it particularly appealing to a Latin American audience. He notes that the rural spirit still permeating Texas poetry has given to it a sense of hope and optimism, an openness to the past, present, and future. He feels that there is not in it the anguish characteristic of so many other poetries of the modern world. This seems to me true even of the work of poets living in the bleaker areas of the State, those who have contributed so significantly to the new Texas writing. Luis has also called attention to the influence of religion on our poetry, even as paradoxically a number of the poems accepts as natural the most unlikely attitudes and practices insofar as religion itself is concerned. The various ethnic and cultural backgrounds in Texas account in part for many of these elements, but the fact that the poets have presented such contradictions of the region as vividly remembered events and responses is evidence of the unique character of their writing and of the sources for it in their Texas experience.

The connection of a work of literature with a specific place has always determined for me much of its inherent value. In recent years this whole idea has perhaps been done almost to death, though without its advocates necessarily understanding the essence of place in poetry. There is more to it than simply naming a location or describing a locale. With the broad migration of teachers of creative writing there has been a tendency to exploit places for their quaint or exotic features. With something of the Southerner in me I find this development comparable to the situation during Reconstruction when

Introduction to *Washing the Cow's Skull / Lavando la calavera de vaca* (Fort Worth: Prickly Pear Press, 1981).

the carpetbaggers descended like a swarm of locusts to take advantage of blacks and whites alike and to pit one against the other. In this analogy the scalawags are those in any region who prefer to promote these flashy types from afar rather than to support their native artists. While this may seem an exaggeration, the effects of a conscious or unconscious exploitation of place in poetry have been to make of the local a gold mine for those who apply to it an opportunist's clever technique, while those attempting a genuine treatment of place, as native or longtime resident artists, are considered inept and out of touch with contemporary writing. For this reason I find much of what passes for place poetry suspect, and remain dissatisfied with the claims made for the work of poets who lack any real ties with where they are or from whence they come. I sense in such work a groundlessness and an unreality, an overemphasis on cuteness and sheer virtuosity. And in contrast to this general state of affairs I find that the Texas poetry collected in this anthology is representative of a vital, authentic expression of what it means to experience the life of a region, to respond to it more deeply than at the level of style or fashionable imagery, and to discover through place one's personal and social history, one's cultural and artistic heritage, however primitive those happen to be.

But again, why Texas poetry in translation? Personally I left off years ago looking to New York or California for artistic inspiration, much less a readership. For me a Texan's natural allies in the arts lie south, where Spanish is spoken and where it is being written with ever greater power. Though the superpatriot still celebrates overloud our independence from the Mexican state, I see our destiny manifest there, our cultural future linked to a chain of nations stretching from the Rio Grande to Tierra del Fuego; and I envision our poets opening a cultural commerce with the descendants of Netzahualcoyotl, to exchange—as the Indians of these continents did centuries ago—our amulets of words for those fashioned by poets we approach ever closer in spirit, having always been nearer to them by land and sea. It is in fact to a Spanish-Indian presence that we owe in large measure whatever claims our poems may lay to such qualities as warmth and vitality. And thus by way of reciprocation have Luis and I labored long to bring into Spanish these handmade beads of a Texas mind and breath.

Generations of Texas Poets

In tracing developments in Spanish and Latin American literatures, critics have relied heavily on the idea of generations of writers as a way of identifying and defining trends within a given historical period, a concept best exemplified by the Generation of '98, which included Unamuno, Azorín, Valle-Inclán, Machado, and even Rubén Darío. This has always seemed to me a useful approach to the continuum of literature and is especially valuable when one would attempt to distinguish between movements or tendencies taking place within a short span of time. Although the distinctions or gradations we observe at close range may disappear over history's longer haul, it is a meaningful exercise to note the ebb and flow of styles and attitudes within a spread of three or four decades, if for no other reason than to recall a few of the more prominent issues and figures of each generation. Such a system of classification may also aid in clarifying the subtle shifts in the poetic strata that exhibit the very makings of a literary evolution. Furthermore, to recognize how a given generation adapts itself to a peculiar environment, which may not exist for the succeeding generation, is to explain in part the reactions of one group of writers to another.

In surveying the brief record of Texas poetry, it is possible to speak essentially of three groups or generations—those of the 1950s, '60s, and '70s. While there has been some overlapping from one decade to another, the rise of basic themes and styles is clear within these three ten-year periods, and each new layer of the record can be characterized by two or three individual poets belonging to that generation. Recent interest in Texas poetry has focused attention, however, on only two outcroppings, as it were: belatedly, the work of Vassar Miller; and disproportionately, that of a group of emigré professor-poets whose presence, beginning around 1976, has received more publicity than has that of any single native poet in the state's history. One emigré poet claimed in 1979 that true contemporary poetry in Texas did not exist until the influx of professor-poets brought professionalism, seriousness, and innovation to the region. I would reply that my own anthologies of Texas poetry, *The New Breed* (1973) and *Washing the Cow's Skull* (1981), amply demonstrate that in fact three strong generations of Texas poets were in existence prior to the arrival of the professor-poets. One review of *The New Breed* questioned my title as misleading, since the reviewer asserted that no other group of writers came before those included in the collection. Yet my introduction to that 1973 anthology clearly acknowledged the importance of a number of figures not pre-

The Pawn Review, vol. 5 (1981-82): 8-17.

sent in *The New Breed* because for me they *did* belong to an earlier generation. Four of those poets are in the 1981 collection—William Barney, William Burford, Vassar Miller, and R.G. Vliet—and one of the major ideas behind *Washing the Cow's Skull* was precisely to preserve their contribution and to present them within an overview of Texas poetry as written by native and longtime resident poets.

The first generation of Texas poets came, then, in the 1950s with the work of Barney, Burford, and Miller. Above all, theirs is a poetry of high seriousness and is marked by linguistic power and mastery of traditional forms. While each of these poets is thoroughly acquainted with the nature of modern poetry, each has established his or her individual voice outside the vogues of the '50s and early '60s. Yet each can be profitably compared with national figures or trends: Barney with Robert Frost; Burford with Denise Levertov; and Miller with the confessionalists Sylvia Plath and Robert Lowell. But it should be stressed that these Texans were creating their styles and ideas independently, and that either they preceded certain trends in the '60s or carried on an existing tradition after a wholly regional manner.

The generation of the middle '60s numbers among its primary figures a poet born before any of those of the previous generation—Joseph Colin Murphey. It was not until the '60s, however, that Murphey discovered his own voice, but by his late fifties he was so successful in achieving a contemporary style and thought that I myself included him in *The New Breed*, not knowing his age at the time that I accepted his poems for publication. Murphey was an early admirer of Galway Kinnell, William Stafford, and Gary Snyder, at the same time that he supported the work of Vassar Miller and other Texas poets through his magazine *Stone Drum*. In general, Murphey first identified with the writers associated with Robert Bly's *The Sixties*, yet his own poetry has always been distinctively Texan in its content and orientation. Another poet who found his voice in the mid to late '60s was Leon Stokesbury, whose 1976 collection, *Often in Different Landscapes*, the first in Texas Press's now defunct poetry series, represented the truly original work of a Texas poet who had already published nationwide in the most prestigious magazines and anthologies.

With the 1970s, some dozen vital new voices began to be heard, although the audience for Texas poetry still remained almost nonexistent. Perhaps the most popular of these 'seventies poets have been Naomi Shihab Nye, Harryette Mullen, Walter McDonald, David Yates, and Sandra Lynn. (See *The Pawn Review*, vol. 4, and *Washing the Cow's Skull* for in-depth reviews of their most recent publications.) Charles Behlen, though not so widely known as the others, has also created a niche for himself with his strongly regional character sketches in poems reminiscent, according to several critics, of those of E.A. Robinson. (A poet from the generation of the late '40s and early '50s, Arthur Sampley, has also been studied favorably, by poet-critic J.M. Linebarger, in connection with E.A. Robinson's work.) Shihab Nye, Mullen, McDonald, Yates, and Lynn have all contributed a new look and sound to Texas poetry. It is even possible— and this is no small accomplishment—for the poems of these five poets to be recognized from among those of the thousands of poets active in the United

States during the past decade. And although an important figure like Barney has gone largely unrecognized since the '50s, the prospects for the generation of the '70s to win a wider audience have been vastly improved, of late, by a growing interest in the state's native poets.

Still, one problem that continues to plague native Texas poets in their search for a proper audience is the attitude that only writers coming from the outside have a real grasp of the contemporary poem. Even though I firmly believe that it is quite simple to document the significant contributions made by three generations of Texas poets, there persists a very real threat to an acknowledgment of or recognition for these poets because of those who would begin a history of the state's poetry with the present generation of professor-poets. The latter arrived with undeniable credentials both as teachers and as writers; nor is the value of their presence to be denied. And yet, if they alone are to reap the benefits of a slowly developing audience in the state, then any true Texas poetry may well be submerged beneath this flood of emigration. The cultural histories of nations that have suffered from one kind of invasion or another are too numerous even to list, so that to name but our native Indians or our neighbor Mexico should suffice to call up rich traditions overwhelmed in the wake of a foreign conquest. Of course, it has been suggested that many cultures were decadent or stagnant at the time of invasion, though this is hardly the case in Texas. On the contrary. But rather than pursue this issue further, I propose to discuss the generation of the '80s insofar as it contains not only a number of emigré poets but a group of native poets which has begun to emphasize another side of the multifaceted crystal that is Texas poetry.

The idea that Texas and poetry do not go together has long acted as a hindrance to a serious readership for the state's poets. Even with the explosion of this popular myth, there remains a feeling among many writers of the '80s generation that anything which smacks of the old Texas is for them and their work anathema. Thus, the school of rough-and-ready, colloquial, or open range writing has been displaced in the minds of these new poets by a need for chiseléd diction, for the plumbing of psychological and mystical depths, and for a type of scientific mysticism. Albert Goldbarth, Jack Myers, William Virgil Davis, and Cynthia Macdonald—all of them emigré poets associated in fact or through influence with the Iowa Workshop school—are proponents in one form or another of such tendencies, but an equally good example of this approach may be found in the work of Pattiann Rogers. Rogers is a convenient representative for several reasons, but principally because her career began, in part, with her 1974 publication in *The Texas Quarterly*.

According to the contributors note on Rogers in the autumn 1974 issue of *TQ*, she graduated from the University of Missouri (Phi Beta Kappa) and returned to writing after a six-year lull. Her poem in *TQ* marks the beginning of an obvious burst of energy that has continued to the present with her award-winning appearances in *Poetry* for April 1981 and in *Poetry Northwest*, most recently in the autumn 1981 issue, as well as with her forthcoming collection from Princeton University Press. What is most striking about her poem in *TQ* is its direct link with one of her latest pieces in *Poetry*. Compare the following lines from her poem in *TQ* (1974)

> How near am I, my brother,
> Three genes removed and that alone
> From the water-fledgling
> Who today for the first time
> Kicked his lovely new-grown appendages?
> . . .
> I am this deep within
> The tiny fur-born rodents
> Who scurry, pause,
> Push their noses thru their wire cages,
> Stop, with glinting eyes,
> And twitching momentarily, my god,
> They wonder

with these lines from "Being Accomplished" in *Poetry* (1981):

> Imagine the mouse with her spider-sized hands
> Holding to a branch of dead hawthorn in the middle
> Of the winter field tonight. Picture the night pressing in
> Around those hands, forced, simply by their presence,
> To fit its great black bulk exactly around every hair
> And every pin-like nail, forced to outline perfectly
> Every needle-thin bone without crushing one, to carry
> Its immensity right up to the precise boundary of flesh
> But no further. Think how the heavy weight of infinity,
> Expanding outward in all directions forever, is forced,
> Nevertheless, to mold itself right here and now
> To every peculiarity of those appendages.

In another poem in *Poetry*, entitled "Discovering Your Subject," Rogers speaks of painting "the same shrimp boat / Every day of your life." It is clear from the two excerpts quoted above that the poet has certainly discovered her subject, not only in the rodent but in the analysis of every "peculiarity of those appendages." Rogers's style has changed for the better, but her subject and diction remain the same, as does her highly intellectual, scientific approach to the mystical. All of this is characteristic as well of Albert Goldbarth's poetry, which draws on the works of Newton (see the poet's *Opticks*, 1974) and Linnaeus (see his poem entitled "Blue Flowers" in *Poetry* for September 1981 —"The lucid, detailed, inarguable, / relentless cataloguing") as a basis for Goldbarth's own probings for a faith in poetry and the workings of the universe. There is much to be learned from Goldbarth and company, though not everything they do can be considered "inarguable."

Both Rogers and Goldbarth now reside in Texas, yet their work would never be taken as regional by any stretch of the imagination. When Goldbarth has chosen to explore "a Texan's mind," he has picked for the purpose Cocteau's male lover, Barbette, who escaped from Round Rock, Texas, and became part of the Lost Generation in Paris. Every generation of Texas poets has had any number of escapees, notable among them Bin Ramke, who shared the 1978 Texas Institute of Letters award for poetry (having already won the Yale Younger Poets Award) for a collection that recounts, in part, the sensitive poet's torment in Texas. (Richard Hugo, who served as judge, found Ramke's escape from Texas a decided plus for his poetry. What is most curious about this and similar cases is that the writer who escapes from Texas always seems to return the book for the applause and prize money.) Though many emigré poets have been, for economic reasons, quite happy to make Texas their home, none has wanted to be identified with the place or its poetic tradition. (The sole exception is Paul Christensen, who in his own poetry and through his fine radio program, "Poetry Southwest," has immersed himself in the region's poetic sources.) The emigré's own writing, like that of Pattiann Rogers, is essentially focused on states of mind, never on the life of a single state of the nation. For this reason, none of these emigrés (with again the exception of Christensen) is concerned with the region as a subject for his or her poetry. In this sense they are closer to Vassar Miller than to any other Texas poet of the earlier generations, and this may explain why Miller and the emigrés are mentioned more often than the other poets of the state. And yet the poetry of both Barney and Burford exhibits a significant use of math and science for psychological and ethical investigation. Barney especially is given to developing insightful mathematical analogies to man's mental and moral problems and his search for understanding of the complexities of existence. Like the epic poet, who utilizes a wide range of sources, styles, and structural patterns, Barney encompassses in his work a variety of elements, whereas the emigré poets tend to limit themselves to painting almost by numbers "the same shrimp boat / Every day" of their lives. Cynthia Macdonald, for instance, has operated on her psyche after the manner of Sylvia Plath, yet only with the result that Macdonald's poems have an anesthetizing effect. Seldom does her work visit, as Barney's does, the great out-of-doors. Rogers and Goldbarth do venture into nature, though frequently what they observe merely serves their obsession with a clinical analysis similar to Macdonald's. Nothing Macdonald has done, however, approaches the brilliance of Plath, not even "Reflections in Stone," which is a mimicry of Plath's "Stones," where the hospital patient sees her environment through a series of ingenious metaphors based on attendants and tools in "the city of spare parts." Nor does Macdonald achieve the depth of a Barney, no matter how completely she devotes herself to self-surgery and personality amputation.

As to native Texas poets of the present generation, they too are inclined, like the emigré poets, to focus on states of mind rather than on the nature of a place as such. Five new poets to emerge within the past year are Diane Bertram, who, with her husband Rex Barnett, has established Sleepy Tree Publishing in Fort Worth; Rob Lewis, with the publication by Sleepy Tree of his *The Green Book*; Prentiss Moore, with publication of his *The Garden in Winter*; Rebecca Gonzales; and Jeanette Burney, the last two with collections soon to be published. Bertram's work is available in *Sleepy Tree I*, an anthology of prose and poetry, and her first poem in this collection, "Habitat," can bear comparison with the best of Lenore Kandel's and Erica Jong's erotic work, and may well go those poets one better. The fish / penis analogy in Bertram's poem is developed brilliantly and the diction throughout is completely right. Her other poems contain flashes of deep psychological insight and extremely controlled writing, especially in "Thaw," which describes a melting icicle as a metaphor for her need for love:

> It's true
> I'll be brittle and fragile,
> I'll break like dry spaghetti,
> but watch this,
>
> just watch: at the instant
> when the light breaks clear
> of that one small lingering cloud,
> see me dive from the tip of the rainspout,
> bare and potent as a pin.

Readers of the selections in this publication will await impatiently the first book by this young "feminist poet."

While Rob Lewis, as a native Texan from La Porte, can allude at times to his presence in or connection with the state, he is in no way concerned with this fact as an issue in his poetry. In "Midnight, a Washateria," the poet refers in passing to "beastly snow pouring down outside / with a will, a puncture in the hot Texas myth." Most of the poets of the generation of the '80s are intent on puncturing the myth that poetry in Texas has anything to do with oil or cattle, though Lewis himself says in the same poem that he wishes he were in these for profit, yet the meaning seems to be that he would prefer even money-making to the painful task of dealing with his memories, his lesions from relationships, "Subtleties to childhood / the networks haven't seen." Certainly Lewis does not back off from exploring the pain of personal relationships. This particular poem includes a very effective insertion of scenes from a Tarzan movie where the ape man is swimming to reach his Jane, a cut water flower in her hand (with a constant play on the film itself being "cut"). The effort to reach someone close—even while touching the person—is a subject treated repeatedly by Lewis. "Interface," for example, is the imagined transformation of the poet into the woman he loves:

> A weight, as of your breasts,
>
> pulls on my chest. I feel
> your hips superimpose on mine.
> My face pulls taut, as if, malleable,
> its clay is worked to yours.

The poems toward the end of Lewis's book show the poet at his best and promise much for the future from this young writer. "Polyphony" achieves just that by its juxtaposition of the sounds of tin on tin, cicadas trilling, freight cars clanging, rush hour traffic, and a linseed gin. The writing here is strong and daring. "For You Or Some Other" is likewise a fully realized poem, where variations on the words "brush" and "blush" yield

> A chord of ripe sonorities,
> awakened heart, it brushed by me
> like a glancing flurry of wings, invisible—
> but where it touched I blush—

Lewis, like Rogers and Goldbarth, reaches to the mystical meeting of natural and human. Another poet of this tendency is Stephen Harrigan, though this has never been the aspect of his poetry that interests me most. While often I find this whole approach too much of an intellectual exercise, there are definitely in the writing of Lewis, Rogers, Goldbarth, and Harrigan many fine moments when we are brought into revealing touch with the mysteries of the material world.

Prentiss Moore's first collection (*The Garden in Winter* from Texas Press) has been hailed as a new angle of vision, a poetry close to that of a Zukofsky or Creeley. What the volume contains, however, is more than anything a borrowing from almost every classic literary source beyond the Texas borders, although in one poem entitled "Texas" Moore does tip his hat (not a ten-gallon, to be sure) to the presence in the state of Moorish fountains "to / honor and enhance / so modestly the sound of water." It is just such a delicate image and sound that Moore aims at in his own work: the calming effect of an artistic design that brings one to a contemplation of natural beauty. One of Moore's favorite sources for tranquility, inspiration, and identification is Zen poetry, with its concern for a still center. But there is neither a new angle here nor an innovative use of the oriental tradition. For an instance of an authentic adaptation of Zen patterns of thought I would recommend rather the poetry of the Chicago poet Lucien Stryk, whose *Selected Poems* from Swallow Press offers the work of a man who has not only translated Zen poetry but has managed to use what he has learned from this tradition for the making of a Midwestern poetry that remains true to itself while it adds the further dimension of a Zen consciousness.

Moore's poems pay homage to every classic poet imaginable, though none of his own can be taken as an advance over or even an equalling of the models. None of the poems in the collection were published previously, and in a number of cases one wonders if reputable magazines would have accepted them, for many are negligible, though this may be my own prejudice against oriental imitations. The diction is frequently archaic, and the straining for restraint or a quiet moment of great intensity grows somewhat wearisome at times and seems a bit self-conscious. Nonetheless, Moore does create a poetry of delicacy and modesty, in keeping with his sources in the Chinese and Japanese traditions. Also, Moore's almost total identification with art itself as a source for his thought and manner may well signal a turning away from the traditional subjects for Texas poetry. (Actually, the desire to repudiate any connection with the cowboy or rough-and-ready image of Texas has served as a motivating force behind much of the work of Robert Grant Burns and, according to Paul Christensen, that of Robert Bonazzi.) In a few of his poems Moore is successful in writing of relationships between others, as in "Divertimento," although the endings of these pieces and of most of the poems in the collection are too often unsatisfying. In "Measure" the poet states that "It is the confusion / of delicacy. / We do not know / where to go. . . ." On the other hand, the risks involved in capturing such delicacy make the poet's even modest triumphs that much more to be admired. It will be especially interesting to note what impact this publication may have on the future practice of poetry in Texas.

Two promising women poets to emerge within the past two years are Rebecca Gonzales and Jeanette Burney. Gonzales may well be the finest chicano poet (*poetisa* I should say) to appear in Texas, even though her poetry is not characterized by chicano themes nor by the more popular and more rhetorical verse forms favored by the leading chicano practitioners. Gonzales *can* write with great power and imagination of field workers in the Laredo area, where she was born and reared, as she does in an unpublished piece on a watermelon picker who labors under the sun like a lover beneath a demanding bitch. For the past twelve years Gonzales has lived in Groves, outside Beaumont, and the watery world of this East Texas area is also rendered with great skill and imagination. Witness this opening stanza from "The Second Time," first printed in *Revista Chicano-Riqueña* (autumn 1981):

> The second time to love
> we avoid absolutes,
> as the marsh refuses
> to be either land or water

The acuteness of this analogy startled me, for rarely in Texas poetry has a poet been able to use nature so convincingly in the service of a human situation. William Barney has done it, but not in the same way. This is original work and presages great things for Texas and Chicano poetry. Another piece, "Beyond Our Grasp," first printed in *New Mexico Humanities Review*, demonstrates further Gonzales's fine use of the natural world:

> Even in the rain
> a good racehorse reaches hard,
> runs clean.
> Need flares his nostrils
> till they bleed a bright red.
> His eyes grow wild,
> never even see the wire;
> his need goes beyond the muddy stretch.

The same poem contains a pair of lines that will indicate in passing the "reach" of Gonzales's psychological insight in this complex work: "We hold each other in our eyes, / practice losing each other." Gonzales has only begun to publish her work in magazines, including three poems in the winter 1982 issue of *Cedar Rock*, but already there are readers anxious to see her poetry collected in book form. Hopefully there will be many books by Rebecca Gonzales in the offing.

Jeanette Burney has published in *Shenandoah* and several Texas publications, and her first book, tentatively entitled *The Opening*, will add to the generation of the '80s another voice given to internal analysis. What distinguishes Burney's poetry is that it represents a valid return to Browning's dramatic monologue. Like Moore, Burney is attracted to classical myths and retells several, à la the dramatic monologue, as in her fine "Leda Speaks After the Bath." "Magdalena" and a sequence of poems on Easter apply Burney's dramatic approach to biblical themes. "Man," perhaps an allegory, is, whatever it is, dramatic:

> I found him drinking rain from the roof, right out
> of the spout, the droplets scattering from his beard
> when he shook like a dog. I am first the virgin—touched
> more by hair on a grown man's face
> than by his wit. I know only that I do not know
> this man, and he is grinning to take me in.
> . . .
>   Can this man carry me
> and all I take? His only baggage is his face—an emblem
> of mistake and find, the skin a telling
> of muscle on bone. His eyes, those bulbs in creases,
> speak oceans to my hands: I want to pull his madness near.
> His face is all that I have learned,
> and like a girl I take him, dumb.
> Every line is earned.

Perhaps the new generation of Texas poets is determined that every line be earned, that no padding, no dependence on the Texas past (on world literature of the past, yes) will interfere with their quest for the grail of a timeless poetry unrestricted by any reference to the region. While I welcome what is to come, I am hopeful that our earlier poets will be remembered for the important role they have played in getting us where we are, even if much of their contribution signifies for the younger writers a basis for counteraction. For it would be a great loss if Texas readers and poets were to miss the sense of tradition that can come from learning the ways in which Barney, Burford, Miller, Murphey, McDonald, Yates, Mullen, and Lynn, to name but a few, have earned every line without resorting to wholesale borrowing or blatant imitation. If our tradition is not so grand as that of Chile or China, it is still ours, and it is up to us to build on it. If we reject it and follow the pied pipers that would denigrate our difference, then shall we be mice indeed, and none that the universe will mold itself to, as in Rogers' mystical vision. Knowing of each generation's contribution will help us to insure our continued poetic evolution. Unfortunately there are still those who find it strange that Texas should have its own literature, but I for one find it even stranger to think that it shouldn't. What is stranger still is the unfounded claim that we have no tradition. The point then is to cease denying its existence and to recognize instead the unique quality inhering in any poetry that belongs to a geographical, historical, and cultural habitation. Seldom has a poetry been divorced from the local, and whatever example is to be brought forward—a Milton, perhaps—must be seen in the end as the exception that proves the rule, for poetry flourishes in the place it knows best, whether it be Greece, England, or even Texas.

Review of *Texas Books in Review*

Originally founded in 1977 by Jim White and now edited by Bill Martin and Tom Pilkington from Tarleton State University in Stephenville, *Texas Books in Review* is back in full swing with its best offering ever. In the last essay of the present issue, Lawrence Clayton reviews three books on Texas art, and in doing so he manages to characterize this entire 1982 version of *TBR*:

> Something in the collection will appeal to the taste of almost everyone. . . . One comes away from the [issue] aware that this is serious . . . not just a casual stroll. . . . The strength of the arts, both literary and graphic, shows marked growth in the state and promises that great things are no longer just on the horizon for Texas.

Nor does this issue of *TBR* stop with literature and art but includes history (natural, Black, *Mexicano*, border, and cowboy), photography, economics, and philosophy. As a survey of 1981 publishing within the state or by its writers through presses outside Texas, the selection is both comprehensive and critically perceptive. This issue is especially notable for the high quality of the writing, the wide variety of reviewing styles and strategies, and the improved layout and design. The editors have done an exceptional job in choosing titles from a broad field of subjects and in soliciting capable, knowledgeable persons to handle the reviewing. Teachers of creative writing and expository prose should make good use of this issue as a sourcebook for the organization and development of effective essays, for examples of how to approach and appreciate the fine publications that are available in the state, and for supplying any writing student with all the appropriate rhetorical tools, including trenchant wit and logical argument.

Approximately half the reviews in this issue concern prose fiction and poetry. In addition, the lead article by Craig Edward Clifford presents a philosophical view of the relationship between literature and place. Clifford's pronouncements sound, however, somewhat behind the times, since his call for a serious Texas literary effort "grounded in our own locale and its peculiar nature" has been under way for a number of years. The essay is also dated in the sense that it is largely a rehash of Clifford's earlier article in *The Texas Observer* (written in response to Larry McMurtry's "Ever a Bridegroom"). In the case of McMurtry's own contribution to this issue of *TBR*, which reviews

Texas Writers' Newsletter, no. 33 (winter 1982): 6-9.

Vassar Miller's *Selected and New Poems* from Latitudes Press, his observations are an important extension of that "infamous" piece in the *Observer* where he first declared that the laurel for excellence in Texas letters should go to this Houston poet. McMurtry's review substantiates his claim through a well-written account of Miller's achievement and by quoting in their entirety four of her poems that demonstrate "her eloquence and her bite." Yet another view that replays an earlier appearance in the *Observer* is George Hendrick's estimate of Betsy Colquitt's *Honor Card & Other Poems*. In *TBR* Hendricks goes further than he had in his useful *Observer* piece—too far in fact—when he places Colquitt in a class with Miller, which is an assertion he fails to support on the basis of the quotations in his review of *Honor Card*. (His reviews of five other poetry collections are generally on target.) The fact that two of these three reviewers have repeated themselves from their *Observer* articles, without adding anything truly significant to what they had already written, may be regretted, and yet with McMurtry's exception as an example of what can be done from one piece to another, it should be remarked that both *The Texas Observer* and *Texas Books in Review* now offer space for in-depth discussions of Texas literature and that this is indeed a welcome development.

In his survey of some of the state's small literary magazines, James Sallis reveals his understanding of what should be the function of such outlets for beginning and established writers. Basically Sallis faults little magazines with incestuous activity, at the same time that he finds such magazines may well offer the only real exposure for worthwhile writing. His assessment seems both fair and judicious, though certain readers and writers will perhaps disagree with him when it comes to specific publications. The information will, however, prove of benefit to all those interested in knowing where to send their latest literary efforts.

As to prose fiction from major houses, this is reviewed with great gusto by Robert Flynn (who humbugs Dan Jenkins's *Baja Oklahoma*) and invitingly by Judy Rigler (who lays before us a tempting look at William Brinkley's *Peeper*). John Erickson fails to convince me that I should read Al Dewlen's *The Session*, while Bruce Gibson, in giving "a legislator's view" of the same novel, disinclines me even further from picking up this piece of "political" fiction. [A fine review of Dewlen's book by Deas Campbell (in a library newsletter from Austin Community College) demonstrates that in fact this is a novel worth a reader's time.] Lou Rodenberg's review of the work of three women fiction writers begins very promisingly, but by two-thirds the way through I have lost interest in hearing so much of Beverly Lowry and Shelby Hearon's plots, which seem tedious and too-too earnest. By leaving more to the reader's imagination, Rodenberg's briefer report on Mary Gray Hughes's short story collection, *The Calling*, has a far greater appeal, which in turn encourages one to seek out this book and read it.

Like Flynn's review of Dan Jenkins's *Baja Oklahoma*, James Lee's "trashing" of what he calls three sleazebooks, published in an attempt "to cash in on the late and unlamented Texas chicwave," is fun from start to finish, for all, of course, but the publishers. Although Lee does make one serious charge when he voices a growing disenchantment with *Texas Monthly*, his is unfortunately a delightful piece of writing based on overpriced absurdities that do not even deserve the space provided them for review. *TBR* may also have erred when it gave over so many columns to cowboy books, yet Elmer Kelton's and John Edward Weems's reviews are both sterling performances, their informative sentences exemplary in phrasing and diction. Judy Rigler's essay is especially impressive in presenting what she refers to as a "border stew"—reviews of autobiography, border economics, military and natural history, "symbiotic relationships shared by the many pairs of border towns," and the novel *Peeper* mentioned earlier. Rigler deals with each distinct topic clearly and insightfully.

Rounding off an essentially balanced issue are reviews of two other novels, a book of E. O. Goldbeck's photography, and studies of Black and *Mexicano* history and of "folk and other art." Russell Long's look at novels involving farm life and the Venezuelan petroleum industry contain valuable generalizations on the nature of fiction, in particular what he refers to as "not quite *roman a clef* and not quite historical novel"—a mode typified by the work of Arthur Hailey of *Airport* and *Hotel* fame. Margaret Culberson's review of the Goldbeck book is the weakest in the issue, and this is owing to the fact that it remains at the level of photographic jargon, a tendency among specialists who employ terminology limited to their own fields of study and who illustrate their ideas with few concrete examples. Each of two reviews by Donald L. Zelman of books on Black leaders and *Mexicano* resistance is to the point and aids in passing on the notion, presented in both books according to the reviewer, that traditional interpretations of the Black and *Mexicano* as docile and apathetic in the face of Anglo dominance have been mythical and misleading. Following Lawrence Clayton's fine essay-review of Texas art and artists, this 1982 issue of *Texas Books in Review* concludes with "brief reviews" of 23 books and a list of publications received.

Once again, the editors of this review magazine are to be commended on a professional and vital addition to the critical evaluation of Texas writing and publishing. News that the next number of *TBR* will appear in the spring of 1983 should be noted enthusiastically and with great anticipation by all those supportive of the future of Texas letters. For through the contributions of *Texas Books in Review*, *The Texas Observer*, and other review organs, the growth and development of a serious writing and publishing tradition in the state will most assuredly be fostered and promoted.

from Foreword to *Two Gulls, One Hawk*

With the title poem of this volume, James Hoggard has achieved a long, dialectical piece that is unique in Texas letters. And while it is the authentic expression of a native poet, "Two Gulls, One Hawk" draws upon a wide range of biblical, classical, mystical, and Southwestern strains in building up and counterpointing its themes of family love, a sense of place, and the creative act. Weaving his motifs and images—of sticks, snakes, birds, the weather, grasshoppers, miracles, and human ties—Hoggard presents a warp and woof that is at once Southwestern and Greek, prophetic and poetic, contemporary and classic. The poem's alternating voices are rich with linguistic play and moving in their emotional responses one to the other. Much of the work's multilevel impact is owing to the poet's skillful manipulation of his image and motivic patterns in a poetic line that is his alone. As a poem that concerns husband-wife and father-son relationships, it is the work of a mature artist who has come to sing of universals in a local idiom that includes the lowly sights and sounds of mesquite and cicada.

On the other hand, "Tornado's Eye" is a poem that recalls the poet's origins, his early journey into the caves of mystery and meaning. In his search for a self-image, the boy in Hoggard's autobiographical piece stumbles over one impression after another, only vaguely aware of a trail that will eventually lead him to poetic invention. The awkwardness of the youth is paralleled by the poem's fumbling effort to discover a voice and a means of recording the significance inherent in the poet's past. Even though such an interpretation constitutes a pathetic fallacy, "Tornado's Eye" serves nonetheless as an important complement to the title poem—the one revealing Hoggard's struggle to create a viable and vital art, the other paying witness to the fact that the poet has, as D.H. Lawrence proclaimed, "come through." Without the first there is not the second, and to have them both is evidence of the necessary ground that has been covered, not only by James Hoggard but by other Texas poets of a generation that promised much and has now delivered.

Prickly Pear Press, then, is proud, on the occasion of the tenth anniversary of its inception, to offer this testament of the strides made in Texas poetry by another writer who has breathed life into a people and place he long since accepted as his own.

James Hoggard, *Two Gulls, One Hawk* (Fort Worth: Prickly Pear Press, 1983).

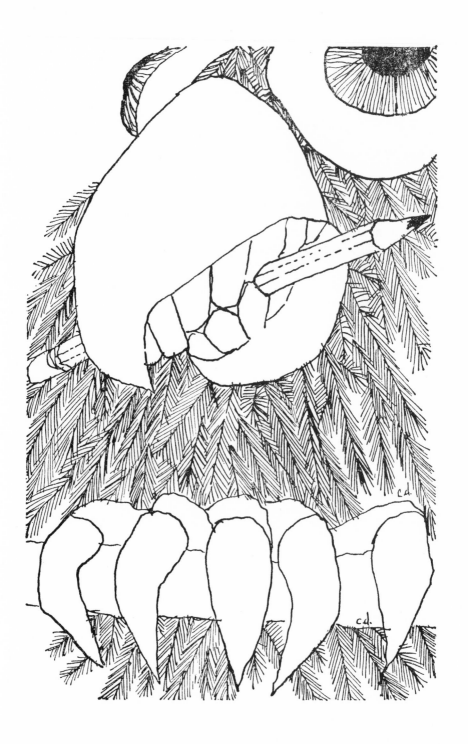

Poems Occasioned by Kennedy

Why poems are written is closely related to why thoughts are followed: where they go may relieve us of our surrounding desperation or lead us into new ways of facing it. Why a poem is not written is almost as thought-provoking a question, and *Of Poetry and Power* (edited by Erwin A. Glikes and Paul Schwaber for Basic Books), a collection of poems occasioned by John F. Kennedy's presidency and death, moves me into this particular question area more than any book I have ever encountered.

For instance, why are such prominent living American poets as Robert Lowell, Richard Wilbur, Denise Levertov, or even Kenneth Patchen not included among the contributors? Did they write poems but not wish to submit them? If so, what could their reasons be for withholding such manuscripts? Perhaps prior publication rights or commitments made it impossible. Still another consideration comes to mind (and one which is obviously self-assuming): why did I write no poem at the time? My reply to myself—that I could not presume the understanding such an event demands—clearly contains a gross misunderstanding of poetry's function. The end of poetry is not necessarily publication, for one of the first purposes in writing a poem ought to be, as Marianne Moore says, to create a place (public or private) for the genuine. Most of us, however, are ashamed of our feelings and try to veil them either by writing obscure verse or, what is worse, by not writing at all.

A question which confronted the editors of this book was whether or not good modern poetry can really serve the public on such an occasion. They believed that it could: "After all, if traditional elegiac forms are no longer available, elegiac feeling and expression still are." It is indeed a high tribute to Mr. Kennedy that, "with the exception of Abraham Lincoln, no President has inspired so much good poetry." Is it so important that our poets write works that will stand with Whitman's "When Lilacs Last in the Dooryard Bloom'd"? Looking at the assassination from a strictly literary point of view, it seems to me (perhaps sacrilegiously) that poetry was cheated. Not only was it robbed of the mature reflections which Robert Frost and William Carlos Williams (already deceased) would have surely shared with us, but Kennedy himself was deprived of the monuments such minds could have erected in his name. And yet, it is both a reproach and a consolation to read the many fine poets who rose to the occasion unashamed of showing their emotions.

Almost every poem in the book utters that most human wish: that it had

The Daily Texan (22 November 1964): 9.

not happened. Many, such as David Ignatow's and Richard Barker's, focus on the sudden emptiness and nightmarish aftermath. Nor is it surprising that to several poets those bleak Thanksgiving days seemed drawn out interminably by the stark black and white scenes on TV. Lewis Turco adds a hopeful note; John Berryman writes several touching movements for the seven children who "play fatherless"; and A.R. Ammons brings back "the caisson / breaking into sunlight / through the crystal black ribbon of trees!" William Burford, associate professor of English, has a fine poem, not included in this book for deadline reasons, that points up symbolically the fact of incomprehension. It was almost impossible to realize that he was dead, killed by "a kind of blunt bud, splintered / Into flower, that could not be touched." And from England, Kathleen Raine writes in her letter to the editors that "the grandeur of the national mourning was upon that level to which he tried to raise his nation."

The feelings of the whole world often seem expressed in the personal grief of one poet. And although their moods and attitudes vary, all the poets here seem caught up, as Professor Thomas Whitbread's poem expresses it, "In the frustration of rage, despair, and grief / At life not being as it ought to be." Fortunately, then, there are such poets as these who are willing to help us recall the politician who "did not depend on cant." And as John F. Kennedy himself said of Robert Frost: "A nation reveals itself not only by the men it produces but also by the men it honors, the men it remembers."

Louis Zukofsky: Knob of Sun

T.S. Eliot, like his poetry, is dead; Robert Lowell, unlike T.S., is alive, yet his poetry is in no better shape than Mr. Eliot's. Fortunately for American poetry, however, there was a movement, begun before Eliot came on the scene (1920) and extending beyond the time he quit writing (1950), which continues to produce much living verse. One of the poets from the objectivist movement to serve as both innovator and link with the past is Louis Zukofsky, whose moving study of Love's eyes, entitled *Bottom: On Shakespeare*, published in 1963 by the Ark Press for The University of Texas, includes passages from such writers as Dante, Thomas Campion, Walt Whitman, and William Carlos Williams. There are no quotes to be found in it from Eliot or Lowell, but then this is only natural, since those two rarely, if ever, see with the eyes of men in love. Praised be it that Louis Zukofsky does.

Although he has never appeared in the popular anthologies such as Untermeyer's, *The New Poets of England and America,* or *Contemporary American Poetry*, ever since he was invited in 1931 by Harriet Monroe, editor of *Poetry*, to edit an anthology of objectivist verse, Zukofsky has been regarded by a number of perceptive readers as one of America's most vital poets. As of this month, Zukofsky's collected poems will be available from Norton. In December 1964, he appeared in *Poetry* and *The Paris Review* with translations of Catullus, and we are most happy to present in this issue of *Riata* another of his translations, one which is previously unpublished.

Of the objectivists included by Zukofsky in his 1931 anthology, Robert McAlmon (discussed in the winter 1963 *Riata*) lived for a time in Juárez and Basil Bunting, an Englishman, reportedly lived in Galveston for several years. It was, perhaps, while on his visit to McAlmon via El Paso that William Carlos Williams, another member of the group and definitely the most important American poet of the twentieth century, saw the scene described in his poem "The Desert Music" as quoted on page two of the present *Riata*. These same men, including Charles Reznikoff and George Oppen (but excluding McAlmon, so far as I can tell), started the Objectivist Press in New York City sometime around 1934. In his *Autobiography*, Williams gives an account of their views on objectivism as opposed to imagism:

> The Objectivist theory was this: We had had "Imagism" (*Amygism*, as Pound had called it), which ran quickly out. That, though it had

Riata (spring 1965): 3-8.

been useful in ridding the field of verbiage, had no formal necessity implicit in it. It had already dribbled off into so called "free verse" which, as we saw, was a misnomer.

But, we argued, the poem, like every other form of art, is an object, an object that in itself formally presents its case and its meaning by the very form it assumes. Therefore, being an object, it should be so treated and controlled—but not as in the past. For past objects have about them past necessities—like the sonnet—which have conditioned them and from which, as a form itself, they cannot be freed.

The poem being an object (like a symphony or cubist painting) it must be the purpose of the poet to make of his words a new form: to invent, that is, an object consonant with his day. This was what we wished to imply by Objectivism, an antidote, in a sense, to the bare image haphazardly presented in loose verse.

In connection with this definition, there are Zukofsky's comments made in his 1931 Objectivist Anthology. What he says (particularly in regard to "past objects" and "loose verse") is even more to the point and helps at the same time to clarify for us his own position, which has expanded in a direction quite apart from Williams'. "It is understood," he says, "that historic and contemporary particulars may mean a thing or things as well as an event or a chain of events. . . ." For Zukofsky this includes "entire aspects of thought: economics, beliefs, literary analytics, etc. The entire matter involves the process of active literary omission and a discussion of method finding its way in the acceptance of two criteria: sincerity and objectification." As illustration of omission in terms of the first criterion, Zukofsky cites Charles Reznikoff's complete poem No. 21 from *Five Groups of Verse* (1927): "The ceaseless weaving of the uneven water." Zukofsky points in this poem to the sincerity of omission wherein the poet has achieved unity by means of "each word possessing remarkable energy as an image of water as action." Each word is responsible to the total impression, and therefore the poet has not tried to gain the meaning in any other than a straightforward manner, has omitted anything that does not contribute to the integrity of the whole. And in turn the reader does not have to go to *The Golden Bough* in order to discover to what the poet was alluding. In speaking of George Oppen's poetry, Williams sees in general exactly what Zukofsky has illustrated quite specifically: "He has never varied in his direct approach to the word as the supreme burden of the final poetic image." Williams says of Zukofsky's difficult poetry—difficult because it demands this same attention to each word—what may be quite meaningful in light of Zukofsky's criterion mentioned above: "Good taste, that's the thing; and not by exclusion, in the vulgar way, but by an inclusion that puts its grace upon common objects, that raises the common to grace."

Taking another of Zukofsky's statements from the 1931 anthology, we can see what he has sought to accomplish over his long career: "Writing . . . which is the detail, not mirage, of seeing, of thinking with the things as they exist, and of directing them along a line of melody." Everything in this statement is pertinent to Zukofsky's poetry as he has developed it with ever-increasing skill. It is especially evident in section 11 of "The Old Poet Moves to a New Apartment 14 Times," published in the March 1963 issue of *Poetry*:

> when the walls
> are dismantled
> realize
> the horror
> of dust
>
> but also
> where a curtain
> kept the dust from
> the walls,
> a white
>
> that with most
> things packed shows how
> little one needs
> waiting for the movers
> to come.

If I understand this section correctly, what Zukofsky is saying, in effect, is that here is some really fresh life; indeed, when it is compared with his own or his possessions' musty state, it moves him so thoroughly that he doesn't have to wait for a Mayflower van (or Eliot's and Lowell's decadent learning) to transport him into an equally fresh view of things; something near and ordinary is enough to startle his imagination to a whole New World of awareness. And listen to the music he makes. These are the ingredients of great poetry, and Zukofsky has them in abundance. Each word counts in the composition, visually, intellectually, and musically. This is more than can be said for 99% of the poetry being written today. As the *Times Literary Supplement* said last August of his eye and ear:

> "Looking" for Zukofsky is bringing into full consciousness and "To see is to inform all speech," which has its Aristotelean provenance: first we see with the eyes, then we discourse of what we see. In an age when print has weakened tactility and the eye, abstracting the message from it, has too often left the ear behind, Zukofsky's defence of the eye is a defence of poetry. For in poetry eye and ear come together in union.

American poetry in the twentieth century begins with Williams' *Spring and All* (1923), at which time Zukofsky was 19. The importance of the work of these two men stems from what the former did in that book and what the latter saw him doing in it. The main achievement, aside from throwing off pessimism, was the development of a daring new line that moves musically with the eye:

> as if the earth under our feet
> were
> an excrement of some sky
>
> and we degraded prisoners
> destined
> to hunger until we eat filth
>
> while the imagination strains
> after deer
> going by fields of goldenrod

Like Stravinsky going over to Webern for security, it is likely that for the same reason Lowell tried to take advantage of the technique which Williams perfected after 50 years of dedicated and slighted practice. Here is what Gilbert Sorrentino says of Lowell in *Kulchur* 5 for 1962 (words which can also be applied to his more recent *For The Union Dead*):

> In Lowell's recent book, *Life Studies*, we see displayed a grudging and embarrassed handling of a "new" line, a "new" freedom. The reviews all praised or damned the book because of its trail-blazing habiliments. Unfortunately, the book is made up of heavy-handed free verse which shows no aptitude whatsoever for the rhythms of American speech. Yet it was greeted as if nothing had happened in American verse since the publication of *Leaves of Grass*.

But then it is to Lowell's credit that he himself once wrote, "It's as if no poet except Williams had really seen America or heard its language."

In their conversation in *Kulchur* 16 for 1965, the English poet Charles Tomlinson and the American poet Robert Creeley discuss which men have contributed most to American poetry. Near the end of the discussion, Tomlinson asks Creeley, "Do you think that Eliot is still available to the American poet as a useful influence?" Creeley's reply is, "No." But in reference to Zukofsky's ability to teach young writers, Creeley has this to say:

> In short, what Zukofsky has done is to take distinctions of both ear and intelligence to a fineness that is difficult. It is difficult to follow a man when he's thinking very closely. And it's extremely difficult to follow him when he's using all the resources that he has developed or inherited regarding the particular nature of words as sound. I think Zukofsky is a very conscious artist; I can't think of another man in the States, with the possible exceptions of Robert Duncan and Olson, perhaps, who approaches the consciousness with which he writes. If

you read his translations of Catullus in which he is trying, in effect, to transpose or transliterate, or whatever the word would be, the texture of Latin sound into American language, it's an extraordinary *tour de force*. No, I find that in this whole thing that Pound came into— the tone leading of vowels, the question of measure, the question of the total effect in terms of sound and sight of a given piece of poetry —these aspects are tremendously handled by Zukofsky as by no one else.

With Creeley's remarks on Zukofsky's translations in mind, we can now come to a consideration of what Louis and Celia Zukofsky have done with Catullus. Their versions are not strictly translations in the sense of a word for word correspondence. And yet, by means of a unique listening and looking exercise, they manage to capture the spirit of the poem as it can be found in a legitimate (which is not to call theirs a bastard) translation. By discovering American words and often American phrases in the sound and appearance of the Latin, they bring to our own language a true contemporary feeling for an ancient author. Here is what Zukofsky himself says of their work: "This version of Catullus aims at rendition of his sound. By reading his lips, that is while pronouncing the Latin words, the translation—as his lips shape—tries to breathe with him." This is basically what happens in reading a Zukofsky poem which is *not* a translation. The following piece, Poem 3 from Zukofsky's *Barely and Widely* (1957), may help to illustrate what I mean when I say that we can breathe deeply the poet's visual and musical atmosphere:

> The green leaf that will outlast the winter
>   because sheltered in the open:
> the wall, transverse, and diagonal ribs
>   of the privet that pocket air
>   around the leaf inside them
>   and cover but with walls of wind:
> it happens wind colors like glass shelter,
>   as the light's aire from a vault
>   which has a knob of sun.

In addition, these lines from a poem written in 1952, "Spooks' Sabbath, Five Bowings," demonstrate how his early concern with an objectivist theory often re-emerges in terms of the felt moment rather than any predetermined rule of composition: ". . . for his part hard objects / became the buttocks of the heart." In poem after poem, there is sure proof that no writer today can surprise and reward a reader in fewer words than can Louis Zukofsky.

This has been meant primarily as an aid to the reading of his translation of Catullus, which appears along with its Latin model on the following page. It is hoped, however, that many readers will be led to read more of Zukofsky than it has been possible to include in this brief introduction, for he certainly lives up to what Henry James saw as the duty of a true poet: "He leads us into his own mind, his own vision of things, and that's the only place into which the poet *can* lead us."

No Perching Allowed

John Milton took a B.A. and an M.A. from Cambridge, but typically of many creative writers he despised his university, believing that it emphasized exactly the wrong approaches to literature. Oxford expelled Shelley, and Faulkner, it is said, flunked out of freshman English. What the facts behind these incidents may be is beside the present point. As a result of such celebrated cases, however, critics pro and con the writer on campus have been inclined through the years to go off half-cocked in every direction: writers are just that and have no business lecturing in a classroom; literary critics waste their time on trivia and deadwood; writers are too many and troublemakers to boot; university faculties are nothing but nests of jealous scholars clinging to the trees of knowledge because the Muse keeps their wings clipped back.

Further, the view taken by most experimental writers can hardly be called sympathetic to the academies, and because of this, their on-campus followers have infuriated the faculties by trying to deny entirely the worth of criticism and scholarship. On the other hand, there are many fine writers, forced into the teaching profession by their families' needs or their own weariness of having to get by on next to nothing, who find a university atmosphere at least more congenial to the dual role of creator and breadwinner than most jobs related to that of writing. In addition to these two reasons, there is the fact that during the forties and fifties many creative writers were also dedicated scholars, and this situation served to locate at American universities a number of the most vital literary movements of the times, creative as well as critical. Finally, then, the question today seems not so much should writers come on campus, since they are already here in force (though I cannot mean by this the University of Texas), but rather, how is the university to make the best of an affair that is distasteful even to those writers able by temperament, but more especially to those reduced by circumstances, to endure the serious drawbacks of an academic position?

At least once a week I walk downtown and mix with the department store crowds, buy a bag of popcorn at a five and ten, then listen to the conversation in the streets. Spending so much time on campus I almost lose track of what "real" people are like. And this perhaps is the main reaction a writer feels when he considers taking up teaching: the environment often strikes him as artificial, divorced from and devoid of life. Because of this, he fears that his work may come to address merely the learned audience at hand, his subject matter be

Panorama, supplement to *The Daily Texan* (9 January 1966): 4.

limited to the struggles of an absent-minded professor, or the trends in university taste influence and frustrate his own peculiar style. The time allowed him for observation, contemplation, and the sheer manual labor involved in writing may be cut into by an overload of courses and committee meetings consequent upon any such position, as is the paper work that may prove so inimical to the activity of creative writing.

There are certainly similar difficulties to be encountered by any working-man, but the writer feels his case demands special consideration. On not receiving exemptions from loyalty oaths, for instance, he raises one hell of a stink. Or if extra allowances are not made, such as more free time for writing and more leaves of absence for research, he complains until the whole school has been split by the controversy. For these and other reasons which have to do with a writer's being universally tagged an eccentric, the university regards him as a menace to the proper functioning of its system. Thus, atmosphere, procedure, and institutional reservations all combine to keep the writer off campus until suddenly the weather has changed.

Once a writer chooses or succumbs to the academic grind, there are actually many advantages he will acknowledge. Access to convenient library facilities can definitely serve as a stimulus for his writing. Not only this, but close association with perceptive scholars and receptive students may well benefit the writer on even more important grounds. Indeed, there have been cases in which a writer's theme or the improvement of a central point was first suggested by a fellow teacher or some inquisitive student.

In considering what services the writer may perform for the university, it should be obvious that an author who is already making a valuable contribution to the field would be particularly well-qualified both to comment on his own work and to encourage new writers and new kinds of criticism in areas he personally considers significant. One example of a very profitable exchange between author and student is the now-famous Iowa Writers' Workshop. It was while a member of the project that W.D. Snodgrass wrote most of the poems later included in his Pulitzer Prize collection *Heart's Needle*, and this highly successful workshop is only one of many operating throughout the nation. In universities from Washington state to New York, under the direction of such writers as Theodore Roethke, John Crowe Ransom, and Hiram Haydn, workshop criticism has helped to develop the outstanding talents of Carolyn Kizer, Randall Jarrell, and William Styron, to mention only a few. Of course, however, none of these names nor not one of these arguments will convince a university that to have writers on campus is beneficial to artist, student, and scholar, when professional jealousy has purposely established there a scholarly birdhouse where no pigeonhole or Zeno Porch will ever accommodate the nightingale.

Randall Jarrell left the Texas English department back in 1942, and since then no major American poet has taught at this "first-class" university. For that matter, I can recall no representative novelists or short story writers either. And yet, with regard to novelists, it is not even necessary to search outside Texas for an artist capable of imparting up-to-date ideas on his own and modern novels in general. Why Larry McMurtry—the best novelist in the state, now at Rice on a Guggenheim—why he is not available at the state university is a question only an administration concerned more with English literature and oil wells would fail to ask itself. Not only does this administration not hire the best in the nation, so far as creative writers go, it has even overlooked the best in its own backyard.

On being asked by several members of the lecture committee (a mistake they will never make in the future) which poet I would like to see visit the University this year, I submitted the name of Louis Zukofsky, a controversial but well-respected sixty-year-old poet who has even been published by the University of Texas Press. My reasons for wanting Zukofsky invited were basically personal, but above those there were more than enough to warrant bringing him here, surely as many as there were for having a lecture by "tangerine-flake" Tom Wolfe and his zoot-suiter's scholarship.

The committee's decision not to invite Zukofsky was based, I am told, on the following reason (which I interpret as extremely narrow and opinionated): the committee, simply wanting nothing whatsoever to do with an author who is difficult to read, took it upon themselves to declare Zukofsky's work not fit for student consumption, thereby leaving the latter no opportunity for exercising their own trained judgments.

In order to establish an example of the type of creative artist most appropriate for putting in an appearance on the University of Texas campus, please allow me to switch horses in the middle of the stream and take an instance from among our recent musical visitors. Instead of being able to witness art in the making, we pay rather to hear a Stan Getz and his cured quartet. The next attraction will no doubt feature the washed-up trumpet playing of Mr. Chet Baker, or some other likely has-been.

All of this is by way of saying that so long as writers and/or musicians are being brought on campus anyhow, why not have the best of the new generation (a Larry McMurtry, or an Ornette Coleman—also from Texas) and, if not the best, then the most sincere of the past generation (a Louis Zukofsky)? I may not be willing to go as far as a reviewer does in the Winter '65 issue of *Kulchur* when he concludes his comments on Zukofsky's collected poems by saying: ". . . there ought to be a flurry of drums a sound of trumpets for Zukofsky, and at the end of a violet carpeted corridor a gold crown: for Zukofsky." All I care is to hear a lecture or a concert once in a while by serious artists whose works come to rest long enough to leave more than a feather at the sill. *He dicho.*

Review of *Dante*

Without ever stopping to consider the reason for "comedy" in Dante's title, *The Divine Comedy*, I often wondered why such a term would appear in a religiously-oriented poem. On this account and many, many others, Thomas G. Bergin's *Dante* (The Orion Press) is a source of useful and stimulating information. Here is how he paraphrases Dante's last letter to his patron Can Grande della Scala:

> "Comedy," Dante states, is derived from "comus" and "oda," and means a "rustic song." It differs from tragedy, which begins in tranquility and comes to a terrible end, and which derives its name from "tragos" (goat) plus "oda," signifying its name therefore, "goat-song," i.e. fetid like a goat (as Seneca's tragedies illustrate), while comedy, though having some early adverse circumstances, yet comes to a happy ending, as appears from Terence. And in style of speech, tragedy is lofty and comedy humble, as Horace remarks in his "Ars Poetica." So the name "Comedy" fits the work at hand: it begins in hell but ends with paradise; likewise its speech is truly humble, for it is written in the vernacular, in which even women communicate.

The "vernacular" is, of course, in reference to Dante's beloved Italian, a language which had not been used up to his time for any outstanding work—all serious writing having been done in Latin. Although Dante himself could and did write in Latin (he is even considered the foremost scholar-poet of all times), he utilized the vernacular because he wanted to write a poem which could be read by those not knowing Latin, for he was primarily concerned that all men should be led in the paths of righteousness.

Aside from Dante's didacticism, Bergin finds that the poet's other main concern was with making a finely-wrought poem that would tell a compelling story. Paraphrasing Dante's early poetry, his political and literary treatises, and his letters, Bergin captures the spirit of the whole man, historically as well as artistically. In discussing Dante's "Commedia," he uses the same procedure with the result that the reader is both informed by the background and delighted by observing the artist at work.

Bergin presents many viewpoints of specialized interest, but only after he has firmly established the poet's two main concerns: "According to Benvenuto, Dante's hesitation [at the beginning of the "Commedia"] in following Virgil [his guide through hell] in Inferno II is not that of a pilgrim frightened by the journey but that of a poet alarmed at the task he has set himself." It is clear from earlier statements that Bergin, although he does not comment on Benvenuto's position directly, accepts the feeling of hesitation both from a poet's standpoint as well as from a pilgrim's. By merely presenting all sides, Bergin has also made a fine case elsewhere against those who would take exception to the poem's many philosophical and doctrinal assertions when the critic moves the reader to see that, although the philosophy and doctrine as expounded in the poem often interrupt the narrative flow, without these supporting walls, which Dante raises behind a foreground of believable characterization, the poem would lose much in richness and in weight. Without laying undue emphasis on any one interpretation, however, Bergin covers various critical approaches to Dante's poem and in an order that makes it clear which are more to the point. In other words, there is no scholarly bickering over dates or pet concepts.

As Bergin states at the beginning of his section on the "Commedia," his intent is not to offer any particular interpretation but rather "to consider what the poet says and his manner of saying it." This is as it should be, for the poem is many things to many different readers. Thus for Northrop Frye: "Of all fictions, the marvelous journey is the one formula that is never exhausted, and it is this fiction that is employed as a parable in the definitive encyclopedic poem of the mode, Dante's 'Commedia'." For Father Kenelm Foster it is "the mind in love." And for Thomas Bergin "no single work of Shakespeare can be compared to the 'Commedia' in scope." Bergin also asserts, and demonstrates by his discussion of the poem, that "There is in truth no better single book for the study of the medieval world."

This year marks the 700th anniversary of Dante's birth. The University of Texas opened the celebration with a lecture by Dr. Carne-Ross, the finest talk I have ever heard. In it he dealt with the various levels of Dante's "Commedia," pointing out that the poet's view of life is not in terms of black and white. This can be readily seen in Bergin's book as well. Treating of the poem's narrative, its allegory, and its doctrine, Bergin gives those who have read the poem new insights, while to those who have not read Dante's masterpiece his study plainly tells the story of growth and design in the work of a poet whose art and thought are as much at home in the twentieth century as they must have been in Dante's own fourteenth.

The only deficiency I find in Bergin's very worthwhile effort comes with the translations, presumably the author's own, which he uses in citing relevant passages from the poems. For one thing, they do not rhyme as do the versions by Laurence Binyon and Dorothy L. Sayers. The most disturbing thing about the translated quotes, however, is that they lose what Bergin has reported seeing in the originals. Fortunately, there are fine translations available (Bergin states that "considering vocabulary alone, Dante is the easiest major Italian author to read") and the rest of Bergin's book should certainly prompt the English reader to check them out for himself. And this alone makes the book an excellent means of marking the poet's birth, for as Mrs. Sayers has written in the introduction to her own translation, "it does not much matter by which road we come to Dante so long as we get to him in the end."

George Oppen: Things & Thoughts

Here at least is one living poet to be read with a will to believe. And any age able to say so much should feel a special joy. For when a generation's poets settle for the easy imitation, it is a sure sign that the society they represent has lost sight not only of itself but of those poets of the past it is ever indebted to for foundations of freedom and truth. Gratefully, then, with George Oppen's *This In Which* we find the work of a man who is totally alive to questions of integrity and ethical thought, speech and the workaday world, silence and frustration, and whose report on these concerns truly deserves a serious eye.

Published in 1934 by the Objectivist Press, George Oppen's first book of poems, *Discrete Series*, has long been out of print. His second book, *The Materials*, appeared in 1962 from New Directions / San Francisco Review. Now, with this latest book in hand (also from ND / SFR), it is high time Mr. Oppen was given the careful consideration his long-suffering work is so worthy of, if for no other reason than this most unusual fact: here is a man who for 30 years has continued quietly producing honest, quality verse of a class wholly unexpected in our day when cheap cleverness and self-publicity are all the rage.

Like so many of the objectivists from the '30s, George Oppen is a highly sensitive craftsman. Also like his fellow objectivists (particularly Zukofsky, Reznikoff, and Williams), Oppen has not been listened to for what he has to say. In discussing these poets, critics have invariably pointed to their use of "ordinary speech" and the "vivid image" but have hardly ever noted the statements being made by means of such mere techniques. It is, perhaps, a commonplace among critics to say that so-and-so has failed to observe such-and-such. Nevertheless, I feel more than justified in contending that, with regard to the objectivists, critics have greatly over-emphasized their techniques while almost entirely overlooking their meaning.

In the first place, it has ever been held a truism that an objectivist's ideas are either marred or completely annihilated by his concern for a realistic description of the object at hand. Quite to the contrary, many a case may be found in which the clearest of statements is drawn from just such a preoccupation with a particular object or environment. As only one example there is the poem "Product" from Oppen's second book:

> There is no beauty in New England like the boats.
> Each itself, even the paint white

Austin-American Statesman (23 January 1966): 17 and 19.

Dipping to each wave each time
At anchor, mast
And rigging tightly part of it
Fresh from the dry tools
And the dry New England hands.
The bow soars, finds the waves
The hull accepts. Once someone
Put a bowl afloat
And there for all to see, for all the children,
Even the New Englander
Was boatness. What I've seen
Is all I've found: myself.

Certainly there should be no real question here of clarity—description moving beautifully to the point. Why critics have not dealt with Oppen's poems
can finally, it seems to me, only be attributed to an attitude established back
in 1934 when his *Discrete Series* first appeared. To wit, William Rose Benet,
once he noted the "parsimony of words," saw no need to discuss further any
statements based on such a non-verbose style—as if the poems of Sappho,
short as they are, were to be forgotten because we have great Homer's epics.

The problem is one of splitting up matter and manner. Here again critics
have chosen simply to avoid the whole issue, thinking perhaps that if, as in
the case of "Product," the objectivist is saying what the critic thinks he is saying, Wallace Stevens has already said it. Admittedly there is a striking resemblance between Stevens' "Anecdote of the Jar," where art (the jar) is seen as
a reflector of the Tennessee hill, and Oppen's poem, where the bowl appears
to serve as a mirror for a typical New England scene. (Oppen is never satisfied
to present images "In which things explain each other, / Not themselves.")
Further, as Stevens was also preoccupied, though more so in other poems,
with the discovery of place and its peculiar relation to the living, our critic
may be thinking that on this point as well Oppen has been beaten to the path.
Yet in the end all of this only serves as an excellent example of how the objectivist, or any other minor American poet, is never allowed on what has
been taken as the posted hunting grounds of a feudal line of "philosophical"
poets, namely Eliot, Stevens, and the like.

So long as this sort of sectioning off is still in effect, the only acceptable
way left to discuss Oppen's work seems to be one of comparing it with that of
his fellow objectivists, who have also been sent to a similar reservation (see
Philip Rahv's essay entitled "Paleface and Redskin"). Thus, when we find William Carlos Williams and George Oppen each greatly concerned with what's
happening on a particular plot of land, such lines as these by Oppen: "At the
roots / Of the grass the creating / *Now*   that tremendous / plunge," will perhaps be permitted their proximity to Dr. Williams' words, "rooted, they /
grip down and begin to awaken," since both poets occupy, so to speak, the
same critical ground.

In an effort to follow up what must be the critics' line of reasoning, I turn now to the problem of poverty as viewed by an affluent poet. Oppen, so far as I can tell, has been well-to-do throughout his writing career. This in itself has been looked upon with regret, for true poets by definition should suffer and starve in rat-infested garrets. But, despite his not having this romantic handicap, Oppen has managed (and chosen, I might add) to speak of the poor with unusual compassion and understanding. Indeed, if their plight may in any way be considered a tragedy, Oppen's "Street" is surely a scene of its en-actment: ". . . I want / An end of poverty / As much as anyone // For the sake of intelligence . . . It is terrible to see the children, // The righteous little girls; / So good, they expect to be so good. . . ."

Above all, the true measure of any poet is how evocatively he speaks of love. Oppen is obviously in love with life, for there are moving moments with his baby daughter on his lap, endearing conversations with his wife, and always the affectionate images of machinery. But seldom is there a "love poem" as such. Whenever he does come to love as a subject, the result is, in more ways than one, a rare flower. Such a poem as "The Forms of Love" would have to be quoted whole, and unfortunately space will not allow for that. A shorter example, therefore, and one which treats of the poet as lover, is this entitled "Boy's Room":

A friend saw the rooms
Of Keats and Shelley
At the lake, and saw 'they were just
Boys' rooms' and was moved

By that. And indeed a poet's room
Is a boy's room
And I suppose that women know it.

Perhaps the unbeautiful banker
Is exciting to a woman, a man
Not a boy gasping
For breath over a girl's body.

To return, as Oppen has throughout the years, to the matter of the world we live in, the first and fourth sections of his poem entitled "Quotations" can, I believe, vividly indicate what it is the poet would finally have us do:

When I asked the very old man
In the Bahamas
How old the village was
He said
'I found it.'

And the child
We took on a trip

> Said
> 'We're having the life of our times'

By means of such a few selected passages it is almost impossible to see that how, as well as what, George Oppen writes is truly, as Dr. Williams has said, of "vast import to the nation." For this reason, those interested in American life and literature should find *This In Which,* or its predecessors, and meet more thoroughly with a living poet who speaks knowingly on such issues as (in "A Narrative") ". . . whether mendacity / Is really the best policy. And whether / One is not afraid / To lie." For as the title of this latest collection may well imply, George Oppen's poems contain more than just a *this*, they also consist of a meaning *in which*.

Following the Chapbook Trail

In reading hundreds of poems a month in the little magazines, one is left with the false impression either that only a few poets are doing distinctive work or that no one is. Perhaps this is just a personal impression, yet I cannot help but feel that it is owing in large part to the fact that chapbooks, which can correct the limited view provided by magazine publication, remain undistributed and therefore unknown. Chapbooks there are in abundance, and healthily so, but bookstores and reviewers have tended to slight them in favor of name press publications. And this is an unfortunate situation for poets and readers alike.

Since magazines too often publish the same poets and only a small sampling of their work—and this not necessarily their best efforts—, the result is often a misrepresentation of a writer's real thrust. Also, any development taking place in the poet's work is usually not evident from simple magazine publication. It is for these reasons, I believe, that to have a number of collections of the quality and purpose of those of Doug Flaherty is to be able to come to a fuller appreciation for this poet's important growth over the past eight years.

As poet, editor, and publisher, Doug Flaherty has rendered as great a service to contemporary American poetry as any young author I know. His magazine, *Road Apple Review*, and his small press, Road Runner, have not only contributed to the dissemination of fine writing but have been instrumental in establishing a climate for serious poetry which re-examines its very *raison d'etre*. Flaherty's publications have set the highest standard for a poetry dedicated to what he has called "the *holy hush*—that feeling created by the poem devised simply and cleanly from the physical experience of our lives. . . ." (in "Poem as Physical Object: Mythic & Elemental," from *Their Place in the Heat*, Road Runner Press, 1971). Flaherty has brought this same critical position very much to life in his own poems, paying witness to a union of critical and creative faculties cited by Matthew Arnold as essential to the writing of great poetry.

Flaherty's earliest chapbook, *The Elderly Battlefield Nurse* (1968), strikes the keynote for his music, imagery, and primary themes. The title poem introduces us to the poet's preference for the world of sensual experience as opposed to the abstract. Despite this dialectical choice, the poem itself is consciously shaped, with an irregular rhyme scheme adding muscle to the statement:

Now, I water flowers, moisture sinks.

Margins, no. 8 (1973): 32.

We plant and never think of roots,
yet all must drink.
My own body, steeped in sun,
sat down stone-hard and closed.

Technically the poem is typical of Flaherty, except for the occasional rhymes, which disappear altogether in his later work. Thematically it is basic. The body and nature are Flaherty's special purview, and have been from the first. In his 1972 collection, *Weaving a Slow Dream of Hands*, this aspect of his work is especially in evidence. Over and over in this beautiful book (both design- and content-wise—having been handset in Ireland) the theme and imagery are of the body's knowledge, learned through

knifing our bodies
against the current
    ("Raspberries")

coffins   those old skeletons
who can dig their way

clean through   feel again
the moist black kiss of loam
the love tangle of roots
    ("Kilcoole")

Roots, raspberries, strawberries, and shells all lead Flaherty to the "secrets of flesh," which are for him the "guts of words" and what "The throat learns" that is "more than words."

For his initiation into the natural world of berries, birds, and the "Ant People" with their underground life "in dry rooms / amid stored nuts & fruits," Flaherty received his magic from a close study of legends and songs contained in the *US Bureau of Ethnology Reports for the 1890s*. In *The Tomb of Skulls* (1970), the poet has given us the taste and touch of his mythic and elemental nature. The union of flesh and earth imagery results in the birth of a poetry faithful to the prose accounts of Southwestern, Wisconsin, and West Coast tribal myths and rituals, at the same time that it breathes a timeless life into what before were mere government documents. This book is a must for all those who would appreciate where Flaherty has come from in order to create his own language, vital with the flow of a maple syrup blood (see "Maple Syrup" in *The Tomb of Skulls*), bright as firewheels but lean and spare as the "Ant People" who

have learned to eat
the god of word & vision
have traced the world
and found it empty

          the slender people
          [whose] eyes have taught
          how to take in our belts

  Flaherty meanwhile has moved beyond even the basic message of these trib-
al-inspired pieces to a poetry of pure image based on certain surrealist principles he has developed and which he sees as necessary for his continued existence as a poet. These new poems will be appearing in yet another chapbook,
and this fact is particularly significant now that his poetry has exceeded the
bounds set by the current tastes of magazine editors—of those same name
magazines, such as *The Nation, Poetry Northwest, The New Yorker*, etc., that
earlier published what he considers his dated (circa 1971!) efforts. It is difficult to keep up with the development of a poet such as Doug Flaherty, but
for those interested, fortunately the chapbooks are an inexpensive passage to
the testament of his stringent but fertile imagination.

Poetry, Verse & "Out of the Human Way"

In her statements on "Poetry and Form," the coeditor of *Concrete Phoenix*, published in Seattle by Spring Rain Press, lashes out at "cut-up" or "found" poetry and asserts that the editorial policy of Spring Rain Press will always be to print poetry with "some value to the human part of us." Karen Sollid concludes by declaring that "For poetry to last it must be more than clever, it must matter to people." I should think that even writers who never quite manage the creation of a true poem, who continue struggling with words and images which have meant something to them, with ideas which are either popular or timeless, who yet recognize none of this necessarily makes for poetry, such writers I believe would agree with Ms. Sollid that a poem must involve more than form, more than cleverness, and must be related to our humanity.

The problem, however, is not one of preferring more or less form, more or less humanness, nor of having the best resolve in the world. Since poetry is the unique (even W.C. Williams, who *found* poetry everywhere and employed the cut-up method at times, knew it was a matter of both magic and mechanics), verse is in fact what we find written all around us, by us, and offered to us as the real thing because it conforms to such and such an editorial policy. I applaud the efforts of Spring Rain Press, like their publication's format, and even find among their pages some few pieces to value, but I have also read poems which emphasized the formal part of man, against their policy, and which still worked as poetry. Using their criterion will, nonetheless, serve me well, I trust, in reviewing five very different collections. I propose, then, to distinguish between poetry and verse, basically in terms of this idea of "the human part of us" as it exists in or is absent from these five recent publications.

First, anything may be humanized, and this is essentially the function of metaphor when it links matter and spirit, animate and inanimate, man and his environment. Today, of course, the approach is to demonstrate how the animate has more soul than what was previously considered spiritual and meaningful: religious, political, historical, and aesthetic ideas or modes of being. In his "Editorial Notes" to *Concrete Phoenix*, coeditor John Sollid pits the lyric against the formal poem, and reports happily that the lyric is winning the battle and is "enjoying an energy right now which assures that it will continue as an important cultural force." Perhaps, though I tend to feel Auden was nearer the mark when he said that poetry makes nothing happen—certainly not by fighting over two valid kinds of utterance.

Margins, no. 12 (1974): 35-37, 78.

There is no doubt that lyrics are everywhere making us feel as individuals through songs or through verse, and this includes the two collections, *Concrete Phoenix* and *Other Season*, from Spring Rain Press. In *Other Season*, there are pieces on a stray dog, a doghouse existence without your love, a cleaning woman life, something entitled "Upon the Poetry of Ivor Winters," many moon verses, several pieces in Norman H. Russell's imitation Indian style, and three "Bel Etudes" by David Berry. All of these pieces are about human emotions, but unfortunately they have the ring of Emmeline Grangerford's work, the effect of a 19th-century Southern versifying that was performed because it was part of being genteel.

At least in *Concrete Phoenix* the editorial policy is applied with better results. Along with a number of verse lyrics (the title of the collection comes from one of these), Marjorie Luckman manages an interesting myth in "One Whiff of Brimstone":

> in a black box
> Grandma kept her buttons,
> the phoenix on its round lid winked
> to tell me it knew I knew it
> came from otherwheres
> into this
> through holes in round buttons kept in a box

Imaginative, but then the piece rambles on and on, losing even this limited appeal that is so entirely wanting in her other verses.

One piece which does achieve a sense of unity (something almost wholly lacking in the work of both collections) is Jon Bracker's "J.L." Traditional in its handling of the elegy form, the poem yet touches the "human part of us" by its simplicity, control, and poignancy:

> And now she, too, is dead
> who liked to live.
> She died still young
> who would have not complained
>
> about the sun today
> which beats on heads
> and helps the grass to grow
> that covers graves.

The irony is natural, part of the "human condition," and the author does not make a grand production of it. Certainly there is a place for such verse, which partakes of tradition and renders its theme plainly and with feeling. If this is not new, it is at least honest and clear. In that sense it is forever fresh.

The one piece I find effectively done in James Sprouse's *Methane* happens to be, coincidentally, on the same elegiac theme as that treated by Bracker.

Sprouse, however, works in a more contemporary vein, while achieving a similar control and directness of approach:

these are the kind
I want on my grave
you told me   holding
your handful of wildflowers
to my nose
            /
bending over a sky blue corn flower
tugging hard to pull it
up by the roots   (we use for tea)
the stalk broke
you fell back   laughing
            /
watching you today
I wondered
        can anything die

As to the rest of the chapbook, very few of the pieces strike me as more than self-conversation or observations without any subtlety or point. Word-play and sheer cleverness make the work basically verse, no matter how contemporary the idiom may be. Cleverness is not a human quality which rates high enough to allow it as a measure of true poetry. It may and does have its place, but used for its own sake, as it appears to be in much of *Methane*, it cannot stand alone, needing a more serious side of man to lean on or be carried by.

As a rule I prefer not to read—or write—reviews that can find little or nothing to praise. Still, it is often possible to determine the positive by setting it off against its opposite. Also, there are certain tendencies in publishing which I resent enough to register against them now and then a few critical remarks. By and large, I would label *Poems*, a collection of work by three women writers, little more than verse. It differs from the writing in the Spring Rain collections partly because it labors at being modern. In Judy Bolz's words (from "String Game"), *Poems* attempt a "soft / unsounded industry" in some pieces, while in others one is too aware, as Charles Ives said of Tchaikovsky's music, that the butter is being churned. The themes of the collection are either feminist or identifiably feminine in their choice of observations and style (the former true principally of Diane Ackerman and Nancy Steele's work, the latter of Bolz's). I call attention to this fact primarily because the book makes an issue out of it.

Ackerman's "Quixote" is a sonnet which asserts that "in my quixotic way I can do it better than you." This piece sets the tone for all her work, but is particularly in keeping with her response to a poem by A.R. Ammons that she finds below her. The language throughout her writing is talky and even strikes me as dishonest. "Full Moon" tries the same lyric-elegiac statement as do the poems by Bracker and Sprouse, but unlike their pieces, which are both successful in their separate ways, Ackerman's is talky and clever, and its conclusion is simply inane:

> I just can't get over
> so round
> a monstrosity. Imagine something that big being dead.

"Menstruation Rag" is as tasteless as its title. I have the distinct feeling that the writer is bending over backwards to be clever, pressing to take advantage of a women's lib posture, and using the writing of poetry as a way of dropping a surprise tampax on a bank president's mahogany desk. Ackerman's other contributions are equally talky and tasteless. Only the list of places where her work has appeared would indicate that she writes better than these selections suggest, although I suspect that many editors who have printed her work were very much taken with just these sophomoric practices.

Bolz's work is unexceptional, quiet, and finally not very clear. The pieces simply fail to work as linguistic or emotive units. There is no sense of sharing with the reader what she sees or feels. Instead, she whispers to us a "pageantry or incantation" which never comes off. As she says in "Proposition,"

> There is something here,
> a closing off of sense
> or loss of memory—
> verses out of reach

Like many poets today she seems more interested in feeling than in thinking. Shades of e.e. cummings, although he did not in reality divorce the two.

Finally, I cannot help sensing that Nancy Steele's pieces are written from a popular point of view which the writer seems to believe will make them consequently popular. That is, the woman is giving her view for a change, showing the male up for the "Brute" he is, as in her piece so titled. Of course, she has the last word and conquers the masculine ego both physically (he comes in the end to "reek of me") and intellectually (she makes a "poem" about the act). Perhaps this makes for interesting reading of a sort, but not a poem, despite the fact that it deals with various human attitudes, hangups, reactions, etc. Even though the car-drag-rubber-skidmarks-on-the-breasts analogy is tight and clever, the piece is ultimately meaningless in terms of poetry and of what I take to be "the human part of us" that seeks to curb our instincts for revenge and self-acclaim.

In considering what makes verse a lesser form of poetry, I have tried to suggest that there are appropriate ways of handling language, feelings, and themes so that the result is not mere cleverness. Good writing involves more than simply choosing a subject that is currently accessible or popular in the marketplace. Although Harley Elliott's *All Beautyfull & Foolish Souls* may not always come up to the "standards" I have set forth here, it is truly the work of a poet who is lyric, who touches "the human part of us," who writes of matters close to his experience which are meaningful to him, and who, through a control over cleverness and sensitivity, communicates such meaningfulness to his readers.

Elliott's is one of those books to be read in its entirety in order to appreciate the unity of its rich variety. Personally, I find the book grows stronger from halfway through to the end. Nevertheless, I do not think the first part is weak, nor could the book do without what I assume is Elliott's earlier, more tentative work. One excellent piece in the first half is "Out of the Human Way." As if in response to the Spring Rain statement, Elliott exclaims:

> How good to be out
> of the human way this long afternoon.
> The primitive soup slowly turns once more
> jackrabbits skirt the tattered snow
> and the snakes have begun
> to unwind in the long sandstone wells
> working up to the skys blue ring.

Humanity or art? Can the two be separated in poetry? What does the "primitive soup" or the "tattered snow" have to do with man? There are the metaphorical links: men are primitive or not—animals are wild or housebroken; soup men eat or sail through; clothes are tattered—snow melts, etc. But does the real poetry not lie in the sound, suggestiveness, and thematic development (a contrast of human and nonhuman) found in such inventive phrases? The poet makes the world human even when he would escape into an uncomplicated animal state. Of course, this is not the point nor even an intended irony of this specific poem. Yet insofar as the question of a relation between humanity and poetry is concerned, this piece does bring the two together by presenting us with the human joy of entering the "primitive soup," and with such artistry that we too leave our all-too-human (inhuman, in the sense of unfeeling, complicated, joyless) existence and participate in the poet's vision, which takes full advantage of our faculties for being alive and for knowing it.

For instances of clever poems which yet maintain a serious intent, I can recommend the tour-de-force pieces "Evidences" and "Orange Poem." In both cases the poet plays with a series of related images, shaping them into penetrating portraits of, in the first poem, his wife, and in the second, of an October night on "an orange porch swing." Other favorites of mine are "Two Hearts in a Room," a tender piece on the poet and his daughter reading a children's story, and "Small Misfortunes," a poem painfully human and containing, incidentally, the kind of image and in the sort of context that demonstrates how man is capable of more than brutality:

> those bruises I've seen
> on the shinbones
> of beautiful women.

There are many fine poems that I could mention. What impresses me most about this book is how consistently positive it remains, even in the face of so many "small misfortunes." It reminds me of Greg Kuzma's best work in this sense, but there is in Elliott's writing a more genuine warmth, less dependence on cleverness, and a deeper concern for the people and places he brings to life. This concern is apparent in the poet's focusing on his subjects for their own sake, not his own. In this regard there is only one piece which I do find unsatisfying, and this is a longish poem entitled "The Geese Like Bombers." What I recognize as an attempt at autobiographical narrative has its moments, but finally the sections do not cohere. As a lyric nature-poet, however, Elliott is superb. Certainly he has plenty of competition, since most young poets today, following the lead of Wright, Stafford, et al., tend to fall into this category. For John Sollid is correct, lyric poetry *is* enjoying an energy right now, although not necessarily in the pages of Spring Rain's publications so much as in those of John Gill's *New: American & Canadian Poetry* and his Crossing Press series, of which Elliott's volume is a fine example.

Personally I still read such epics as *El Cid, Beowulf,* and *Paradise Lost* with never-ending pleasure, perhaps because in those works there is not only lyricism and nature, but to a greater extent than in any other type of poetry, more of "the human part of us," at the very least in terms of volume. Too, I am interested in the long poems of such a contemporary poet as Enrique Lihn. Yet I can still admire the work of a lyric poet like Elliott whose humanity keeps shining through, even in such a "beautyfull & foolish" image as the one in his poem "Songs and Lights," where "constellations of fingerprinted gum" float beneath the tavern tables. It occurs to me here that Elliott has captured in the phrase "beautyfull & foolish" the two aspects of man which, when seen in interaction, produce the fallible, precious part of him we think of as human. The book cover is of the poet-artist's own design and the photo on the back by his wife shows Harley Elliott as silly in his top hat and shades as his daughter is ingenuous standing with her fingers lightly resting on his shoulders. All in all, a family affair adding a further human dimension to a book well deserving of publication.

Goldbarth's Vocabulary Banquet
& Treatise of Sand

Surprisingly, from the pens (or typewriters) of a number of the youngish lyric (or neosurrealist) poets have come of recent some fine longer poems. It is surprising mainly because the lyric today does not usually offer the kind of complexity of, say, a song by Blake or one by Yeats. There is not the possibility of building on such foundations a larger work, for long stretches of surrealist writing numb like an endless bus ride. Even Frank O'Hara's often enlivening "Second Avenue" lacks a controlling force that can save the whole from ultimate dullness. Galway Kinnell in "The Last River" works with a limited group of images and colloquial phrases in order to create a dramatic long poem in 27 sections. Here imagist and objectivist principles gain added power and endurance from being drafted into the service of considerations larger than the lyric can normally handle. Another valid long poem of the last few years is William Kloefkorn's *Alvin Turner as Farmer* (Road Runner Press, 1972), which combines narrative flow with earth imagery as a means of revealing insights into the lives of the sequence's rural speakers. With *Opticks: a poem in seven sections* (Seven Woods Press), Albert Goldbarth has also achieved success with the long form and has employed for the purpose both imagist and surrealist techniques, as well as some which sound a Shakespearean note in America. This book-length poem releases lines with the jollity of the *Henry IV* plays and even at times comes close to the beauty of *King Lear*.

On one level Goldbarth's *Opticks* is simply delicious as a linguistic offering. The first section not only establishes the theme of "how glass came into my life," but it sets the driving rhythmical and tonal power of the whole poem. Using asterisks as breaks between run-on stanzas, Goldbarth weaves a "latticework of crosses," telephone poles, and barbed wire, which is at once imagistically intriguing and shot through with internal off-rhymes. The poet's ability to spin an endless array of interrelated images is quite amazing. This could, of course, become cloying if it were not for the accompanying sound, and for the awareness on the reader's part that all of this cross imagery has something to do with glass, though *what* remains for the moment unclear. And thus the question near the end of section one brings us back to the vague connection asterisks, swastikas, "a trellis of crosses," "a crystal lens of snot," and "an assasin's cross-hairs" have with "how glass came into my life":

Margins, no. 15 (1974): 37 and 58. Excerpts reprinted in *Contemporary Literary Criticism* 5 (Gale Research, 1976), p. 143.

What is it

*

that makes us believe in the eye, how,
if the intervention were clear enough
our vision would never fail, be symbiotic inch by inch
with starlight?

Section two, as the headnote and Notes at the back of the book indicate, is based largely on Sumerian myth and liturgy. This is a re-creation story, with interpolations of the creation myth of Enki (of Gilgamesh epic fame?) and a "colloquial translation" of an oriental "personal document." Here a reader could easily object to too much scholarship and not enough poetics, if that were in fact the case. Goldbarth, however, manages a piece of writing which builds and builds, is rich with striking similes ("I moved like a milkless dug") and colloquial phraseology:

The light pus scent—my wife, and a blindman would know
better than to suck there! I felt dead to watch her, dead
to pace the pit's-rim of her dying.

The repeated motif, "I felt dead," is handled to good effect, and while this theme is reminiscent of Prufrock, the colloquial humor makes it new:

The oarsmen sang
Egyptian women have teeth in their twats; but I felt dead.

Sand, sight, and the desire for something "to take beyond dying"—all are central to the poem's argument, and the colloquial metaphors are to become an integral part of the later sections.

As a Chicagoan writing of glass, Goldbarth does well to work Frank Lloyd Wright into the poem, for as the poet's quotations from the architect show, the latter dreamed of a city

"woven of rich glass.
Such a city would clean itself in the rain, would know no fire alarms;
no, nor any glooms."

This section (number three) is especially important thematically, cataloguing as it does many of the qualities of glass, such as the paradoxical one of its being cold as ice, and yet able to collect "enough of sun to set this page on fire." Inserted in this section is a short, one-page piece, rhymed in quatrains, which uses the Kenneth Patchen and Robert Creeley technique of alternating two extended conversations every other line. As a list of glass containers (and illustrative again of the theme "And so I put my life in glass"), this is a meaningful part of the poem, but otherwise it is one of the work's few lapses from a high level of performance. On the other hand, it is also in this same section that Goldbarth inverts the perspective and gives to the idea of a glass container a surrealistic twist, the feeling of a "whole 'nother world." Breaking his glasses, it seems, the poet finds he has a shard lodged in his skin:

> And I stood, glass
>
> *
>
> in me, an anomaly, the blood sample
> holding the bottle. Oh
>
> *
>
> once glass is intimate with your body
> you're never the same, a part of you, some nodule's
> pricked with the closest thing it's ever known
> to true invisibility; and
>
> *
>
> glass is changed.

Alliteration serves as the unifying device for section four, just as imagery does for section one and repeated motifs and colloquial phrases do for section two. The occasion is a Medieval Guild's making of a stained glass window. A-. side from its thematic interest, this section offers the fun of a rollicking Falstaffian sound:

> And I don't know who flicked what first, how
> or why: but, flash! 'n suddenly the sky's all fist
> and flung oven-forks, and the hermitty-thin limbs of the Brothers
> and hamhock-hanging arms of the Winemakers Group meet
> clenched-n-clawing in a tumbled heap of noses slammed askew,
> cloaks wound round molds for chamber pots, bald heads
> bedecked in buckets, drench-n-dust-n-ruckus. . . .

In section five, Newton's prisms serve as a way for Goldbarth to comment on his own technique. This section also begins to raise questions of transcendence and a type of poetic ethics: "what we live for's the sun / in the grapes." The first part of the section is taken up with a car accident, the windshield necessarily a key image. A difficult section, it is also a highly significant one.

With section six Goldbarth presents a brilliant monologue of a G.I.'s discovery of a stained glass window, himself, and a sense of God:

> and prayed
> to our God, and asked the words cased
> in my breath be safe as another god kept
> his believers' bodies in bandage.

The desire to "save something," which is nominally the Eshcol window (actually preserved in a church in Iowa), carries with it the moving undertones of "Death / And Resurrection Through Glass."

Unfortunately, after six superb sections, the seventh and final, I find, represents a serious falling off. Allusions to Galileo, Kepler, and Leeuwenhoek are fitting, and many of the lines are certainly up to the poem's overall majestic sound and sense. I suppose what I object to most is Goldbarth's appending to *Opticks* a clever critique of his own as a conclusion to the poem. Perhaps I dislike being preempted, as the poet says he intends, but what is more disturbing is such cleverness after so much intrinsic humor and high seriousness. This prose commentary detracts from a poem which needs no "fresh air" of the sort that comes from heaving "a rock through [yes] the beauty of Goldbarth's precious stained-glass window." This is not, however, a weakness without remedy, since it merely requires the exclusion of section seven or a conclusion more in keeping with the tone and tremendous power of the preceding sections.

In *Opticks* Goldbarth has seen, as Blake says, a world in a grain of sand, although to the Chicago poet's credit he has not gone to this or other such well-worn quotes for his sources. Instead, he has ranged far and wide—Egypt, the Illinois tollway, Germany of World War II, a Middle Ages glass makers guild—to demonstrate that "everything's in the window." Other than the specific inspirations mentioned in the poem itself, I wonder what poets Goldbarth was reading at the time of composition. This fine poem makes me think of Lear after he is blinded, of Louis Zukofsky's *A*, with its variations on the I's (pronounced *eyes*) and its blend of colloquial and scientific languages, without there being any suggestion of direct influence.

Despite a surrealistic playfulness and an often derivative type of recent inclination for exhausting the possibilities of single images, Goldbarth's sources are finally and essentially very personal ones. The result is a long poem with a singular impact. Many voices speak, some with excitement and some with concern, but the ultimate force of the poem comes from the poet's sureness of touch in working his almost epic loom. Or, to change the metaphor, *Opticks*, for a treatise of sand, is a banquet so heaped with juicy treats that it proves Goldbarth's is truly one of the most fertile imaginations going.

Review of *Tarot Poems*

On first receiving Karl Kopp's *Tarot Poems* (The Three Herons Press), among several other volumes to be reviewed, I was completely put off by the title as well as by the cover (a view from below, up through a spiraling well, with roots growing out of its bricks), which is in keeping with a type of pseudo-mystical tendency the whole tarot business represents for me. Only glancing at the first few numbered poems I felt that my early impression was fully confirmed. Later, however, I returned to the book and began a thorough reading, from beginning to end. Although I still felt the opening poem weak and was somewhat discouraged by the typographical tricks (CAPS, quotes, and placement of words to suggest dissolution), I found the second poem quite to my liking, in fact entirely to my taste: the portrait of Charles Drury Cooling that of a person I would have wanted to know the way Kopp knew him, though in many ways it's the effective use of language which makes him known, perhaps in a way he never was nor ever could have been. It is this highly imaginative reality, achieved through an often offbeat rhythm and typography, which marks the work of an original poet who recognizes that the making of a poem depends both on faithfulness to the subject and to the poetic art itself.

In section number four of "Death," from the "Tarot Poems" (which are organized under the headings of "Death," "Magician," "Fool," "Tower," "Sun," "Lovers," "Strength," and "Star"), Kopp offers his intensely moving use of a newspaper account of a 25-year-old's suicide, into which he weaves an appeal to friends that they set up for him a poetry reading. An inclination to compose from found objects is common in this book, especially in the long "Death" section, which takes up half of the book's 55 pages. In this particular poem, the juxtaposition of found material (a newspaper article) and the poet's own correspondence serves to reveal an undeclared acknowledgment of the somewhat absurd situation of his request in light of a greater need experienced by the suicide, at the same time that it makes a telling commentary on the poet's perennial and almost shameless dependency on some kind of literate and financially supportive audience. In the newspaper account of the suicide's having waited for a ride on a highway for 11 hours, after which he took his life with a .22 caliber pistol, the father of the boy is quoted as saying that his son "was waiting all his life—he wanted help without / having to admit he needed it and without asking / for it." Such statements and reports of facts in the suicide case are paralleled or alternated with sections from the poet's own letter

Margins, nos. 28/29/30 (1976): 133-35.

asking if there is a possibility for a poetry reading. The poet's awareness of the near relation of his seeking assistance to the needfulness of the young man, at once a laugh next to the desperation of the hitchhiker and yet so very close to the poet's own need to communicate, makes for an extremely dramatic piece. The two situations gain in reality from the poet's skillful weaving of the found and the invented. Though the letter requesting consideration for a reading is real enough, it is essentially an imaginative projection. The combination of the two worlds—Coleridge's imagination and fancy—heightens the effect and achieves a wonderfully sad irony.

This same poem also indicates something about how the poet sees his own art: "False modesty aside, I read well. In fact, I / write *to* be heard aloud—with even, occasionally, / rock rhythms. / Anyway...." While this may sound destructive of the serious tone of the whole, the closing comments on a failed marriage and "I don't cost much" add to the analogy and make of what might only seem a clever use of shuffled texts an authentic dramatization or portrait of the artist as dependent. Again, this piece reveals much about the poet's techniques, in particular those which coincide with his concern to be heard. Kopp's poems seem to overflow with words and phrases that fit together in an unending, strangely cohesive manner that recalls F.S. Flint's directive "to compose in sequence of the musical phrase." Overall there is a subtle sound system constantly at work in Kopp's unstopped, plunging lines. And though his poetry sends the reader's eye and mind reeling headlong from one right observation and association to another, there is ever the poet's sure touch to hold to—everything he says seems appropriate in itself, even as it drives deeper toward a meaning only grasped in passing and through the sheer accumulation of the poet's "rock rhythms."

Sections 6 and part of 7 are also "found poems," the former a letter to the absentee-landlord-poet from a poor Ozark family and the latter a newspaper story of a couple in Santo Domingo who voluntarily crucify themselves for more than 24 hours "to promote world peace" and to demonstrate "that the spirit [is] stronger than the flesh." In section 6 the poetic reality is once again recognized and recorded by Kopp with no fanfare (though the arrangement of lines and words suggests that the real has been rendered by artistry). Characteristic also is the touch of self-deprecation that goes far toward making the poet more human and the poem a lesson for all concerned:

> You no You was here & could see
> We didn't have anything much.
> But we haft to make out on what
> We do have Would you Please
> Write us soon & let us no when
> You want us out....

Section 7 is primarily a war-story poem, of a boy's becoming intrigued by his father's captured enemy weapons. This too is apparently a true-to-life account. Kopp tells it the way it is and yet in a manner that reveals repeatedly the poetry where he found it—in the everyday life of children and adults. Between the war story and the poem's conclusion falls the crucifixion report. This imitation-of-Christ account gives rise to the concluding lines that are a type of prayer and seem to refer indirectly back to the war story of the first part of the poem. The final stanza is Kopp at his most characteristic:

> You who drowned to sin in the
> muddy Jordan You who hushed
> with your lily feet the lash
> of Galilee You whose wounds
> never won for you the Purple-
> Heart KEEP Mr. Gorman safe
> > > > will you?
> long dead but found beneath a heap of
> poisoned corpses in World War One
> who taught me how to swim till I could
> hurl myself headlong from the pier
> again and again to the waves
> some thirty years ago
> in Buzzard's Bay

Not to leave the impression that Kopp's range is limited to "found poems," it is necessary to speak briefly of a number of the other pieces offered in the poet's first book. Section 8 of "Death," for example, is a beautifully-developed poem that includes sights of Lebanon, where Kopp spent time teaching at the American University in Beirut. The image of a lighthouse is superb: "it cancels stars in its sweep." Many of the poems in "Death" are portraits or character sketches, including number 9, which presents the poet's grandfather, dead of cancer:

> so strong so dashing once
> so brown of eye   played doubles
> against Bill Tilden   in his prime

Section 10 of "Death" is a romping piece that moves from the Alamo (San Antonio, Texas) to the Potomac and back to Nuevo Laredo (on the Mexican side of the Rio Grande). Kopp's ear for bits and pieces of conversation and typical phrases from Army lingo (he was apparently stationed in San Antonio) is extremely accurate. This poem is similar in style to "The Tower," a fascinating piece with a little something for everyone. I myself admit to envy of Kopp's having seen and gotten down so brilliantly a scene I could have used in a sequence I wrote two years ago, concerned with Indian mounds of North America and the Nazca lines of Peru, though I feel certain I would not have managed the job Kopp has done:

> Vanished long

before fathers mound-builders patted earth
to fantastic shapes: serpents   bears
geometrical intricate arcs and circles
and never saw the whole design. No mountains
in Ohio   no tower high enough
saw only through the mind   and yet so perfect
now as aerial photographs show
parks   mostly kept by the State   though
at least part of one in Newark some forty
or fifty miles from Centerburg is a golf-course
the mounds handicaps   perfect traps

As for love poems, Kopp has those too. "The Lovers" is a fine example, making use once more of a personal letter, as well as of a quote from Chaucer. It is a homecoming to love:

two continents an ocean then
to a wire fence at the end of a pier
Customs pried for dope or diamonds
in my gear   found nothing of value
and so released me home to you
that pier became a garden
                              New
Yorkers disappeared to tunnels
as we sped to the farthest edge
of the island
alone and but we two

Kopp's use of internal rhymes, inversion, and displaced words—it all works. The sound is taking and the sense is both real and imaginatively charged. And finally it is this winning combination of real and imaginative that makes of the book a rare find, despite any superficial prejudices I or anyone else may have against tarot cards or clever typography. In short, I highly recommend this and any other work by Karl Kopp that should hopefully be forthcoming.

Thomas Whitbread

Ubi sunt? is a poet's constant question, not only the romantic's but the classical and the contemporary's alike. In a Spanish version of Heraclitus, the philosopher states that no man bathes in the same river twice. Tom Whitbread has both lamented and celebrated this fate of things, standing, poetically speaking, where he "half-reaccepts the intricacy of living." His own poems are simple-sounding but intricate designs which "seem greatest [when] some major change / Comes of the evening, such as a reformed mind, / A new sense of limits and of wider range." As a former student who has returned often during fifteen years to fruitful re-readings of such poems as "Motorcyclist" and "Breakings," I acknowledge the enduring lessons Tom Whitbread has taught me: to accept limitations of our own making or those imposed by nature, while yet believing it possible "to change the music of the stream / By dipping an idle finger into it." Ringing his changes on the mutability theme, Whitbread has achieved a body of poems full of sympathy for the common fate of place and flesh, forming thus in his poems a bond between the two. The sonnet form is made for such a meeting of mutable and immutable, and in Whitbread's crafted stanzas there is grasped an understanding and acceptance of time's sculpturing hand.

Perhaps the truest paradigm for Tom's method and meaning is found in one of his favorite images, that of the pond. As a poet, Tom is the captain in his "Captain's Pond," the man who believes "when there's nothing to be believed," one who dives into the muck of romance, of a bloody Argentine rite, of the rubble of war, of suicide, of any pond where "antagonisms meet," bringing back to life "credence as our constancy." Despite his questions as to "who can bare / scar-piercing changes in his central cells?" Tom Whitbread has long been willing to risk the depths and dangers awaiting just below the ordinary surface where "extremes meet," breaking from poem to poem the "bloody pond" and the "silent miles" in hopes we grow "reminiscent," "to feel whole," to find our ways "Towards warmth again, away from emptiness." This is much, and we are fortunate indeed that this Connecticut Yankee came to Texas to share with us how at Fresh Pond "as the world grew dark" he and his friends "drew together."

Lucille, no. 10 (summer 1978): 8-9.

Review of *Eye-to-Eye*

Like her earlier chapbook from Texas Portfolio, *Tattooed Feet*, Naomi Shihab's *Eye-to-Eye* is a catching piece of work—infectious as laughter and as welcome. Not that these are comic poems. Many touch on the dark side of our lives—the death-in-life of the elderly, the slide show where "lives pull apart like old cloth. / You mend and mend so long, then make rags." Yet always the theme of darkness "like a heavy coat / I didn't want to put on" is balanced by the lighter one of "breaking into song." A number of poems attempt to survive "all those dark hours" by dreaming, remembering, or dancing:

> We danced. And everyone loved us
> because we did what they maybe felt,
> but didn't do. I carry this with me,
> that sometimes things happen
> which no one could have planned
> and they are, beyond everything,
> true.

In another piece (dedicated to William Stafford, who took the cover photo of Shihab) she speaks of how her poet-photographer-friend can "Leave us that small place where a stone / enters the water, / the feel of a chair in our dark." Much of Naomi Shihab's work concerns itself with just such a search for small places (of integrity, of feeling, of "a delicate enterprise / of eyes") within a larger world of darkness or unseeing.

Aside from the thematic content of the collection—though significantly linked to it—there are the stylistic and technical aspects of Naomi Shihab's work which merit mention as well. Even when the piece is a playful love poem, as in the case of "How It Is," the poet by means of fine understatement makes the lightest subject carry a fairly heavy load, ending this piece on separation of lover-friends with "Now comes the hard part." Similarly, in writing of an "Address Book" she creates an analogy between book and house so as to achieve in the final stanza a more serious statement than the subject might have seemed capable of offering:

> You handed me a pencil and let me move in
> O what an intimate evening, you and I,

Lucille, no. 10 (summer 1978): 68-69.

propped in the same catalog like fence-posts
linking the distant regions of the earth

Although many of her metaphors (or similes) are quite fresh and engaging, others seem too easy, too sentimental, too catchy, as in "San Antonio":

I remembered the old men
in the west side cafe,
dealing dominoes like magical charms.
It was then I knew,
like a woman looking backwards,
I could not leave you,
or find anyone I loved more.

The metaphors of the first and last poems of the collection ("Eye-to-Eye" and "Arriving at a Fish") are some of the strongest, but the analogy of westward movement in "The Saddest Cowboy in Texas" strikes me as too surrealistic in a cliched sense—a reaching for the ineffable solely for effect. At such times the effort fails to convince, despite the value of the object reached for.

On the whole *Eye-to-Eye* is an easy book to read—the lines moving as smoothly as the rivers that inhabit Shihab's poems, with water being equated with the free flow of feelings (though at times the poetry gagging us like her "stick caught halfway / between a river and a sob"). What is most attractive in her work is Naomi Shihab's ability to maintain an openness to the simplest events and to celebrate them with a matching candor and with an uncommon freshness of expression. And while her poems move in the mind with a natural ease, her openness to her subjects and her accompanying naturalness of treatment are not at all easy for a writer to manage, and for this reason we cannot help but find her performances infectious, something like the child's brief vacation-providing illness that any sibling would love to catch.

Review of *Running in Place*

Running In Place by Robert Lietz, from L'Espervier Press, is a book which, as its title indicates, goes nowhere. The lines of these pieces are not only "like boulevards / threatening to collapse / on their hollows" (in the title poem) but in fact do fall flat on their monotonous faces and are empty of all music, meaning, and of even a single striking metaphor. It is one of the saddest excuses for a book that I have come across in recent years, and yet to judge by its magazine credits, it should be a strong collection. *Poetry Northwest, Shenandoah, Seneca Review, Epoch*—these are top-notch publications, but I'll be snookered if I can find a single piece in Lietz's collection worthy of appearing in those pages. But then again, this book is an encyclopedia of all the worst habits encouraged by some of these same magazines when they continue to publish so many pseudo-surrealists, what I unfairly refer to as the Iowa Workshop imitators of the Iowa Workshop School, a kind of writing which is characterized by "smoke in the room like a presence" (in the clever but pointless "Trying To Second-Guess The Gypsy"), by a vague spiritualism assumed to reside in everything such writers do or say, their analogies always suggesting that "the news / will not be good" (in "Post-Partum") because that's the fashion. This school of vagueness, of a "face without features, / its surface giving way," still dominates the minds of those who send out a call for another vague graduate to teach the Iowa Workshop fourth-rate versions of Breton and Char.

Although many other books will serve better to inform teachers of creative writing on current trends in the contemporary poem, this collection by Lietz may perhaps exemplify a predominant and altogether overrated manner. Every popular cliché from the Iowa handbook is here. There is the irritating use of "you" to tell me that I am doing things that I have never done nor ever wanted to do:

> You study
> the span across the baseboards,
> the fogged mirror in the foyer,
> obscure and tilted,
> like the breath-touch of someone
> who cannot be there.

Here too is the penchant for mixing a grubby image with a fake profundity:

Texas Writers Newsletter, no. 21 (spring 1980): 6-8.

"She shakes disaster like dandruff / from her sheets of flesh") in "Sailors' Knots"). And if you miss it in one poem you will find almost the exact phraseology in another, because, of course, it's even better warmed over—a workshop byword:

> She scrubs formica
> in mustard-colored sleeves.
> He envies storm-reddened single men.
> They shake off disaster
> like a law-suit, so close
> they project a singular future. (in "Two")

The irony is as heavy-handed as my own. Apparently about a couple hating their life together even though they "share" a symbolic mustard-colored vision, the vagueness of the matter is so dense that few readers will penetrate to the significance of parking meters singing, of gloves that "peer from puddles / with soil in their eyes"—yet certainly we know the news is all bad, as it should be according to the handbook. Envy, the staleness of a relationship, and "welts on his wife's back" unify the writing, but for what meaning other than a journalistic-"spiritualist" record I remain hard-put to say. Only in a piece like "Listening To Freights At 10:30 P.M." do I sense a living mind struggling with something other than its own overworked fantasies (here the birth or death of the speaker's daughter), and doing so in language approaching poetry, though inevitably, it seems, the writing falls apart in the last lines with their flatness, their total lack of music.

I have never liked negative reviews, for they do little good. And yet this publication deserves to be singled out as representative of a tired mannerism, the epitome of pointless writing perpetuated by too many programs in creative writing and even by some of the most prestigious magazines in the country. *Texas Writers Newsletter* can help discourage this kind of textbook manner and will thereby render an invaluable service to creative writing throughout the state and region.

Review of *The Tramp's Cup*

David Ray is one of the contemporary poets whose work I most admire. And for many reasons, among them a maturity of sensibility, the technical range, and a fresh, open feeling the poetry leaves me with. This new collection is vintage Ray, speaking as it does of many of the familiar spirits the poet has tried for years to exorcise. Fortunately for us he has not been able to; instead, he manages once more to make a poetic peace with such demons as "desire / [that] burns small / like rust," an obsession with the knowledge "that they had no use / for me," and resentment that "the pinball machine / our fathers won for us . . . [is] all lit up / with hamburgers, cars, blondes and the Milky Way." And though there is still bitterness and irony in his voice, Ray attempts understanding and a remaking of history through his subtle imagery and music:

> We sit down to play at our rusty bridge once more.
> This time I accept your hundred thousand Jews,
> and charm you into peace with ten thousand trucks,
> all winterized, as your Nazi uncles asked—
> with tiny toothless skulls for gearshift knobs.
> ("For Nicolas Born, German Poet")

The irony in Ray's work comes through most clearly in the poem he has been rewriting so powerfully all his career: of the father who sends "his son a stone / when the boy had cut his wrists and asked for a loaf." In "The Barber," the latest version of his central theme, Ray brings a bitter indictment against the man who

> kept his nose clean the next twenty years
> and died without sorrow
> only because he didn't know how
> to feel it.

The lack of feeling in his own father has resulted ironically in Ray's unending "array" of deeply felt poems. "Words at Midnight" also treats of the barber-father, but in this poem the poet is somewhat reconciled with the man who "No doubt gave / to others ample love, so long as they were not / your sons."

The Tramp's Cup (The Chariton Review Press), reviewed in *The Pawn Review* vol. 4, no. 1 (1980-81): 171-74.

Ray ends the piece on a positive note that indicates his ability to see beyond personal pain to those moments of renewed enthusiasm that may be shared by all the living:

A life's a life
so long as hope for change can send us
running, for a haircut or the alameda fireworks.
This you somehow knew, and so, Dear Dad, do I.

Ray's poetry is not always easy to take, and in some poems ("On the Circuit," for example) the tone and attitude seem overly critical. But even in the harshest poems Ray presents the undeniable fact of our failure to give "ample love." The poet reminds us of the simple lessons we all need to learn—and practice. One of these is contained in the book's title poem:

All one really needs
is to keep out
the damp.
He had learned that well
and had not an enemy
in the world, had nothing
to fear, nothing
to lose, nothing
to stop loving him.
And thus his cup of tea was sweet.

Despite much resentment and a good deal of criticism of our unfeeling world, Ray's book offers numerous poems of love—for one, the beautifully shaped piece entitled "The Monastery in Scotland":

Once more your
eyes take me back, nowhere else can I
truly be at home who am not wise—
nor elsewhere be alive
at all. How

close I am
to you, yes, I am crawl-
ing upon you now. I am the fly,
the dragonfly, skimming, suffering,
I am the waterdrop.
I am you.

In addition to these amorous lines, there are innumerable phrases that render "rainbows full of promise out of our fog."

Romantic to the core, Ray yet knows that the past was once the present and that our responsibility is to live now, not just in memory. While the past is recalled in "Stopping by the Roadside in Indiana Hills":

> the International Harvester
> truck grill with its one headlight
> stand[ing] in its elegance in grass
> saying This is what happened
> to us . . . Ah, we were happy here!

in one of my favorite pieces, "Written on a Bus," the poet summarizes our tendency to look forward to a time of freedom and self-realization without recognizing that *now* is the most fulfilling period we shall ever know and that in the future *now* will be recalled as the only true paradise. Overhearing two bus drivers discussing plans for retirement, Ray imagines that time when the one driver, who plans "to fish and cure his bacon," will find himself after a year of his dream

> cured, like his own bacon, of more than one notion,
> and wishing he were six years younger,
> bored, on a Texas highway, talking to Fred,
> just being the one who turned the big wheel,
> watching for cities, ahead, behind.

In most cases I have excerpted the conclusions to Ray's poems, but what is most impressive about his poetry is the way it arrives line by line to these overwhelming insights—nothing new, yet all so tellingly constructed in paradoxical, ironical, or symbolical language. And what he does best is to reveal these truths through everyday events and objects. In "Poe's Anvil," Ray speaks of a man named Poe who wants to sell his anvil at a junk auction. As in other such poems Ray is quite ready to purchase the unwanted item (natural symbol of his own childhood, when his two parents gave him away to an orphanage). Nor is he interested in the anvil just to resell it at a higher price (as the buyer is who outbids him in "At the Auction"). David Ray wants to have the anvil "to go on / hammering on." Here again the poet has managed not only to make peace with his past but to turn it into a solid basis for symbolic utterance. For Ray has learned to hammer out on the cold world of his past lines of beauty and love discovered in the "useless" things our lives have too readily rejected. From the reject, David Ray has produced a poetry like "heaven's rainy rapture," an art that, perhaps like all true poetry, is a recycling of life and language and those throwaways they contain.

Reviews of *Repairs,* "Prayers," & *Songs of Cifar*

Two books could hardly be more dissimilar than G.E. Murray's *Repairs* (University of Missouri Press) and Naomi Shihab Nye's *Different Ways to Pray* (Breitenbush Publications). The one is almost totally negative in its view of life: "Assured of disaster"; the other is nearly always positive, open, and accepting. While Murray's diction is characterized by the repulsive (infection, sweat, grease, contamination, soot, "some swollen finger of land at the tip / of [a] continent, in a casket of sun"), Nye's is marked by the "regions of kindness" ("A policeman gives me / half his breakfast and we smile, clear signals in the traffic," "a therapy in fields," "the comfort of wood," "I'm lost, you moan, I have no idea where we are. I pat your arm. It's alright, I say. Surely there's a turn-off up here somewhere"). Murray finds no hope anywhere:

> we wait by the window with house plants,
> our fears
> Nearly realized, a salt lick of faith turning to stone
> in our bowels[;]

Nye encounters it at home and abroad:

> More and more I understand what people do
> I appreciate the daily braveries   the clean white shirts
> morning greetings between old men
>
> . . .
>
> And she handed me one perfect pink rose,
> because we had noticed each other, and that was all.
> One rose coming into Cuzco and I was thinking
> it should not be so difficult to be happy in this world.

Everywhere Murray goes (mostly to bars or where fish or animals are being caught or slaughtered) he finds dissipation and "All things pedestrian." The result is that his words, as he says in one poem, grow thicker: "the chunky arms of a wheelchair rider." Murray especially likes simile, which serves to bring in another grisly image in case we've forgotten the last dozen or their

New Letters, vol. 48, no. 2 (winter 1981/82): 105-107.

effect has worn thin: "Like a new bruise"; "like tetanus / In a dripping wound"; "Wars blend like seasons"; "Our young like acne"; "like a pouch of slag"; "like a scalpel." Reading his book, I was never certain what reason he had for writing, except to report how bad things are. Which is not to say that there isn't a place for this kind of poetry. I continue, however, to find it fashionable, and because such presses as the University of Missouri's support this type of writing, it remains in fashion. If you wish to know how disgusting we are, *Repairs* will make that clear in rather dark, hard, and gruesome lines.

The other side of the coin may be too sentimental for some. Nye's travels (to Palestine, Latin America, bakeries, and into the lives of volcanoes, fish, tables, streets, or relatives) discover for her the miracles of small events and memories:

> I found the table at a store called
> "The Hand and the Heart"
> I was not looking for tables
>
> The table sat in the center of the room
> leaves like wings folded at its sides
> a single drawer with a runner that stuck
>
> Now I am learning the comfort of wood
> as I place my head on the table
> as I fold my hands over the scars

Nye can also use simile, but it is to make things appear sacred rather than pathetic. But comparison is rare in her work, for she seems intent on presenting objects and people as they are. Nye's people are essentially loving, yet the poet does not at all ignore the ugly or sad:

> Before you know kindness as the deepest thing inside,
> You must know sorrow as the other deepest thing.
> You must wake up with sorrow.
> You must speak to it till your voice
> catches the thread of all sorrows
> and you see the size of the cloth.

Her metaphors are integral and aid in her effort to make the emotional or philosophical statement. The most impressive poems are too long to quote: "For Mohammed on the Mountain" (a fine piece on an uncle in Palestine who chose to go alone and live on a mountain for the rest of his life); "Negotiations with a Volcano" ("We need dreams the shape of lakes, / with mornings in them thick as fish"); and the title poem, which contains a passage that may serve to sum up Nye's poetic vision:

> There were the men who had been shepherds so long

they walked like sheep.
Under the olive trees, they raised their arms—
Hear us! We have pain on earth!
We have so much pain there is no place to store it!

But the olives bobbed peacefully
in fragrant buckets of vinegar and thyme.
At night the men ate heartily, flat bread and white cheese,
and were happy in spite of the pain,
because there was also happiness.

Nye may write only to report that it doesn't seem to her "so difficult to be happy in this world," and for some this may not be reason enough. If it's not, her readers can still enjoy in her work a freshness of expression that will whet even the dullest of appetites, grown so from a surfeit of the negative view toward "All things pedestrian."

Songs of Cifar and the Sweet Sea (Columbia University Press) by Pablo Antonio Cuadra, a Nicaraguan poet translated by Grace Schulman and Ann McCarthy de Zavala, belongs to the same school as does the work of Shihab Nye, or vice versa, since Cuadra was born in 1912 and Nye in 1952. Nye is attracted to Central America and would certainly identify with many features of Cuadra's writing: its simplicity, its focus on peasant life, and its emphasis on the positive and loving. Stylistically the writers are also comparable, since both Cuadra and Nye tend toward the lyric, the celebration of the small moment. In her introduction, Schulman claims that Cuadra writes with "a vocabulary that is plain and also elevated to an epic tone." More often than not, however, the language is flat and uninteresting linguistically, both in the English and in the original Spanish. Cuadra is at his best in very brief haiku-like pieces that eulogize or elegize, as in "Fisherman":

An oar floating
on the waters
was your only epitaph.

"In Memoriam," a longer poem, is basically on the same theme and ends: "His only / shipwreck / on land!" Here the writing does not achieve any real elegiac impact. The facts from the life of the fisherman are not presented effectively and the conclusion is an attempt at cleverness that seems out of place.

While both Nye and Cuadra celebrate the lives of "the people," Cuadra is more bent on creating the life story of one man, Cifar, and his relationships with other fishermen, though more often with several women who seem simultaneously both to reject and to seek him. As a hero Cifar does not come off as a particularly attractive personality, despite the efforts of a sage figure to enlighten him by means of bits of wisdom interspersed throughout the poem: "The master smiled and said: / 'That which is known / is the unknown'." Schulman exaggerates in suggesting repeatedly that Cuadra's poems are concerned with the real and the people. Her introduction is a typical piece of propaganda that gives us a hard sell on how Cuadra is a representative of political and social awareness when the poetry does not evoke this feeling at all. Schulman's commentary reminds me of a Mexican edition of Alejo Carpentier's *Los pasos perdidos* (*The Lost Steps*) which advertises the Cuban author in bold red letters as the writer most representative of the Cuban Revolution. The novel has absolutely nothing to do with Cuba or the revolution, and in Cuadra's case as well there is little or nothing in the poetry that calls our attention to politics. So that Schulman has used the opportunity to preach at us, directing us away from the poet's art to considerations which, while they may be significant in themselves, do not relate to the work at hand. More than concerning himself with political realities, Cuadra in his poems attempts the presentation of the life of a man "taken over / by the child he was / who still is / towing him along / to dreams." As Cuadra's persona remarks, "I prefer / the strange to the known." There is reality in Cuadra's work, but as even Schulman notes, it is often transformed into the mythical.

If a poem such as "Written by Cifar about his Daughter, Ubaldina" is representative of Cuadra, and shows him at his best, as I believe it does, then Schulman has misrepresented the Nicaraguan's work:

> Give her a gentle bay
> where her boat will be reflected
> as if hatching another,
> a peaceful inlet
> where the sun
> will dry her nets.

The translation here and elsewhere remains faithful to the original, though frequently the Spanish offers the translators little to work with and the results are necessarily uninspiring. The range of the poetry is extremely limited and Cuadra's work in no way deserves the accolades accorded it in Schulman's introduction. Certainly Cuadra is not a poet of the stature of his fellow countryman, Ernesto Cardenal, and does not belong to the grand tradition of Neruda, Vallejo, and Paz, as Schulman asserts. Nevertheless, Cuadra's vision, modest yet authentic, merits a reading by anyone interested in Latin American poetry, as well as by those attracted to the positive and empathetic rather than to their more popular opposites: negativism and the cult of the pathetic.

Place

is a theme common enough among singers of the Americas, & now I too would
take it as my own, seeing as how it does lie ever-so-close to home. And besides,

who has told
of a spot to know,
like heaven of old,

that where to go
for viewing it all,
no mind or heart

throwing up some wall
to hide a part?
Why not bring them here

like quarreling brats
you keep all day
in rooms apart?

Can't you hear
their sincere drats
promising so for true

how yes they'll play
fair as fair,
never again to argue,

or even give a dare,
just let back in
the other's ken?

Like the bark of the birch, as a subject it has been once & again remarked upon. But anyhow, Chihua, bear with me and this turgid Texas style. Recall the
skins of trees we saw on wending our way up the statued hill, San Cristóbal,
favorite haunt of the romantic & the suicide. Thin & white they were, rolled

Tide, no. 2 (Catholic University of Chile, 1967): 64-90.

paper sheets, each with its set of letters joined by pluses, all enclosed by ar-
rowed hearts. Living walls, I thought, tempting the knife of the mind to come,
carve, & initial them. Rather I would have the very groves engrave our love
with a shade can feed & free the eyes.

Here below, our range of vision limits the field for good, so much there is
to munch on by the inch. At times we're starved, from staring into space. With
all restrictions removed, the strength of form has fallen away, as did the power
of the Lord from the Nazarite, his sacred locks shorn by Delilah's lovely hand.
The imagination's mischief has pulled me out of socket. Let me plug back in
& feel the season's juice again.

Working within, the housemaid waddles to the window and throws the shut-
ters back, to air the room, to let the orange tree's fragrance in. A camera myself, I climb on the crowded bus for town & carry with me the photograph of
her cleaning from inside out, shaking the dusty rug, the sheets & spreads still
warm with love. (Elsewhere I have snapped a shot of the transit system, its
world within a world, entrance & exit / life & death, the driver a god who moves
the earthbound where they would or must WE'RE COMING AT IT OR BUST!

What is all this talk I hear, of margins defining an inner growth? Each office
worker hunches over a dark varnished desk, feels chained to pen & paper. The
mind moves out, no matter. Or should it just stay put? We stand in line—what
here in Chile they call a "tail," and to tell the truth, most of us look a horse's
before the worrisome waiting's done. Across the counter, behind the seated
official, atop the index file, four large letters identify this section as the one
for persons whose last names start with:
The workers all resent their jobs. Their
low pay as indecent as a neckline in New

H I J K

Orleans. An ink pad with its thumb-print
roller is parked on a table passed the livelong day by every bored. Over it all
has settled a fine dust that dulls every finish. Hidden too by black clouds of
tedium is any gleam of a human smile, though a sign big as life reads SONRIA.
Seen no longer one at a time, the endless faces offer no *bon voyage*. On the
walls posters of a field of blue cornflowers, of Paris, France, of medieval cas-
tles along the Rhine alleviate the dismal. Here they dispense (with) certifica-
tion, of residence. In thong sandals, weighted down by her crammed woven
plastic shopping sack, a number waits her turn. Humbly, evidence enough she's
lived here all her life. Is unaware of the foreigner's way of stomping about in
an unknown tongue, bitching that time's a-wasting. Like TIME itself, she's
never seen the enemy as ever the hour or day.

Then it was that the Reverend Elijah P. strutted right in where we all lan-
guished in line. Says he, "See these uncivil servants, they're missing out on
treasures landed, so to speak, at the shores of their own doors. Golden voices
from over the seas. Silver hair from Wisdom Bay. Coined words & phrases the
self-important assistant might pick up, worth far more than all the nights she's
dying to spend in bed with a pocket edition of *Free To Love Again*. She could
easily sample that poor fellow's priceless wares in the five minutes she's argued
on to keep from doing what little he needs done—proof his record's washday

clean. Time. Freedom. For all the use she's put them to, she should have locked herself away. A wearied spirit comes of not slamming our distant selves in a solitary cell. One close thought leads to another, once the start is made, to inspect what comes to visit—Bird Man of Alcatraz. She just might see him later. Handsome chap. Such things happen, you know. And not alone in movies. Take it from me, while wings may be true things of the mind, in the end all means of flight must come to roost on a limb or in among the droppings of some chicken coop. Find a face and rest upon it your wornout wandering dreams." Chihua! I've found a feather—stuck it is in my bluegreen sweater. It must be from the couch, the one where . . . AIR!

> Come, numb lips,
> from too much
> suavity,
> enough's enough,
> you're tipsy!
>
> This,
> the mahogany neck
> pored over, kissed,
> skin of smooth
> Araucanian age
>
> mixed with Spain's
> sanguinity,
> may indeed
> be the flavor,
> the bite, yes,
>
> & as some say,
> the after-taste
> of a straight
> Kentucky whiskey.
> But come away,
>
> dumb lips, & let it
> for now your lesson be,
> that just to touch
> her Chilean blend
> has you intoxicated!

Falling in love is another. Remains in bounds to reach beyond he who senses the might of restraint. The arc of the eyes a rainbow, the iris enrichens like a pot of gold. But blinders would help at times. Flowers bloom unseen, behind the red brick wall. Deliciously they scent the walk. The passerby, free to wander far abroad, at last wishes he grew rooted as they, to give off such aroma, the kind anchored ever in place.

Still half-asleep, the rhythm of the bus bumps me till my eyelids drop. Now I feel the sun, now the shade, but never know what causes either one. Trees, stores, spaces? The dark, the light, comes & goes, like the man who feeds the pigeons under watchful eyes of the palace guard. Kernels of corn scattered, they gather, peck, mount the parapets. I pass beneath & feel—splat!—a good luck charm. Or so they say it is. Their guess is better than embarrassment. Makes the cleaning bill less of a shame to pay. The old man empties his seed-bag & moves back into the anonymity where all exist, our deepest needs unknown & only fed on grains we none of us can quite digest.

DOWNTOWN MY LECTURE ROOM IS COLD & DAMP AND LITERATURE BEING WHAT IT IS—AN OLD HORSE DRESSED UP BY A NEWSTYLED RIDER, AN ACCUSTOMED ROUTE TRAVELED BY UNCOMMON MEANS, A ROAD THAT ARRIVES THOUGH DELAYED SOMEWHAT BY DETOURS FROM OFF THE BEATEN PATH—THE PROFESSOR OF SUCH A FAITH LOSES HIS MOMENT FOR INSTRUCTION. THOSE OBSERVATIONS HE MUST FEEL MOST APROPOS COMING ONLY ONCE THE SURVEY CLASS HAS LONG MOVED ON, TO THE NEXT REPRESENTATIVES OF PERIOD, PLACE, & THEIR PECULIAR CONCERNS. MUCH LIKE THE LOVER, WHO HAS LOST FOR AYE THAT GOLDEN OPPORTUNITY FOR SETTING THE WHOLE THING STRAIGHT AGAIN, OR THE LAW-YER, WHO MISSED HIS MOMENT FOR MAKING THAT MOST DRAMAT-IC POINT, THE TEACHER, THOUGH FEELING HIS BELATED DISCOV-ERY UNWORTHY AN INTERRUPTION OF CHRONOLOGY MERELY FOR THE SAKE OF BACKTRACKING, TO A SUBJECT HAD ALREADY BORED THE STUDENTS HALF TO DEATH, REMAINS STILL DEEPLY DESIR-OUS OF COMMUNICATING, NOT JUST ONE MORE FACT—FOR WHAT LITTLE IT WOULD ADD TO AN UNDERSTANDING HOPELESSLY HAND-ICAPPED BY THE LIMITS OF AN ANTHOLOGIZED VIEW where did I say we should look to each tree, each poem, as if it were the only in sight? those famous words, shoals the lookout never spies in time, the breakers of taking it on himself to guide the ship aright BUT A PERSONAL DELIGHT, RESULT OF THE REVELATION ITSELF. LEFT THEN, STANDING STARK STILL, NAKED BEFORE MIND'S EYE, EVEN AS THE WORLD ROLLS BY, THE TEACHER FINDS RELEASE AT LAST, PUSHING HIMSELF TO SUBSTI-TUTE FOR BLACKBOARD CHALK & A QUAVERING VOICE, THE PEN WITH ITS RETRACTABLE TALK. And to think this a sad state of affairs is not to appreciate that here at least a man may have his say, regardless of time—truth his one & only watchpiece. THIS

> that is admitted
> permits the mind to move,
> a proffered hand

or the very band
inviting a couple
to up & dance

takes the fault to
waltz it
round thought's hall

to limber wrong
with the rhythm the song of
forgiveness   no!

that forgetful sway—this
of giving way, of
letting whirl

remembrance the while
stepping right
where toes would go

I've known readers to joy in the foreign author's cutting down of his own
hometown, seeing no more in this than lambaste of a distant wrong. Criticism?
It starts at home & stays there, no matter to whom the property belong. Though
the owner live in another locale, what faults are housed in the domicile, so described, inhabit the reader's house as well. Surely there is but a negative kind
of comfort to be had in finding creaks in the other's floors when in effect it is
where & how we pass our days. To continue, not seeing the life as our own,
since the book or title's in another's name, bespeaks a people will take a leak
on the very campfire whereon their meals are laid & this *porque ¿cómo que
se llama?* the flame is believed to have come from HELL. Know then, those
stains the author paints on his personages were first condemned in him. "Thy
love afar is spite at home." The product of a shrimp & his bottle of rum dedi-
cates these next few lines to the poet Nicolás Guillén:

At an unsafe distance—
     here is where we spend our days.
     Romance of yesteryear

a past account
     out of which to us
          the shame alone is paid.

O friend, can you? I cannot hear
     the happy songs of heart-free slaves
          nor now my own race shouted down

by righteous voices lift a black man's cause,
him, could be, my own forefathers cast
on Cuba's New World shores

in role still lower than pariah dog's
or one would prove him better off.
O earth, what debts are we too soon

to set on those your unborn sons?

Dr. W.C. Williams speaks in a normal tone of voice, from Paterson, New Jersey ("How could a poet come from such a dirty slum?"), and is heard now round the world. "But Doc," the impatient ask,"ain't it just this sort of local anesthesia deadens a man to everything outside his own city limits?" Aristotle & things, he replied. Not Plato, with that notion of forms (the one, the many), who placed it all in paradise, out of reach. Poe wrote to the One there too. O.K., but dialect. It too's an issue. Plain speech, where you come from & where you're going identifies your starting place, is carried with you clear to the grave. The tongue is in the head, & has a distinctive taste. Even a universal, eternal thought's flavored by lips that give it birth, by labials formed from getting the lay of a land. Bohemian, Basque, British, all bear in mind the local & leave the foreign parts as ports of call, trade for what can spice a daily diet, while ever the heart's true hunger's fed on good old homestyle looking.
"BUT IF, DURING THE FIRST THREE YEARS OF THE EIGHTEENTH CENTURY, THE NEARLY TWO HUNDRED CHURCH MEMBERS WHO CROWDED INTO THE MEETING HOUSE AT WESTFIELD AWAITED TAYLOR'S PORTRAITURE OF CHRIST WITH 'KNOWING ANTICIPA-TION,' THEY WERE PROBABLY NOT PREPARED FOR ONE DOCTRI-NAL VARIATION OFFERED BY THEIR MINISTER—THE POSITIVE AS-SURANCE NOT ONLY THAT THEIR NATURE HAD BEEN DIGNIFIED AND HONORED EVEN ABOVE THE ANGELS IN ITS UNION WITH GOD IN CHRIST, BUT THAT IN A WAY THEY TOO PARTOOK OF THE NA-TURE OF GOD—A PROUD AND EXULTANT DOCTRINE RECONCILED WITH DIFFICULTY TO CALVINISTIC DEPRAVITY. TAYLOR, IT MUST BE REMEMBERED, HAD SERVED THESE PEOPLE FOR THIRTY YEARS, AND HAD BEEN RESPONSIBLE FOR THE SPIRITUAL FORMATION OF PERHAPS HALF OF THEM; THE RAPPORT BETWEEN THEM AND THEIR MINISTER MUST HAVE BEEN FIRM AND COMFORTABLE." What comes back most is how that poet-preacher's church committee voted to prepare 4 or 5 barrels of beer, to be made available at the building of his congregation's new meetinghouse. "Thou mayst as easily toss away the earth as a tennis ball" as to tackle the erecting of a house of worship without a drop or two of a town's own homemade brew.
Walking the after-Xmas streets, living in the aftermath where I've tried my best to summarize what goes down before time's blade, putting on my grade-

school thinking cap, but alas! all that comes is childish distraction: a military band on parade. Halt. Salute to tall, big-nosed Frei. And now they've broken out with the Chilean national anthem. The ceremony concluded, forward march. With what grace the drum major signals a half-column right! By his reddish-brown moustache, British, but for all that Chilean, now that he is here. I too skip into step, shoulders pulled back, propelled once more by the pride of place.

In the end land is the possessive one more than man, entering him by sights & sounds, till at the last interred he is in her, & that, so far as he may know, for eternity. At times even, a *terremoto* trembling with desire, unable to wait a decent spell, she opens right at the pedestrian's feet, closes shut again his short story over even before he ever thought . . . .

Two strains run in me, of NORK & the Puritan hymn. SPEAKING OF THE ENGLISH, I KNEW A BOBBY BEEN RIGHT HERE IN CHILE FIVE AND THIRTY, YEARS THAT IS. HAD NEVER LEARNED THE LANGUAGE. TOOK LONG WALKS OF A MORNING 'RIGHT TO THE TOP OF THE HILL.' WATCHED THE SEA & HEARD HIS NEIGHBORS GOSSIPING, ALL SO MUCH TO HIM LIKE THE SOUND OF THE WAVES CRASHING IN BELOW. HIS WIFE, SHE WAS SIMPLY FLUENT. TALKED A BLUE STREAK, OR BLOODY, AS HE WOULD SAY, WITH THE MAID, OR ANY VENDOR CAME ALONG. BUT ALWAYS SHE WAS THE ONE SPOKE TO HIM OF WANTING THE DAYS OF LONDON AGAIN. NOT HIM. SAID HE 'WOULDN'T GO BACK FOR ALL THE TEA IN CHINA.' BET YOU STILL CAN FIND THEM ANYTIME OVER THERE IN VIÑA. All this what you say may be true & all, but the love of a land gets out of hand. Fatherland, super-race, & a clannish bunch of rot. What's here eludes the tourist and the visiting research scholar, never gets in the movies either. But then, it's always ANOTHER THING WITH GUITAR, like a

> female friend of mine
> who's never married
> always says
> when a man is down
>
> don't you help!
> just put foot to head
> till he lift it up
> himself.
>
> Now should she ever
> take that fatal step,
> sure hard to see her
> pregnant as a cornsower
>
> out in Temuco,
> seedbag cross his waist,

dropping kernels to earth,
& then,

just for the
growing upright,
stamping them down
in the furrow!

The occasion is the ordinary: a late spring afternoon, drinking beer at a neighborhood cafe. Both doors open upon the street, though, as ever, one is with the iron fence down. The sky stands warm blue against the heavy wire. Two rats sun on the sidewalk running along the muddy canal. Across it, back from a foot bridge of wood, a newer building, than the one next door, holds the keyholes to lives we would we knew. Those seated near don't interest. I'm so mad I could kick an apricot. We await the dark, when windows lit by lamps within will at least reveal the color, the cast of a walled-in life. Back here I eye an unknown leg, who sashays in through the threshhold frame, a pink ribbon pinned to the bun of her hair, believing she hung the moon. Thinking to despise such self-conscious airs, I wish her inspite of my "better" self. Other youths arrive, in snow boots, from the long & dusty trip down from the ski resort, Farellones. Skiis stood outside, they sip their suds at the counter. The waitresses wear, as usual, their business-like blank looks, serve the same menu of food & drinks: beer on tap or bottled, pure nectars, raw ground meat with lemons, onions, white bread or pumpernickel, hot dogs with homemade mayonnaise, & sliced pork with choice of avocados or sauerkraut. The landlord's a flaxen-haired *alemán*. I myself am a "Yankee Go Home" from Texas. On paying their bills, his patrons, most of them darkhaired Latins, see in him the Hitler type. To glance my way, they see a land of oil wells & millionaires, and Dallas that killed a president ('why do you *always* resort to assassination? we accept them good or bad'), state where everyone wears a gun, where blacks and mexicans are murdered on sight—yes, these are facts known by all discerning eyes, & easily observed in me. For my own mistaken part, Santiago is a city of dreams, one cradled by the cordillera. From here visions of north & south visit the citizen's every waking hour. Nearly none of them would choose this spot were it not for the benefits of a paying job & the pastimes a pop. of 2 & a half mil. has made come true. For daily, their thoughts return them to the southern rain or to the deserts they deserted up north. Even now another Moses, Mahdi, or Mohammed may shimmer forth from the latter's sands like a mirage dancing on the dunes of the Egyptian Sudan—the north of Chile with its mystical temperature. The wet south the while grows moldy & slow in its unchanging season, a kind of classical heaven, for some, with rain falling thirteen months per year.

The occasion is one of many—a thought worthy as any when enhanced by a frame of mind. And so to repeat: a late spring afternoon drinking beer at a nearby pub, both eyes opening upon the street. As ever, one is locked inside itself—in it at least the poet's by tradition blind, at once to look inside & out—

both of mine are near sky blue, this by fate, but nonetheless I have sought to see the likeness here: of the scurrying rats, of my murky thoughts sent to run with them beside the scummed canal. What a sure cure is there here for what dad called a pure case of optical rectosis, translated comes down to a real cruddy view of life! None, until it happen that EL AFILADOR

> blows that indian whistle
> while pushing his shop
> from street to street—
>
> all now shaded by cottonwood,
> its leaves like arrowheads,
> green hearts, what have you,
>
> the tree that followed sharply upon,
> flowering in the face
> of dull winter's wit—
>
> for on it he announces
> with special interval & scale
> he's come to grind
>
> carving knives,
> scissors,
> what you have—
>
> I've this edge of the mind
> beyond his wheel's repair,
> but listen intent on the indian tune
>
> & find it keen,
> feel it fresh & clean,
> paring away this cheesy rind

In the days when love has come & gone, what to do? I enter the edifice of spring, where each & every room, seen from the surrounding dark, is lit by an inner light, its enamel a perfect match. Sights, blooms fall away from their sprouting out too soon, my views, their fragile pink, chaff now to winter's bitter return, by every passing foot the cement stained, my vision trampled down. Yet in their stead a thousand green hands are reaching for the sky, & soon the fruits of a patient wait will be held up by her orange tree arms. Persephone putting on a fresh & fragrant coat. By extension a typical western phrase: got you covered. Don't move. The only thief is you. The land belongs to the slow but sure to look, to read the life-lines on every river-branching leaf. But what comes of KEEPING TABS ON THE OTHER GUY'S TAKE?

For several months running, both
in dark from that time of birth,
the two musicians played apart,
two cold blocks of Moneda street
trafficking between their songs.

Today, in the shade, in the shadow
of a branch of the Banco del Estado,
here where, for better or worse
harmony's ranks have gathered,
arrayed in winter's uniform

of castoff toboggan & army coat,
the blind are warming the banking day
with fiddle & Spanish guitar,
cups hanging from instrument necks
to catch what coin we "rich" discard.

And yet can such a wedding last?
Or shall I out of good intent,
dropping my trifle
to just one tin,
return each tone

to lonely battle, when,
even with eyes
for seeing the sight,
elsewhere jealousy's making me
to play the beggar again?

How give the land back to those who till & plant? Since when did they,
living upon it, loving it as we do the bodies none can keep, not own it for
their own?

We travel out of the city, to pay the country a visit, just for its quaintness'
sake. On the bus with us the landsmen are heading home from morning shopping in the capital, a place to them unfeeling as a butchered calf. Never will
they ever be themselves but in the unconfusing cornfields. We take the familiar out of them, to return it on documents officially signed & sealed. In the
evening, coming again into the city's littered streets, our memories move back
to the walking hand-in-hand, barefoot along the road, where with each step a
fine dust shot up, warm between our toes. Afterwards the splashing of feet in
a cold clear stream, all the time knowing how out of place we were. Our hearts
are in the crowded, vulgar town, theirs in the country with its mud & rutted
ways. This day closes with S U N S E T P E T A L S , A S F R E S I A ' S H U E
S E T T L E S

with one diffused by the lumberyard
drying uncorded stacks of pine
while last snow spots the cordillera,
faintly, a spattering of paint

from an unseen scaffolding in the sky,
& just from these few scraps
& the orange & banana peels pitched
to the street at market's edge

mind builds up what might be there
beyond the yellow light, bears down
on the next intersection, as if to say
with warning signs of green & gray,

no turning to either side allowed,
leave to chance what's up ahead,
proceed, let go that presence come,
collision anew with the here & now.

THAT SUMMER IN AUSTIN WAS EXTRA HOT. BUT THE WINDOW FAN, the kind with a rubber hose for dripping water down through straw, kept our second-storey room damp all day and with it on come night we damn near froze to death. As the midday heat was filtered through the wet, we lay on the soiled bed sheets, stripped down to our dirty underwear. Socks worn for a week and more at a time were piled in the walk-in closet, along with Blackie's sandbox. I had moved to the boarding house first. When the Beast arrived later, we connived with the cleaning lady and continued only paying rent for one. Jenny couldn't read nor write, but tried. She dusted the desk, leaving scraps of paper with words copied in an all but illegible scrawl. Or have I mixed her up in my distant mind with another maid was as poorly paid? The one in the house on Whitis Street where Andy roomed in '58, was joined there by good ol' George, who used to pitch in with the other students roomed with them & buy her a bottle of her favorite wine, Thunderbird, at $1.79 a fifth. Was it she or Jenny fell asleep on the front steps in a February freeze, and never woke to clean another lazy student's toilet bowl?

The Beast was sure he could sell an article on the battle at Goliad, to *True* or some other rag. Every morning he went bright and early to take notes from the tombs at the Texas History Library. Returning at lunchtime with juicy tidbits of treason or choice cases of cowardice, he ranted and raved that the bastards had sold out, let the Mexicans murder Texans. All his talk of bravery began getting on my nerves, and with the very next worship service in honor of he-man Hemingway, I couldn't resist reading to him how W.C. Williams had held the foreskin while Ernest's son was circumcised, the father unable even to watch. Not that I ever held anything personal against "Papa" myself, even imagining how he must have felt. But my object gained, a mild furor the result of the reading, lasting three or four days, things settled back down to normal, though the Beast never forgave that point and I still regret having made it. In any case, with less talk of courage, and the black cat continuing scrawny as the day the Beast had sneaked him in, we suffered on from the tortillas and beans lunch and supper—a diet sufficient unto those accustomed even from birth but pretty trying on any other system. The same goes, I suppose, politically speaking. Some people accept a meager meal of monarchy.

The nights were taken up with bumming a pitcher of beer at Scholz's Garten, before bed and just before the Beast did his 25 push-ups. Economics had us both by the ying-yang. Every morning after the he-man left I checked the mailbox for replies from the hundreds (or so it seemed) of high schools I had written in search of a teaching position   ᘯ ᘰ   Dear Sir: We have decided to hire someone with more experience. Sincerely yours, etc. Thus it was that without it, and where to get it without a start I'll never know, each morning staring me in the skinny face were thinner hopes and cheeks, the closer it came to Sept. 1 and the beginning of public school. And with it all, Beast and beans daily increased in their powers of irritation.

Ah, where are the important issues of '63. I recall the Beast here and now not because time has swept away, as ever it does, the sands that grate, though it has indeed, but rather because it was precisely of South America the Beast was ever dreaming: to make it down to Colombia, marry an indian beauty, have a dozen mestizos, and rule a fundo from horseback with whip and a wide straw hat. His last epistle (we both had our heroes) was postmarked Placitas, New Mexico, telling of how he was living with a philosopher cousin, next door to Robert Creeley, and if and when it rained again and Creeley came out in the clay, he would get a set of the poet's hoofs and mail them on down by muleback.

First time I met the Beast was on the Texas coast, in Beaumont, where we both were taking the same geology course. Naturally neither of us cared the least for a conglomerate, metamorphic, or any fault in the earth, except the ones come by social pressure or injustice under the weight of the law. So we soon turned to jokes just to while away the endless days of trilobites. Our lab instructor had only one arm, the source of many a snide remark. Naturally too, our own unkindness was fully justified on the grounds we were forced by degree requirements to take such a crusty course. Our idealism never went too far.

One day one-armed Charlie, in front of a class three-fourths female, informed us to put our rocks back in their boxes. The Beast caught it right off. He snickered aloud and Charlie realized his verbal displacement. Then he doubled the whole class over by correcting himself to say I mean you can put your rocks back in your drawers. Nevertheless, under that crude, rude layer there was a sentimental core that wouldn't have taken a geologist to uncover, for the Beast was anything but a prehistoric monster. He, like Hemingway, developed a hard shell to protect a tender heart. When I think about it now, it all falls into place.

On our first talking together over contour maps of a submarine volcano in central Texas, he told me of a story he had written and had had rejected by *Atlantic* or *Harper's*. It seems he invented a version of "The Emperor's New Clothes." Caught by the editor with his own pants down, the Beast insisted he had never even heard of such a fairy tale before. In telling me the story he erupted right over the contour map, as I am certain he had on reading the customary rejection slip. At least the editor had appended a note explaining the secret of his genius, or so he interpreted his denuding. At any rate, interested in his writing, I agreed we should try our hands at starting a counter-literary movement against the existing order. Since the college magazine was called *Pulse*, we christened ours *Repulse*. The ususal thing for those still believing in the undiscovered brilliance of their wits. And, of course, where would a couple of bums like us have ever come up with the mon? To make up for this puncture to our pride, we put on the outward signs of an inner strength, criticizing all published efforts while remaining immaculate ourselves within the excuse that had we had the wherewithal we certainly would have done a better job by far. In the end all objects worthy of ridicule avoided us like the plague. And so we could only look to take it out on each other.

It was one hot weekday as we swam in a rain-filled sandpit, near the lair of the Beast, his deceased father's house on the outskirts of Beaumont in a community known as Rose City, on a street named Azalea, in an area overgrown with pine, sweetgum, and Baptist churches. After cooling off for an hour or so in the sandpit pools, we lunched on the back porch and played mechanical baseball. The Beast had been trying to sell that penball machine for months, in order to pay off the ticket he had picked up as a result of a car wreck for which he was necessarily not to blame. Since I was winning on the machine, the Beast began with the requirements most essential for the making of an honest-to-God poet, none of which qualifications I could ever hope to meet. Though naturally *he* could, being in and therefore loving the Cassius Clay tradition of the greatest. Following that futile attempt to rub me raw, he passed on to Christian Science, a religion he resented by instinct and one to which he knew I was then attracted, by the exact same power in reverse. That unique American movement received from the Beast a barrage of epithets to the effect that anyone taken in by Mary Baker Eddy and her anemic key to the scriptures ought to be tied and drug behind horses. The Beast and Mary Baker! two grand *gringo* institutions taking each a side of the road to glory.

While we lived together that summer in Austin, I kept my copy of Mark Twain's *Christian Science* well out of sight when the Beast was around, so as not to supply him with additional ammunition. Besides, one of the groups in America, listed by Twain in that book as suspiciously inclined toward radical religiosity, was none other than the Scottish sect Mark labelled and libelled Oliphantism! The Beast was truly beautiful in his humor and in his sense of what is best for the next guy. But for me to have furnished him with more artillery would have just been asking for an all-out attack on my defenseless character. Not that I don't take myself much too seriously. Some will say it's a necessary evil, but with the Beast around it was safer to keep such moral zeal well underground, unless of course the self-indulgent need special outside help to inflate the ego by blows, in which case hot air would have done it or one long seige of his laughter morning till pushup time at night.

That summer I was saved from his finding me out by finally getting a teaching job, at which time the Beast and I parted company for more of the same but without the other as witness. On several trips to Austin I did visit him, though by then he had moved to a room the ceiling of which was covered with egg cartons, across which huge cockroaches ran their foot races round the clock. All in all, a den befitting the Beast. Not that the one we shared hadn't been. The only reason he removed himself was on account of that skinny coal-black feline. For, one day, two weeks or so after I left for the Texas deserts and the Beast had forgotten during all that time to empty Blackie's sandbox, Jenny opened the closet door. Next day, to the landlady, she let the cat out of the bag! On discovering how we had all through the summer cheated her out of double the rent, she made life so miserable for the poor Beast that he finally moved in with the roaches. You might say his kindness caused it all. Chihua, the Beast is a living fable.

More often, to meet the earth, takes many a fall. For that there are at dark the roots of trees & by day the polished floors. Viet Nam is our longest war. I only fight that one the Greeks began: Is the actual our furniture or the golden chair of paradise? The stakes I think must be the same: dying with things as are or death for what the change may bring. Life is the woman loved without having once our way with her.

He sits in shade without his legs, shining shoes not even for a living wage. In his chosen place sun rarely comes, AND YET

> call him
> a mountain,
> his head
> among the clouds,
>
> neither need
> be denied him,
> nor divine
> nor human side,
>
> even though from time to time
> we find him
> face downward here at the corner
> of Los Leones & Hernán Cortés
>
> on steps lead up to church remains—
> a paintless door with its peeling frame

closed on the vacant lot behind—
at the knees his trousers doubled & pinned

O still like a poem it lasts for me, the lustre he gives to the man with a shoe.
And even though Haydn's "Mass in Time of War" arrives at the pub by radio,
is here on tap same as the brew, it makes no one mellow but me. "Miss, do
you mind turning down that noise? " I drink, strain my ears, and make another start, another go at READING THE SUN, for

Ever local in nature
each work opens
on rooftops & trees
of a feature
fitting the nation.

Author for a day
of the place to
which he warms,
even now, with early
morning, he's passing

the political rally,
rolling as a trolley bus
silently by,
flashing when a
line connects,

casting comments
on a speaker's specs:
light!—
for what utility
the land elect.

Eating One's Words

Back in 1965 when I was editing the University of Texas' student literary magazine, *Riata*, I wrote an article on Louis Zukofsky in which, as one professor put it at the time, I used my favorites to whip those poets I found wanting. My heroes, the influences I wrote under from the beginning, as with many a college student of the late fifties and early sixties, were Williams, Creeley, and Olson. The objects of my ridicule were, necessarily, Eliot and Lowell. Since that time, however, I've noticed at least one characteristic of my writing which places it in Philip Rahv's "pale face" camp—and this the very thing about the Eliot-Pound school that I came down on the hardest: literary allusion. Even though I have always attempted to achieve naturalness of diction, to treat of the everyday event as Williams preached & practiced, I find that unwittingly I now rely heavily on reference to other writers, to jazz & classical music, and to little-known facts about my home state of Texas.

Starting with an interest in description of the near-at-hand, trying to allow it to reveal its own inherent poetry, I looked at the region I lived in and sought to coax a spirit of its earlier days into the language of the present. It got to where I couldn't write about much else. Even love poems turned into studies of the western landscape instead of the other way around. I felt stuck with a subject that kept repeating itself like an endless drive across West Texas. I love such a journey myself, but I saw that few readers outside the state would share my enthusiasm. And then it struck me that the possibilities of language were also limited by my repetitious treatment of native scenes. What I've since discovered is that, fair or not, I do better to come at my home state as a foreigner (which I've actually ended up doing geographically)—almost to see it through the eyes of an alien.

One recent example of this is a poem I've written about Armenia, a subject of which I had only a passing knowledge, had even to research, of all things. But through looking at my old stomping grounds from the perspective of an unknown land I was able, I feel, to say about the Southwest what I never would have without the distance provided by this approach. Not only has another point of view aided me in gaining new insight into an obsessive subject, but allusion to other writers & other fields has also given me the authority I believed to be lacking in my own voice, as well as a greater sense of the usefulness of this literary method I earlier scorned.

Their Place in the Heat Contemporary Poetic Statements, ed. Doug Flaherty (Road Runner Press, 1971), pp. 46-47.

Through the association of subjects seemingly so unrelated I find I have created for myself a fresh way of presenting qualities I have long admired in the persons & places I've known the best. Perhaps this is more illusion on my side than anything else. Nevertheless, the pleasure I take in linking up sophisticated positions with supposedly hick parts or people is quite a far cry from my editorial pronouncements of the mid-sixties. And I don't see this as a clever way of showing off semi-bookishness. On the contrary, it's probably just a sentimental need to say that my real subjects are too good for me. In any case the moral is clear. And I like morals. Not the kind that tell us not to do it, but rather the kind that lead us to laugh at ourselves for being so pious.

What I mean is—I wouldn't have anyone quit forming judgments just because they will most likely return to haunt him forever. All I care to see happen is that once it's time once more for me to eat my words I hope I can realize what a good way it is to know how wise I'm *not* when I won't leave myself open to the joy of having a change of heart.

Forms of Exile

When faced with exile, Socrates made it clear to his judges that he preferred death. The philosopher's reasons were many, including both the practical consideration of his age and the more highly motivated view that such an alternative would contradict his very life and teachings. In the case of Joyce, exile seems to have been self-imposed, apparently because he felt objectivity to be essential to his art, one in which the presentation of deep passion required distance from the beloved object. The political exile of Solzhenitsyn is an example from one socialist camp, while the mass exodus of leftist writers from Chile following the fall of Allende represents the shifting sands of that same struggle —this time those who would have ousted the Russian have themselves sought refuge in the very system they once condemned, namely this of the United States. The pains and paradoxes of exile are evident throughout the history of ancient and modern literatures. If there is a lesson to be learned from this history, perhaps it revolves around the fact that some form of exile is often part and parcel of the literary life, whether it be the result of social or political reaction, creative necessities, or simply, as is the case more often than not, of economic forces. In today's world there has been a marked increase in the number of educated persons who are seeking positions as teachers; add to this the influx of intellectuals living in political exile who occupy posts in academic institutions, and the result is a dire shortage of jobs, not only for graduates in general, but especially for those hoping to remain close to their native ground. As if this were not enough, there is yet another form of exile which affects the writer of every age and nation, and this is his or her separation from a native readership as a result of generic and stylistic banishment. Specifically I am referring to a simultaneous disregard for a native vision and voice and to a rejection by editors of all but the poetry which fits a magazine's ready-made image.

In Texas there has been an effective ban on native poetry, and particularly on those poems which either exceed the thirty-line limit or attempt to deal seriously with regional topics (and I do not mean by this merely poems on stereotypical western settings). This form of exile is partly related to political and social pressures, as the minorities are well aware when they try to publish poems on their own predicament. A magazine like *The Texas Quarterly*, for example, has degenerated drastically from the issues of the late fifties and early sixties when it published such seminal figures as Louis Zukofsky and James Dickey, and such a regional poem as R.G. Vliet's "Clem Maverick."

Tawté (May 1975): 48-51.

It is my understanding that this heavily-endowed journal has become principally a means of attracting donations to the University's already burgeoning business enterprise, the University of Texas System. Contributions, it is said, are from those who want to see articles published in exchange for a university trust fund being set up in the donor's name. Perhaps this is not at all the case, but rumor most likely has grown from the very real fact of the magazine's dramatic decline in quality.

Recently, *The Texas Quarterly* (Autumn 1973) published an anthology of contemporary poetry which included most bloodless examples of verse imaginable. Among the several University of Texas (Austin) faculty members represented (almost the only Texans included) are two of my former professors there, Thomas Whitbread and Ambrose Gordon. Whitbread's contributions are an all-time low for his work, which has steadily fallen from its high level of achievement in his Harper & Row collection, *Four Infinitives* (1964). Whitbread's "Love of Life," with a title that not even irony could rescue from triteness, is typical of a majority of the pieces in the anthology with their presumptuous profundity. His "Poor Death" employs another outmoded approach to poetry with its nineteenth-century allegorizing: "Death cannot entertain the life, / Even if He exist. . . ." This indeed is a sorry development, for Whitbread's power was once in abundant evidence. (I long debated the inclusion in *The New Breed* of a number of his poems on Texas scenes which back in the mid-sixties appeared on the front page of *The Texas Observer*. But feeling the poet was no longer really writing, I chose to exclude him.) One of Gordon's poems, with its use of controlled fishing imagery, is unusual in being worth the expense incurred in the always beautifully-printed *Quarterly*. Most of the pieces are written in dated techniques, with pounding iambics and archaic language: "He grew to manhood ere his heart had found. . . ." At the other extreme is prose broken meaninglessly into stanzas: "because pleasure for them // either had to do with / the church, or else you / didn't talk about it." The attitude of the editors toward the art of poetry is epitomized by this contributor's note on a poet originally from San Antonio and now married to a Mexican banker: "She lives in a beautiful San Angelo estate, the perfect place to entertain guests, raise a family, and write poetry." Another poet from San Antonio, on my pointing out this note to her, encouraged me to print it as a found poem. I prefer to try and discourage such aristocratic attitudes toward poetry (and of all places in Texas) and to encourage such poets as Whitbread, as well as his editors, not to foist upon the Texas reading public a non-poetry that continues to give the state's literature a bad name.

Obviously my criticism of the *Quarterly* is too extreme to be of use in suggesting the true nature of exile and its relation to a failure among editors to support an authentic regional literature. Yet neither do I restrain myself from criticism any longer simply because I sense that sour grapes have played a part in the formation of an otherwise justifiable evaluation. For too long writers like myself have been inclined to ignore the publishing situation in the state, choosing rather to go elsewhere to find outlets for our native expression. The unfortunate result has been that much of our literature has either become the property of other regions or has perished for lack of pages where it could gain the needed exposure to a native region's hot winds of opinion or its cooling rains of praise. While political and social attitudes have in the past hampered publication, oftentimes in recent days a pseudo-political poem or a self-serving piece of social criticism has found its way into Texas publications more easily than the genuine work of a dedicated artist. And it is finally the prejudice against certain genres and styles (mainly longer poems that deal with the dreams and realities of modern Texas life and do not fit into the predetermined molds or categories acceptable for publication) which has perpetuated at this date the most serious form of exile.

Ezra Pound left this country with a belief that it was culturally ignorant, and in exile he exhorted Americans to wake up to their artistic aridity. Many of Pound's teachings are still applicable to our present circumstances, but with the rise of regionally-conscious poetries, it seems to me that there is a new life being breathed into the body poetic. A magazine like *Margins* (Milwaukee) is giving vital review space to poets from every section of the nation, including chapbooks by Texans and the collection from Doubleday by El Paso's Ricardo Sánchez, *Canto y grito mi liberación*—the latter reviewed by *Tawté*'s Jim Cody. From Minnesota to San Francisco, from Chapel Hill to Fayetteville, younger and older poets are joining together in support of regional writing of a new kind. What makes non-academic poetry in the Midwest so healthy is the fact that such an established poet as Robert Bly is encouraging and publishing the younger and older regional poets of the area. In the *American Poetry Review* (vol. 3, no. 3, 1974), Bly has collected poems by eight fellow Minnesotans, among them Franklin Brainard, a 55-year-old poet who, little known outside Minnesota, has been active for thirty years. There are several established poets in Texas, but not one has taken any interest in poetry in the state, sticking rather to their own isolated publishing careers. Nor has any press in the state been consistently dedicated to Texas poetry. In Illinois, on the other hand, a state university press is now bringing out a second anthology of Midwest poetry (*Poets of the Heartland II,* edited by Lucien Stryk). The first volume sold widely and served as an introduction to a rich regional heritage. No Texas university press has attempted either a Southwest or a Texas anthology of poetry. Yet both the quality of writing and the demands of a growing poetry market make it a natural publication for any university press in Texas worthy the name.

Although the type of exile I have been discussing may not seem to follow from the normal meaning of the word, the fact of the matter remains that exile from the printed pages of his state is the most deadening form of exile experienced by the regional poet who would survive as such in his own mind and in those of his native readers. Certainly there are equally or more serious forms of exile in our nation demanding attention: the Black or Chicano living invisibly; the housewife divorced from her being by a chauvinistic male; and the sensitive mind estranged from itself by a guilt-ridden conscience. I do not deny that exile may be a state of nature to be endured by every man and woman. I only know that the form of exile which concerns me most intimately and which that exile may be a state of nature to be endured by every man and woman. I only know that the form of exile which concerns me most intimately and which I feel can be treated realistically to the benefit of those exiled inside or outside the state is this of divorce from a regional audience, estrangement from a meaningful relationship with those who would be able to and are in need of sharing the native poet's utterance.

Another magazine in Texas which seems to me to have renounced its role in the development of native ties is the *Southwest Review*. While some Texas writers are welcomed to its pages, these seem ever a select few. Overwhelmingly the *SWR* is a magazine devoted to poems on esoteric or sentimental subjects, written by persons who have little or no interest in a regional poetry, or for that matter in true contemporary poetry. And yet it was no other than J. Frank Dobie who wrote that "The *Southwest Review* of Dallas has announced a policy of asserting the Southwest in literature." Apparently "literature" has never quite included poetry, for the *SWR*'s record in this regard is poor indeed. Even when the editors accept a poem by a Texan, it is almost invariably among his or her most inconsequential work.

Considering this state of affairs, it would seem that the only answer is to found a new type of publication dedicated to encouraging Texas poetry. Who will do this, and within the state, remains to be seen. Thanks to *Tawté* a start has been made in this direction. Without a well-funded organ, and without the support of established poets in Texas, the need for developing a regional poetry and of relieving the pangs of exile experienced by so many native poets will not soon be realized, and Texas will continue to suffer from a lack of elevating poems. Of course, there are those like Robert Grant Burns who see a regional poetry as nothing either special or necessary. His own poetry derives perhaps from a different source of inspiration, but this may not be true of all Texas poets and is certainly not of me. Perhaps, also, it is the exile who most longs for a link with his native ground and with a tradition from which to draw his strength, something the printed page can alone provide. Only communication will close the gap between the exile and the land he loves. As poetry is the most sincere form of expression, so it is necessarily the most authentic answer to any form of separation.

It is a curious comment on our North American culture that few of us ever speak of exile, while most of us experience it even living within the nation's borders. Leaving the country is thus not so disrupting as it is for natives of nations where a sense of isolation does not infect their entire sensibilities. One reason for the isolation experienced by Texas writers is the almost total indifference within which they create their work. Pound once wrote that a national literature is such only when it does not need to apologize for its existence. In the case of Texans, we still feel ashamed of our poetic heritage or what we take to be a lack of same. As a result, readers in the state rarely take an interest in any writer who would claim the title of Texas poet. By contrast I think of Chile, the home of my wife María, a land to which I have long been attracted romantically and intellectually, where the grand tradition of Huidobro, Neruda, and Parra has created a deep understanding of and appreciation for native and regional poetries. (In a sense every country to the south has developed a regional poetry within the larger Latin American culture.) Because of this greater appreciation for regional writing, my own work as a Texas poet has greatly appealed to Chilean poets and an article on its backgrounds and growth by the Chilean poet Oliver Welden has appeared in *Revista de la Universidad de Chile*. I mention myself as an example simply because such interest in a Texan's poetry is rare, and I am aware of no study of this sort published in this country, where a Texas poet within or without the state has been considered in his regional light. Not that my own work is exceptional. The point is that Texas poets have not received from their own readers the kind of serious consideration that will prompt them to identify with their region or its poetic destiny.

I feel bound to acknowledge one personal factor with regard to exile which both inflates and punctures my ego. As I mentioned, my wife is a native of Chile; she has exiled herself for my sake, never having intended before our marriage to leave her land, particularly not for life. This sacrifice on her part is a form of exile which I enjoy daily, and yet I find my own exile from the printed page quite unbearable. On the other hand, there is no doubt that exile endears me to a place whose many slighter blemishes have been removed by distance, and even some of its more glaring ones. Nor is this exile a complete one, since magazines outside the state have generously taken me in—although this is not at all the same, even when some of these publications have reached readers in Texas. Irregardless of the paradoxes and contradictions involved in my position on exile, I continue to contemplate a means of prevailing against the most seriously stifling aspect of exile: the inability to keep in touch poetically with my native inspiration.

In the publishing state that I envision for Texas poets there will be a closer look not only at the younger artist but at poets of the past or those like Minnesota's Franklin Brainard who have worked for years with little or no recognition or encouragement. The poetry of R.G. Vliet, that of William Barney, and the work of William Burford, among others, should be presented in critical contexts which can serve to establish an appreciation for Texas poems. There is much to be done in this area and no one person can hope alone to make more than a dent. Instead of making this call-to-action, I should of course begin the job without so much ado. But then I fully intend to take up my own gauntlet and can only hope that the Texas literary exile will soon receive in the pages of his native publications half the reception accorded the Bible's prodigal son.

Inspiration and/or Artificial Insemination: Remarks on the Teaching of Creative Writing

Despite a feeling of inadequacy, even inability, on the part of those of us who accept the responsibility for conducting courses in creative writing, it seems that we all go about this business with an undying faith in its efficacy. What weighs heaviest on our minds is not so much the thought of an impossible task we are expected to perform, but rather of how at best we can only hope to avoid interfering with the creative process while, for purposes of academic credit, requiring a set amount of writing, generalized assignments, and the strictures of deadlines, not to mention the pressure—even if only an unconscious one—to conform to our own personal likes and dislikes. In addition to the difficulties imposed on us by a need to arrive at a final grade and those we ourselves erect by having the class hew to an almost indefinable standard we as writers have long labored under, the student comes to us for that most insubstantial curriculum: Inspiration. To his or her appeal for divine motivation I find that I have tended through the years to respond with little more than the boards and bricks of a highly mundane instruction. And yet the results have continued to amaze even me, for never having had a single course in creative writing myself, I cannot quite believe that I would have been moved to fulfill my own uninspiring demands, let alone today's student-writer, who seems to expect more from educators than I ever did—nor had I ever intended to become one!

After teaching the writing of prose and poetry off-and-on during ten years (in a junior college, in a maximum security penitentiary, in a Mexican university, and now here at the University of Texas), I have come to formulate a number of artificial assignments designed either to serve as a means of inspiration or to substitute for it in the meantime by preparing the student's vocabulary and technique for the moment when heaven or whatever it is deigns to pay that special visit. Although I have never considered my approach particularly original nor even wholly satisfactory, I did find it of interest that Kenneth Koch, author of several works on the teaching of creative writing, has employed the same method, a fact I was unaware of until he spoke here in Austin on 12 April 1977, outlining his practice as applied to workshops with children, the elderly, and university students. I was especially struck by Koch's comment on the validity of assigning such a complicated form as the sestina, a saddle with which I have often strapped my own unsuspecting charges. For the pre-

Introduction to *The Poet Trap* (spring 1977—privately printed, The University of Texas at Austin).

sent semester, however, I chose something a bit different—the terza rima form with its not quite so repetitive rhyme scheme (merely three words carrying the same essential sound, whereas in the sestina six end-words are repeated in six 6-line stanzas and one 3-line stanza, usually with different meanings for each appearance of the end-words, according to the changing context). In both cases the response has been similar: initially the class resists, later it curses its fate, then flounders around in the form, and ends frustrated yet extremely elated. Even though the levels of success may vary, the results have been both entertaining and edifying. And given the artifice required, the products have especially surprised and pleased me by the naturalness, and at times the urgency, of their sound and sense. When a student has managed to make each word count in 25 lines that he or she has invented purely to flesh out a form, I feel as proud as if I myself had fathered the poem.

The role of the creative writing teacher is clearly problematic, since he may be and often is accused of screwing up what was a perfectly beautiful creation, by probing about with his blue pencil or scarring with the forceps of a due-date. The most serious complaint concerns a belief that he stifles the creative urge by enforcing such artificial rules and regulations: assignments of traditional forms, pat subjects, and the specification of off-rhymes or the prohibition of "that" clauses and every so-called cliché. And then, when all is said and done, the teacher himself gets caught not practicing what he has preached.

Nevertheless, despite a certain trepidation on entering the classroom, I find that my experience with asking students to create according to prescribed forms and with requiring them to treat of the most unimaginative subjects has proven an exciting exercise and even at times has accounted for a moving poem. Examples in the present collection include several pieces which were written to fulfill a call for either a suite of poems or a theme and variations; others came from carrying out an assignment which involved a class trip to the newly-opened student union in search of poetry that would arise from any sight or sound. In the case of the required ode, I asked for poems on unlikely subjects and was delighted by paeans to Stuckey's, a cockroach, and toes. The terza rima assignment also resulted in daring combinations when I asked that the student employ objects with movable parts as a way of working an idea through the 25 lines of preferably off-rhymed tercets. And likewise in the requisition of a self-portrait I was gratified by poems of fine insight, garnished with fresh images such as Sharon Sans's volcanic baked potato and Linda Kerr's opera ticket like an exiled prince (not included here, unfortunately). If such artificial fields can yield these highly imaginative if hybrid harvests, I dare say that once these student writers have found their own special terrain it won't be long before we the readers will reap a crop of truly mature and musical works.

Along with their own writing I also required that the class choose for discussion contemporary poems by other writers, as a way of presenting to themselves an idea of what they were seeking to achieve in their own work, criticizing the how and why of poems they found closest to their present taste and needs. A similar exercise involved the translation of a poem from another language, whether the student knew it or not, suggesting that a friend who did or a dictionary or both could serve as an entrance into the mystery of foreign poetry. In each case the results seemed as stimulating for me as they did for the students themselves. When taken as seriously as this class took them, all such unknowns can lead to fantasy and, as Jacob Bronowski phrased it, to a greater "reach of the imagination."

Finally, having delivered the poems, the time came for completing the creative process by giving them to the world on the printed page. While this last step is often the most painful, since it normally depends on the whims of editors or the space limitations of a magazine, it need not be so in our age of self-publishing (to be distinguished from the vanity press on the grounds of one's openness and the sheer joy of doing it oneself). I am and have long been a great believer in published anthologies of class work because they, perhaps more than anything else a teacher can do (though again artificially but nonetheless), inspire the student to polish more conscientiously and to work with a deeper dedication, knowing there will be something more rewarding than a grade to show for the effort. And too, the entire activity of making a book goes hand-in-hand with the fullest creative expression, since to give the work a life of its own, to receive comments on and reactions to it from an objective audience, and to have it as a permanent marker for memory—all are necessary parts of writing the road to improvement.

It is with self-renewing pleasure as a teacher that I add this latest collection to those made along my own path of creative writing, inspired always by students who in return for a specious lecture have offered the genuine refrain.

Creative Writing as Myth & Mystery

To my utter consternation, I discovered on the first day of spring classes that the course I had been assigned was not poetry, my longtime friend and confidant, but rather prose fiction, that untrustworthy bag of wind. What to do? Out of desperation I turned to legend. Or to be more precise, I asked my students to rewrite a myth, a folk or fairy tale. Before that I assigned them a task equal in impossibility to the one the department had set for me—write a mystery. To my amazement, they responded in both cases with the genuine article, not merely another through-the-motions exercise. And so I found once again that, no matter how artificial the requirements of a course, students can turn them into the stuff of a real and vital writing.

It seems that as a teacher I still haven't learned my lesson. But I can very definitely report that my faith has been restored once more, in students, and in the courses they take, which I have had the privilege these thirteen years "to teach."

Although prose fiction is something I have only dabbled in myself, there was available to me as a "resource person" the fine Texas short story writer, Tom Zigal, upon whom I called on two crucial occasions during our discussions of myth and mystery. Tom visited with us on his own time to share two of his stories and his special enthusiasm for detective fiction. We all thank him here for his very valuable insights and for his own inspiring craft.

Many of the stories selected for this anthology are admittedly an outgrowth of quite basic exercises:

> characterization——through a description of objects identified with a person or by means of an association of ways of dress with thought processes;
> point of view————told from that of the author's opposite sex;
> simultaneous
>   talk & thought——dreams or memories in the midst of conversation;
> symbolism—————three types within a single story: conventional, universal, and accidental;
> traditional
>   plotting———————repetition but also reinterpretation of well-known myths or of the mystery-clue-solution model.

Introduction to *Bernie Feldman's Detective Cookbook* (privately printed—spring 1978, The University of Texas at Austin).

The examples offered here, however, deny in many ways their beginnings as mere classroom assignments. In several cases the reader would probably not notice the underlying myth, since the story becomes so urgent and contemporary that he is not concerned to recognize its source in antiquity. (This seems to me particularly true of Cordie Harwood's "Chariot of a God.") Other pieces play more openly with a familiar myth, yet they still manage to create a fresh story by adapting the traditional plot to a present circumstance. (Both Mark Pearce's Socrates-Frankenstein remake and Zetta Young's beanstalk transplant are notable in this regard.) And while some mysteries can be parodic, as in the case of Alan Bishkin's title story, "Bernie Feldman's Detective Cookbook" (of which unfortunately only an excerpt could be presented here, yet even this contains his remarkable denouement and suggests a summary of the whole ingenious plot), other tales will surprise as convincingly as any fictive work worth its salt in suspense (see for instance both of Trey Goldsmith's intriguing contributions).

It is to a writer's imagination and to his or her determination to turn the archetypal into a personal artistic property that any credit for success is ultimately due. If the teacher can feel a part of this accomplishment, it is for having seen the student-writer through, for having attempted the best he could to keep out of the way or to render aid when necessary in assuring that each student *present* what it was he or she wanted or needed to say.

The object or motive behind this modest publication is essentially practical —to force the teacher into closer editing and to encourage the student to achieve a more thoughtful revision. Within the time-limits of a semester, perhaps it is unwise to rush such writing into print, yet revision may continue beyond appearance in such an ephemeral publication. Meanwhile, we have the proof of our efforts, something to remember and to measure our diction, structure, and invention by, and, most hopefully, a story or two to share with friends, with fellow readers and/or writers. And even though the teacher must at last assign a grade, we all know that in the end the real test of creative value is reserved for our gentle critics, for the connoiseurs of the art of fiction, for you gourmets of such cookery as is served up here from recipes for mystery & myth.

On a High Horse

It may have been simpler for Pound's generation to speak to the question of where poetry was in their time and where it should have been or had to go if it was to achieve a meaningful role in the twentieth century. More likely the explanation for their seeming ease in expressing themselves to the point on so many occasions lay with their deep understanding of the nature of poetry in all ages and their deeper urge to move the art beyond its rather outmoded practice. In our own day, owing largely to those poets' promethean efforts, there is such a diversity of approaches open to the poet that for any one person to make prescriptive statements is not only presumptuous but unrealistic. Too often in recent years, however, the tendency has been to identify all contemporary poetry as either in the Iowa School tradition or outside it, with the latter elements relegated to a misled preoccupation with regionalism rather than with working out the "new" American Surrealism.

While the major poetry publications have settled into a custom of heralding one look-alike after another, the nation's stock of real poets has fallen to an alarming low. I personally would point an unpolite finger at a type of industrial complex known as creative writing programs for having turned out writers with no personality, no roots, no grasp of literature beyond the narrow range of their professors' own poetic nepotism. The result is a stream of unconscious image-makers who rarely if ever penetrate even to the level of the modernists' minor poems. What is lacking in our poetry is strength of character, a willingness to take risks for the sake of touching base with more than a deep image, with a vision of more than cuteness and clever lines.

At the same time that the drive to make a tight subjective poem is limited by the poet's own thin experience of any world other than that of the academic classroom (even those with wider knowledge of a workaday existence having had it shaped and shrunk by the habits of the writing program's heartless exercises in how-to-turn-every-fact-into-a-symbol-for-sale to the *in* magazines), the carelessness of those who write without regard for any rhythm or diction more engaging than those of *Sports Illustrated* (and even the latter's are superior to most word choices and sound patterns to be found in the leading poetry journals) has left most lines and narratives far below the interest level of football journalism.

Except in very rare cases, poetry today is no longer a challenge nor an inspiration, and the unusual instances are encountered most often in the littlest

Seems, no. 14 (1981): 29-30.

magazines or are only seen in chapbooks that go unnoticed by reviewers, undistributed to bookstores, and hardly ever acquired by libraries. The sadness of this is that those with special talents quickly give up attempting anything more than a marketable product and thus fall into the academic/commercial bog of the indistinguishable and the basically undistinguished.

What I miss is a body of poems that has been earned through true dedication to the art. Rather than another celebration of another ingenious self or another cultivation of another clever simile, what American poetry needs is a poetry that reaches down to subjects larger than the poet's experience, to themes that put to the test his or her hold on language and all its tools for understanding. I submit that the academy will not supply this profundity that can only come from being dissatisfied with the formulae mouthed in the classroom. Not that I have been able to achieve the measure of discourse I myself dream of creating, which gives me pause in mounting this high horse. Even so, something has caused our present recession in poetry, and whether it follows from the nation's economic stagnation or from overcrowding in the classroom, it seems to me critical that all of us seek the difficult, that we reject the cleverness that has plagued our notions of the nature of poetry in this or any age, and that we search first and foremost in our own regions for those touchstones that will lead us back to local and enduring facts which can give rise to interpretations more substantial than those ready-made responses to gimmicky headlines the writing programs have sold us on.

To work out our own lonely and irrelevant meanings will prove more profitable in the long run than the best-paid shallowness with its hollow recognition accorded those who have met a prescribed academic regimen. And this is not to feel sorry for ourselves, but to face up to the real and essential demands the art of poetry has ever made on those who would suffer its glorious burden of bringing language to life and life to language.

Index